The Battle of Thermopylae

A Campaign in Context

A selection of Greek arms, including shield, spear, sword, sheath and greave.

THE BATTLE OF THERMOPYLAE

A CAMPAIGN IN CONTEXT

by

Rupert Matthews

SPELLMOUNT

British Library Cataloguing in Publication Data:
A catalogue record for this book is available
from the British Library

Copyright © Rupert Matthews 2006
Maps Copyright © Rupert Matthews 2006

ISBN 1-86227-325-1

First published in the UK in 2006 by
Spellmount Limited
The Mill, Brimscombe Port
Stroud, Gloucestershire. GL5 2QG

Tel: 01453 883300
Fax: 01453 883233
E-mail: enquiries@spellmount.com
Website: www.spellmount.com

1 3 5 7 9 8 6 4 2

Printed in Great Britain by
Oaklands Book Services
Stonehouse, Gloucestershire GL10 3RQ

Contents

List of Maps

Acknowledgements

I would especially like to thank the Hoplite Association (www.hoplites. org) for their assistance. Any mistakes that remain are my fault for not consulting these expert re-enactors properly during my researches. I would also like to thank Kelly Ostler for her support and assistance on my visits to the places mentioned in this book – and especially for her excellent mapreading skills when finding the more obscure locations.

Preface

This book is the story of perhaps the most famous military campaign of the ancient world. It has everything that a writer could want: action, adventure, mystery, heroism and much more. As a story, it is thrilling. As an exercise in military history it is fascinating.

The Greeks later claimed that the entire future history of the world hinged on this one campaign. As they saw things, the vast and powerful Persian Empire was a brutal dictatorship in which nobody had any rights except by favour of the monarch – the King of Kings, or Great King. All individuality was stamped out by the autocratic system which stifled trade, the arts and freedom. In the Greek city states, the arts and sciences flourished as individual freedom was celebrated and allowed its full rein. Each of the many small states was free to choose its own system of government. This Thermopylae campaign was a war between the Free World and a Slave World.

That, at least, is how the Greeks saw it. It was an apocalyptic vision in which the stakes were high and the world trembled on the edge of an abyss. Many modern writers have followed the Greek lead and viewed the wars of which the Thermopylae Campaign formed a part as being a struggle for freedom.

As ever, of course, things were not quite that simple. Slavery was an accepted part of life in all Greek states: the much vaunted freedoms were reserved for the privileged citizens. Nor was the Persian system of government quite as brutal as the Greeks liked to maintain. Subject peoples were often allowed to run their own affairs according to their own laws, so long as they paid their taxes on time and caused no trouble. And the war was very definitely not a conflict between Greeks and Persians. Many Greek states were already within the Persian Empire, or owed allegiance to it, and their men fought on the "Persian" side in the conflict. Many other Greek states, cowed by the awesome might of the King of Kings surrendered promptly rather than fight.

But in many ways the old, Greek view of this conflict does hold true. The issues may not have been as black and white as they pretended, but this was very definitely a war between rival and incompatible cultures. It was a war in which there could be no compromise peace or diplomatic accommodation. Either Persia would conquer Greece or it would not.

In the event, of course, Persia did not conquer Greece for reasons that will be explored in this book. It was Greek culture and learning that came to dominate the Mediterranean world. Passed on by way of Rome, this Greek culture still pervades the Western World to this day. As I write in England in the early 21st century, I live in a democracy – a Greek concept – and I write in words formed of letters from an alphabet – another Greek concept. Our buildings are adorned with Greek-style columns and works of art that clearly owe much to those of Greece. None of this would be the case if Persia had conquered Greece.

The story of the wars between the mighty Persian Empire and the states of the Greek League is relatively well known. The events were dramatic and far-reaching in their importance so they were well recorded at the time and have been much explored by historians since. Of all the incidents in these wars, which stretched over several generations, none was so dramatic as the Thermopylae campaign, the subject of this book. Again, the outline story has featured in numerous books and articles.

What marks all these accounts is that they tend to concentrate on the political side of the conflict. Battles and campaigns, though they are often dealt with in some detail, are seen as background to and results of the intrigues and machinations of the rulers and politicians who fill the pages of these writings. This is understandable, for the ancient sources that we have, focus on pretty much the same things. When Plutarch wrote his Life of Themistocles, the Athenian leader, he was interested in how a man from a relatively humble background could rise to be leader of his state and what he did with that power once he got it.

For a military historian, this can all be rather frustrating. The reasons for battles in the Ancient World are given clearly enough and who won them, but only rarely is there any discussion about how the battles were fought. We read almost nothing about weapons, tactics or logistics. But how were the armies kept supplied with food? How did a Greek soldier fight? What made the Spartans so special on the battlefield?

In some accounts this is inevitable. Herodotus, writing only some 30 or so years after the events described, simply did not need to tell his readers many things that we, reading today, want to know. He did not need to set down detail on the weapons of the time, for his readers would have seen them for themselves. He did not need to explain how troops formed up for battle, as his readers would already have known.

The effects of this assumption of knowledge on the part of the reader can, in places, be unfortunate and lead to some serious misunderstandings. To take one example, Herodotus mentions clearly and specifically that the battlefield at Thermopylae was dominated by a defensive wall built by the Phocians. He does not, however, give a description of it, nor does he say much about its role in the fighting; for the simple reason that his contemporary readers would have known the type of wall he was talking about and exactly how it would have been put to use by the Greek army.

Unfortunately, many modern writers have assumed that because Herodotus does not mention it often, this Phocian Wall must have been unimportant. It was not, it was crucial to the conduct of the battle. Herodotus does not mention it often because it was commonplace. He goes into detail only on matters that were unusual and needed explanations to his audience.

Imagine a modern writer producing an account of the Allied invasion of Normandy on D-Day, 6 June 1944. He would not need to explain what a tank was, nor an aircraft. He would not need to explain that Hitler was dictator of Germany nor that Churchill was Prime Minister of Britain. All this he could assume his readers would already know. He could just get on with telling the story of what happened. But for a reader in the 40th century, unfamiliar with the situation in the mid-20th century, all this and much more would need to be explained for events to make sense.

This book is an attempt to explain to the general reader the reality of warfare in the year 480BC. It seeks to give a plausible re-creation of the tactics used in the Thermopylae Campaign and to put them into the context of the time. It explains what the weapons were like and how they were used in action. It describes the usual tactics of the different military units involved and how these would have impacted on each other in battle. I have walked the battlefields on foot and have handled replica weapons at some length. I have then used this information to put together an account of the campaign itself.

It is usual for a historian to explain something of the way in which he has treated his sources. Footnotes are the usual academic way of doing this, but I find that the constant flicking and back and forth can spoil the flow of a work for a reader. Instead, I have mentioned my sources in the body of the work and how I have interpreted them. But I have done so only when dealing with a contentious issue or when I felt it necessary for one reason or another.

The main source for the history of this campaign is *The Histories* of Herodotus. Herodotus was born some five years before the Thermopylae Campaign took place and wrote his monumental book some forty years later. He is quite open about his motive in writing the book, saying as the very first sentence "Herodotus of Halicarnassus here displays his inquiry, so that the human achievements may not become forgotten in time". He also makes it clear that his main method of discovering what had happened was to go and talk to people who had been there. He was writing at a time when the veterans of the war would have been in their 60s or 70s.

Unlike some modern writers, I see no reason to disbelieve what Herodotus tells us. But it is important to be clear about his sources where possible. He will preface some sections with words such as "The Athenians say that ..." or "The story told in Syracuse is ..." So what we have in his book are largely the remarks of old men speaking with hindsight. Occasionally it is clear that Herodotus is drawing on government archives or official accounts of one kind or another, but most often he is dealing with human memory.

Inevitably, old soldiers like to dwell on their victories and to make light of their defeats – or at least seek to blame them on somebody else. And by the time Herodotus was collecting his evidence the members of the League had fallen out with each other. Men in Athens would have had good cause to blame Corinth for anything that went wrong and vice versa. All this must be borne in mind when dealing with Herodotus.

It is usual for contemporary sources to be treated with rather more respect than later histories. I'm not sure that I altogether agree. To return to an analogy from World War II, the newspapers printed on 7 June 1944 will have been carefully checked by the government censor to ensure that nothing useful to the Germans was included in their accounts of the D-Day landings that took place the previous day. A book written five years later would have been free to detail exactly which units landed where and how strong they were. But it was not until the 1990s that top secret government files were released that revealed that the Allies had cracked the code used by German military radio operators. This provided the Allies with precise information on where the German forces were and did much to explain why the Allied commanders behaved as they did. Clearly, the contemporary account was incomplete compared to that of 50 years later. Plutarch was writing his account of events 400 years later than did Herodotus. He used different sources and, at this distance in time and without any evidence to help us, we have no way of knowing if Plutarch's sources were more or less accurate than those of Herodotus.

We must also be cautious when ancient writers claim to be telling us what happened at secret meetings or that certain people had ulterior motives for their actions. Writing within living memory of the events he describes, Herodotus could not put down something that was transparently false as the mistake would soon be pointed out and his writings lose credibility. Imagine a modern historian claiming that the Mustang was a German aircraft of World War II. But when making claims of secret deals or motives, the writer strays into territory where his claims could not be so easily disputed. Who knows what secret negotiations go on behind the scenes? Herodotus may be right when he tells these stories, or he might be wrong. We have no way of knowing. All we can do is compare the "secret" events to the public ones and try to judge if they have the ring of truth. It is not often that the ancient authors factually contradict each other. More often they give different, but not necessarily incompatible, information. It is the role of the historian to compare the different accounts and try to match them together to present a coherent and credible account of what really happened.

Finally, there is the problem of dates. All the ancient sources tie their accounts of the events to the Carneian Festival. Their readers would have known when this was and so would have understood on which dates the different events happened. However, the Carneian Festival was tied to the cycles of the moon and our understanding of exactly how is incomplete. Basically, the Carneian Festival of 480BC may have fallen on the August full moon or the September full moon. As will be seen, I favour the August date. This is not because of any great understanding of lunar cycles or ancient Greek religious festivals. It is simply that so many military events happened after the Carneian Festival and before winter weather closed in on Greece that I think that the earlier date is far more likely.

There are many other deductions that I have made in this book, some of which I explain in detail and others that I do not. No doubt some readers and scholars will disagree with me, but for better or worse, this is my interpretation of events. It is based on what I believe to be sound logic, on an understanding of how war was organised and fought in that distant age and on my understanding of how men thought back then – which was very different from how men think today. I have done my best to produce a readable and yet well researched account of a military campaign that took place some 2,500 years ago.

Checklist of Individuals, Legendary Heroes and Deities

The names of the Greeks, Persians and others who will be encountered here may be unfamiliar to many readers. To aid the reader in making sense of the sometimes convoluted relationships between them, here is a checklist that may be referred back to as necessary.

Achaemenes	Brother of Xerxes, governor of Egypt and commander of the Persian fleet during the Thermopylae Campaign.
Ahuramazda	Chief god of the Persian Zoroastrian religion.
Alexander I	King of Macedon. Alexander the Great (356-323BC) was Alexander III.
Amyntas	King of Macedon, father of Alexander I of Macedon.
Antidorus	Sea captain from Lemnos serving in the Persian fleet, he defected to the League.
Antipater	Treasurer of Thasos, a Greek city within the Persian Empire.
Architeles	Senior Athenian naval captain.
Ariabignes	Half-brother to Xerxes and a commander of part of the Persian fleet.
Aristeides	Athenian politician and opponent of Themistocles.
Aristodemus	Spartan soldier who left Thermopylae.
Artabanus	Uncle of Xerxes, he opposed the invasion of Greece.
Artemis	Greek goddess of hunting and wild country areas.
Artemisia	Queen of Halicarnassos, a Greek state within the Persian Empire.
Atachaees	Cousin of Xerxes and military engineer.

Athene	Greek goddess, patron goddess of Athens.
Arthimius	Athenian who worked as a secret agent for the Persians.
Boreus	Greek god of the north wind.
Cleombrotus	Spartan prince and military commander, younger brother of King Leonidas.
Cleomenes	Former king of Sparta who died in suspicious circumstances just before the Thermopylae campaign began.
Cobon	Priest of Apollo at Delphi.
Croesus	King of Lydia, defeated by the Persians in 546BC.
Darius	Father of Xerxes, he rose to become King of Kings after organising a coup against the previous ruler of the Persian Empire.
Datis	Persian nobleman, killed by the Spartans soon after the Marathon campaign.
Demaratus	Former king of Sparta ousted after a scandal. In 480BC he was serving as an advisor to Xerxes on Greek military matters.
Dieneces	A Spartan soldier at Thermopylae and celebrated wit.
Dionysius of Phocaea	Greek naval commander during the Ionian Revolt.
Ephialtes	Greek peasant and traitor from Malis.
Ephorus	Greek military historian who wrote in about 350 BC. His account of the Thermopylae campaign has been lost and only fragments quoted by other writers have survived.
Epicydes	Athenian nobleman and famous orator.
Euanetous	Spartan nobleman and general.
Eurybiades	Spartan admiral, during the Thermopylae campaign he was the official commander of the combined League fleet.
Eurytus	Spartan soldier at Thermopylae.
Gelon	Powerful ruler of Syracuse, willing to help the League, Gelon was unable to do so because of an invasion of Sicily by the Carthaginians.
Habrocomes	Half-brother of Xerxes and officer in the Persian army.
Habronichus	Athenian sea captain, he commanded the fast galley that carried messages between the League army and fleet.
Heracles	Legendary Greek hero and supposed ancestor of the Spartan royal family. Also known as Hercules.

Herodotus	Greek historian who wrote an account of the wars against Persia some 40 years after the Thermopylae Campaign.
Hipparchus	Athenian nobleman, exiled for political reasons, Hipparchus served with Xerxes as an advisor on Athenian affairs.
Hippias	Former dictator of Athens.
Hydarnes	Persian nobleman and commander of the elite Immortal unit.
Hyperanthes	Half-brother of Xerxes and officer in the Persian army.
Leon	Greek sailor, the first man to be killed in the Thermopylae campaign.
Leonidas	One of the two Kings of Sparta, Leonidas commanded the army of the Greek League at Thermopylae.
Leotychides	One of the two kings of Sparta. During the Thermopylae campaign he stayed in Sparta to attend to domestic and religious duties.
Lycomedes of Athens	Greek sea captain.
Mardonius	Son in law of Xerxes and Persian nobleman. He commanded the Persian infantry during the Thermopylae campaign.
Megabazus	Persian nobleman and a commander of part of the Persian fleet.
Megacreon	Citizen of Abdera, a Greek city within the Persian Empire.
Megistias	Greek seer and priest.
Miltiades	Athenian soldier and victor at the Battle of Marathon in 490 BC.
Ocytus	Commander of the Corinthian ships within the League fleet.
Pantites	Spartan soldier, used as a messenger by Leonidas.
Perialla	Priestess of Apollo at Delphi.
Perseus	Legendary Greek hero and supposed founder of the royal family of Argos.
Phanias of Lesbos	Greek historian, his account of the Thermopylae campaign has been mostly lost.
Philaon	Commander of the 150 Cypriot ships in the Persian fleet.
Pindar	Greek poet who wrote an epic poem about the Thermopylae Campaign, now mostly lost.
Plutarch	Greek historian writing in the 1st century AD, he wrote a biography of Themistocles.

Prexaspes	Persian nobleman and a commander of part of the Persian fleet.
Pythia	Title of the priestess at Delphi who delivered the pronouncements of the Oracle.
Pythius of Lydia	A Greek merchant and landowner of legendary wealth living within the Persian Empire.
Scyllias	Sculptor and professional diver, perhaps of Athenian ancestry, employed by the Persians. He defected to the League.
Themistocles	Athenian politician and military commander. During the Thermopylae campaign he commanded first the Athenian army and later the Athenian fleet.
Tritantaechmes	Persian nobleman, cousin of Xerxes and officer in the army.
Tyrtaios	Greek poet of the 7th century BC, he wrote a number of famous marching songs used by the Spartans.
Xerxes	King of Kings, the Great King, ruler of the Persian Empire.
Zeus	Chief god of the Greeks.

CHAPTER 1
The War Begins

The sack of Sardis. It was Athenian involvement in the destruction of this Persian provincial capital that led to the Persian invasion.

The actual spark that started the war between the Greeks and Persians came in 499 BC, almost 20 years before the climactic Thermopylae Campaign. The underlying tensions had, however, been growing for some time.

At this period, Greece was not restricted just to the modern country of that name. Greek-speaking cities and states were scattered from southern Italy and Sicily in the west across to what is now Turkey in the east. Nor were the Greeks united. Far from it. The Greek peoples were divided into a large number of states ranging in size from a few hundred citizens up to those that numbered hundreds of thousands among their populations. Each state was independent of all others and hostilities were as usual as friendships.

Each Greek state was free to choose its own form of government. Some were ruled by kings or military strong men, others by groups of nobles and a few were democracies. Slavery was common, even in the democracies, and society was far more rigid and hierarchical than in the modern western world. There was, however, an underlying recognition that the Greeks were a people sharing a single culture that marked them out from all others, who were generally dismissed as barbarians.

In 546 BC the powerful Persian Empire conquered the land of King Croesus of Lydia, in what is now western Turkey. Many of the smaller Greek states around the coast of Asia Minor, the area then known as Ionia, had recognised some form of overlordship by Croesus. The Persians took over this relationship. At first all was well, as the Persian monarchs made no attempt to enforce taxes or obligations on their new Greek subjects that were either novel or onerous. But gradually things changed.

In 522 BC a coup took place within the Persian Empire. The details of exactly what happened are shrouded in propaganda, but the result was clear. The throne was seized by Darius, a remote cousin of the previous monarch. Darius was a bureaucrat of genius. He thoroughly modernised the administration of the Persian Empire, introduced a standardised coinage for the first time and set about ensuring that he drew the maximum benefit from his various possessions. However, he came from an agricultural society in which all wealth derived from crops and livestock. He did not understand how commerce and trade worked, nor how to tax it without damaging the wealth-producing elements.

Inevitably the self-governing Greek states on the periphery of the Persian Empire began to feel the impact of Darius' reforms. Darius not only created a new basis for taxation, but was fearsomely efficient at collecting it. Those states that proved recalcitrant about paying found the Persian army on their doorstep. Darius' usual tactic was to abolish whatever form of government the Greek state had and replace it with dictatorship by a Greek he could trust. The Greeks denounced this arrangement as the rule of tyrants. Unlike the modern implications of the word, this did not imply that the rule of the tyrant was cruel or despotic, merely that it was illegal.

In 499 BC a wave of rebellion swept across the Greek states of Ionia. The tyrants were expelled or executed, as were local Persian officials and tax collectors. The Ionian Greeks sent messengers to the other Greek states asking for help against the Persians and offering the rewards of plunder as an inducement. Athens rallied to the cause, sending a powerful naval squadron and some soldiers. The high point of the Ionian Revolt, as it is known, came when the Greek insurgents captured the Persian provincial capital of Sardis. The town was looted and burned.

The success of the revolt was short-lived. Once Darius mobilised the vast resources of the Persian Empire, it was only a matter of time before the Ionian cities were recaptured. In 494 the rebel fleet was defeated at the Battle of Lade, whereupon the rough alliance that had held the various Greek states together fell apart. Each state rushed to make the best terms it could with the Persian monarch, who used the proud title of King of Kings. Darius did not allow every rebellious state to make peace. An example was made of Miletus, the first state to rise, which was sacked and burned.

When Darius learned that Greeks from outside his empire had helped the rebels, he was furious. Unable to wreak his revenge on them for the time being, he took a symbolic arrow and dedicated it to his god, Ahuramazda – Darius was like most Persians of the time a Zoroastrian. He shot the arrow westward and made a solemn pledge to take his revenge on the Athenians. To keep his vengeful frame of mind alive, Darius ordered one of his servants to whisper in his ear "Master, remember the Athenians" every time he sat down to dinner.

In 492 Darius was ready to take action. He sent his son-in-law Mardonius with a powerful army to conquer Thrace. This the able young soldier did with skill and speed, though he had the misfortune of seeing his naval support fleet almost wiped out by a storm as it rounded the cape of Mount Athos.

The following year, the King of Kings sent envoys to the Greek states in what is now Greece. Each state was asked to deliver to Darius a small box of earth and a flask of water as tokens that they acknowledged the

Persian King of Kings as their overlord. Some Greek states, cowed by the sheer military might of the Persian Empire did so, others prevaricated and delayed sending a reply, hoping that Darius was not really serious. The Athenians kicked the envoys out without ceremony. At Sparta, the strange, proud and ferocious Spartans threw the envoys into a well and told them to get the earth and water for themselves.

In 490, Darius sent an invasion fleet under the command of a nobleman named Datis to destroy Athens. The Persian force captured a few islands along the way, and landed on the southern end of the island of Euboea to establish a forward base. They reduced the previously impregnable cities of Eretria and Carystus in less than a week. From Euboea, the Persians landed at Marathon ready to march on Athens. They never made it.

Led by Miltiades, the Athenian army, supported by some local allies, attacked first. Despite being heavily outnumbered, the Athenians won the battle and killed some 6,400 Persians for the loss of just 192 citizens – though no doubt some non-citizens died as well. It was a remarkable victory. The Persians retreated back across the sea. It was clear, however, that the Persians would come back. The questions were when, where, and how to defeat them.

At first the victory of Marathon seemed to show that the way to ensure victory was to rely on the heavily armoured hoplite infantry, which had composed most of the victorious army at the battle. However, one faction in Athenian society disagreed. Led by a talented young orator of humble background, named Themistocles, this faction thought that the Persian expedition of 490 had been merely a fraction of the military might of the Persian Empire. They argued that if Darius mobilised his entire resources, not even the combined armies of all Greece could defeat him. However, they reasoned, logistical supply would be a key weakness of any such massive Persian invasion. Darius' supply lines would inevitably involve merchant shipping. Cut those supply lines and the Persian invasion would be stopped.

Themistocles argued constantly that the prime need of the Athenian state was to increase the size of the navy. In this he had the support of the poorer citizens, who could expect to earn good wages from the state as oarsmen and sailors, but was opposed by the richer citizens who had to pay the taxes. The deadlock was broken in the autumn of 484.

Athens had some small silver mines at Laurium. These were leased to a private company which paid a percentage of the bullion extracted to the state. As 484 came to a close the miners suddenly and unexpectedly broke into a new seam of ore that was breathtakingly rich and large. In the first year of production the new seam produced five tons of silver, and expansion was under way. Suddenly the Athenian treasury was overflowing. After some complex intrigue and political manoeuvring, Themistocles got the money allocated to shipbuilding. Athens would have its fleet.

The Laurium strike came not a moment too soon. Disturbing news was reaching the Greeks on the mainland of events in the Persian Empire. Darius had died in 485 and his son, Xerxes, had been kept busy touring to ensure the loyalty of his subject peoples and their governors. But in the spring of 482 Xerxes sent messengers galloping out across his vast empire. They had orders to put the complex, but superbly efficient bureaucracy of his father into motion. Weapons were to be made and transported to the city of Susa. Food supplies were to be gathered together, packed into storage containers and likewise sent off to Susa. By spring 481 vast quantities of all sorts of military necessities were ready and waiting on the pleasure of Xerxes, King of Kings.

Now fresh riders went out putting the mobilisation of the armies of the Persian Empire into operation. All across the Empire the men liable for military service were called up and informed of the orders of the Great King Xerxes. Each unit had its own instructions, but by far the largest mustering was to take place at Sardis. There could be no doubt now as to the target for all these careful preparations. The long delayed invasion of Greece was about to start.

As news reached Greece that Xerxes was gathering an army at Sardis, Sparta took the lead. The two kings, Leotychides and Leonidas, sent heralds to every state and city in Greece summoning representatives to attend a conference to be held in the autumn of 481. At this point there was no formal agenda, nor any firm proposals. The meeting was intended simply to discuss the situation.

The meeting was at first intended to meet in Sparta, but was then moved to the Isthmus of Corinth. The move was probably prompted by Themistocles of Athens who rightly reasoned that it would be better to hold the gathering on relatively neutral ground. We don't know exactly which states sent representatives, but it is certain that the majority of mainland states did attend, as did many representatives from the islands.

A question mark hangs over King Alexander I of Macedon, both at this meeting and throughout the campaign. The powerful kingdom of Macedon lay to the north of Greece, astride the route that Xerxes would follow on his invasion. The Greeks did not regard the Macedonians as being true Greeks, but neither were they classed as barbarians. The lowland areas of Macedon had adopted Greek culture and language. The ruling family, the Caranids, were believed to be descended from the ancient hero Heracles, which made them distant cousins of the Spartan kings. It is likely that a message was sent to Alexander, but equally certain that he did not attend. (This Alexander, incidentally, was an ancestor of Alexander the Great, who was the third Alexander to sit on the throne of Macedon.)

Alexander's position was as ambiguous as the Greek view of his kingdom. When Darius had been preparing to attack the Scythians, he had sent ambassadors to King Amyntas of Macedon to request help. Strangers to the northern kingdom, the ambassadors managed to insult the ladies of the court. Alexander, then a rash young man, lost his temper and killed the Persian ambassadors. Only prompt action by his father, Amyntas, and the pressing need of Darius for allies averted a war. When he came to the throne, Alexander maintained close links to Greece. He even competed in a race at the Olympic Games, coming second. Alexander had, however, wasted no time in sending the symbolic gifts of earth and water to Darius, and then to Xerxes. In return he was allowed to rule his kingdom as an effectively independent monarch.

Now that the Persian monarch was marching against Greece, Alexander had to choose. It was typical of this wily ruler that he managed to keep on side with both Persians and Greeks. Publicly he sided with Xerxes, providing every assistance that was asked of him. Privately, he kept in touch with the Greeks and sent them messages and advice when he could. It is likely that he had a representative at the meeting held at Corinth, but took no active part.

Other states leant further toward the Persian invaders than Macedon. Those in Thessaly would be the first truly Greek states to be invaded by the advancing Persian host. The most powerful royal family of Thessaly, the Aleuadae, had long enjoyed good relations with the Persian Empire. They had been offered good terms by the King of Kings, so it is likely that they had already decided to side with Xerxes, or to "medise" as the Greeks termed it. But not every city in Thessaly was ruled by the Aleuadae and even in areas under the control of that family there were other factions. Many of these opposed submitting meekly to Xerxes.

Thessaly sent representatives, though how many is unclear. They came to the isthmus meeting to gauge the likelihood of victory over Persia. More particularly to see if the fighting men of the Peloponnese and Attica would be willing to march north to defend Thessaly. Further south the cities of Boeotia looked to powerful Thebes as their leader. It was widely believed that Thebes favoured coming to terms with Xerxes while this was still possible. No representatives from Thebes are known to have attended the conference.

It was in southern Greece that the opposition to Xerxes was strongest. Athens and Sparta had no real choice in the matter. The total destruction of these two states was the declared purpose of the invasion. For them the question was not whether to fight, but how to fight. The cities of Arcadia and Achaia would almost certainly follow the lead of Sparta, while others would follow Athens.

The powerful city state of Argos sent no representative to the conference. The lack of its fighting men and warships would be a serious blow to the Greeks. Worse, the city stood south of the Isthmus of Corinth, putting it in a position to stab any defence in the back and give victory to the Persians. Argos had been involved in years of intermittent warfare against

Sparta. She might choose to aid Xerxes to defeat her local foe, she might stay neutral or she might be induced to join the defence. It was clear that the attitude of Argos would be crucial, but with no representatives present it was impossible to find out what that attitude was.

Also absent was Corcyra, modern Corfu. This was a rich and populous state which had one of the largest war fleets in the Mediterranean. Like Argos, the attitude of Corcyra was important but there was nobody at the conference to speak up. Likewise, Crete had sent nobody to the meeting.

The discussions got underway at last, and continued for some days. There was a great deal of squabbling and debating. Nevertheless some serious decisions were taken, apparently on the insistence of Themistocles and the Spartan kings. First, all quarrels between the states which had sent representatives had to be put on one side until the Persians had been dealt with. The Athenians led the way by patching up their differences with Aegina. Second, it was agreed that any Greek state that sided with Persia would be stripped of one tenth of its wealth once the war was over.

Then came the difficult subject of agreeing a genuine military alliance. Promises could be made easily enough, and were, but actually putting a united army and navy into battle was quite another. It was agreed that each state would contribute as many men and ships as possible, with each state paying and supplying its own forces. Herodotus says that there was going to be a central war chest into which each state would pay a sum of cash. No other source mentions this, so it may be a case of his Athenian sources misleading him by trying to claim a longer history for the arrangements of their own day.

Then came the vexed question of appointing a commander. Not only was pride and honour at stake – always important to the ancient Greeks – but so was trust. Each state had its own local agenda and motives. These may have been officially set aside for the period of the emergency, but no state wanted to see a rival given the command of a huge force that could then be misused.

There could have been no serious doubt, however, that the army would be commanded by one of the Spartan kings. Not only did Sparta contribute the most effective fighting force, but their kings were raised from birth to command armies. Traditionally, one Spartan king led the army in times of war while the other stayed at home to govern the kingdom. Which king was to march to war had not yet been decided.

Command of the fleet was more problematic. Of the states at the conference, Athens had the largest fleet. A proposal was put forward, presumably by the Athenians, that their admiral, Themistocles, should command the combined fleet. The proposal was voted down by a combination of the smaller states. Athenian pride was hurt and a row broke out. The dispute was solved by Themistocles himself. He stepped forward to resign his command in favour of the Spartan Eurybiades.

In theory, this put the entire military effort under Spartan control; but the forces sent by each state remained under the control of their own commander. While they were pledged to obey the orders of the Spartan commander in chief, it was by no means certain they would do so. In practice, this meant that the commander needed to call frequent councils of war at which his subordinate commanders could discuss and debate what actions to take. It was hardly a recipe for decisive military action, but it was the best that could be agreed. And at least it was agreed by all present.

Beyond that there was no agreement possible on strategy, tactics or diplomacy. There were, quite simply, too many unknown factors for any sensible decisions to be taken. Nobody knew how large the Persian army was. And there were too many key Greek states whose attitude remained in doubt.

The final decision taken at the conference was to delay taking further decisions until the spring. Meanwhile spies would be sent to Persia to ascertain the forces ranged against them. Envoys would be sent to Argos, Corcyra and Crete to ask what those states would do. A fourth envoy was to be sent to Gelon, ruler of the enormously wealthy city of Syracuse in Sicily. He was a Greek ruling a Greek city so it was hoped that he would send some help.

With that the conference broke up. The delegates went back to their homes to await events. Xerxes, meanwhile, was preparing the most powerful army the world had ever seen.

The Persian Emperor Darius from a relief at his palace at Persepolis. The servants carry a parasol and fan to keep the emperor cool. Such luxuries attended the emperor even on military campaigns.

CHAPTER 2
The Persian Host

A depiction at Persepolis of the elite guardsmen who accompanied the Persian Emperor at all times. Each man is equipped with spear and with bow, and would have worn light armour beneath the brightly coloured robes.

No aspect of the Thermopylae campaign has given rise to greater controversy than the size and composition of the army led by Xerxes into Greece. It is generally agreed that the army was very large by the standards of the day, though how numerous the host was is a matter of great dispute.

Some time in 481BC, Xerxes gave orders for his army to muster at Sardis by the following spring. The city had a number of advantages. The city stood on the lower slopes of Mount Tmolus overlooking the plain of the River Hermos. The area around the city offered plenty of water and productive fields from which the gathering force could be supplied. It was, moreover, capital of the province of Lydia with good road links to Ephesus, Smyrna and Cyme on the coast as well as to Ipsus inland, and thence on to the interior of the Persian Empire. When Xerxes was at Sardis supervising the gathering army, he could keep in touch with the rest of his empire by messenger.

Sardis had another overwhelming recommendation as the spot on which to muster an army to invade Greece. This was the city burned to the ground by the Athenian army that had crossed the sea to support the rebellious Greek cities in 504BC. By using Sardis as the mustering point, Xerxes was making it very clear what the purpose of the great expedition was to be: revenge.

Simply the fact that Xerxes was to lead the campaign in person signifies that this was to be an event of paramount importance to the Persian Empire. He had not yet led a military campaign himself, as had his predecessors as King of Kings. Xerxes had been too busy reforming his empire, overhauling the bureaucracy and putting the system of taxation on to an efficient footing to spend time leading armies. In any case, he had not faced a major war against an outside enemy before. Now that a worthy adversary was to be faced, the King of Kings decided to command in person. Such a major expedition would call upon all the resources of the vast empire that Xerxes ruled. Messengers were sent to every province demanding money, supplies and, above all, men. No province was excused contributing to the great project.

This was of course because Xerxes needed the men, money and supplies to put his invasion force together; but there was another motive. By bringing at least some men from every province, Xerxes could impress on each the great power and might of his dominions. Men overawed by the resources of their master were less likely to rebel in future and those who returned to their homes would bear witness to his might.

Xerxes was also playing a propaganda game with the Greeks. Although he clearly intended to extend the Persian Empire to encompass all of Greece, his thirst for vengeance was directed only against the Athenians and Spartans. Persian messengers were busily at work among the other Greek cities. Promises were made of light taxation and wide-ranging self-government to those states that submitted promptly. Some were told that only symbolic gifts of soil and water would be demanded, others that free passage to the soldiers of the King of Kings would suffice. All were told of the dire consequences of standing in the way of the will of Xerxes.

It was to reinforce the last point that Xerxes wanted to gather men from all over his empire at Sardis. He knew the Greeks were familiar with his provinces that lay close to them, but he also knew that countries such as India or Bactria were little better than myths and legends to most Greeks. By confronting the Greeks with very solid evidence of his mastery over such distant lands, Xerxes hoped to intimidate them and convince them that resistance was worse than futile, it was suicidal.

No records have survived from the Persian Empire to help us decide just how large was the force that Xerxes had gathered at Sardis by the end of winter. Herodotus puts the strength of Xerxes' army at around two million men and says that they drank the rivers dry as they advanced. Many historians have dismissed this as a wild exaggeration. Some have guessed that Herodotus was out by a factor of ten, a not uncommon error; but one that Herodotus does not make elsewhere. Few historians have made an attempt to produce an accurate picture of the vast force advancing towards Thermopylae.

And yet there is enough information available to come up with what may be a reasonable assessment of the size and fighting qualities of the army that marched with Xerxes. To understand what happened at Thermopylae and to set the campaign in context it is essential to understand, or attempt to understand, the capabilities of the Persian host. To do otherwise is to duck the issue.

As with so much about the Thermopylae campaign, it is best to start with Herodotus, while always bearing in mind that he wrote with hindsight and that those who gave him his information may have had reasons to add their own viewpoint. Herodotus uses the grand review held by Xerxes of his forces at Doriscus in the spring of 480BC as the setting for a dramatised account of the army and navy under the control of the King of Kings. The information that Herodotus gives about the Persian army is not simply a bald total, he lists all the subject nations that provided troops and how they were brigaded together for active service. This information is best presented as a table (pp 26-27). Herodotus also says that about

11

300,000 Thracians, Macedonians and northern Greeks joined the army as it advanced.

As usual, Herodotus does not tell us where he got this information from, but it does bear all the hallmarks of being an official document of the Persian Empire. The neat rounding of all numbers is typical of the Mesopotamian bureaucracy. We know from other sources that Persian generals preferred to have units of uniform strength for logistical purposes and would group together smaller units to achieve this, as on Herodotus' list.

There are two known sources from which Herodotus might have gained a contemporary Persian document of this kind. The first possible source was Xerxes himself. In the winter of 481/480BC, the Persians captured three Greek spies trying to enter the camp at Sardis where the army was mustering. Swift and brutal death would have been the usual punishment for such men, but Xerxes intervened. He ordered his officers to take the spies on a guided tour of the camp. They were to point out the many different nations gathering for war, their weapons and their numbers. Xerxes's motive is clear. At the time he was trying to win over to his side as many Greek states as possible. No doubt he hoped that reports of the overwhelming nature of his army would prompt some undecided states to opt for collaboration with the Persians.

Secondly, it should be remembered that Herodotus was a native of Halicarnassus. In 480BC, when the historian was a child of about five, this city was part of the Persian Empire. Indeed, Queen Artemisia led the Halicarnassian ships to war on the Persian side. It is more than likely that Herodotus could have acquired his list from contacts in his home city. At the least, his older contemporaries who had worked with the Persian bureaucracy could tell him whether or not a document was genuine.

Whatever the source of the information given by Herodotus, it is quite clear that the list is not an accurate record of the army Xerxes led into Greece. It would have been physically impossible to march that many men along the roads available, and to keep them supplied. However, the document on which Herodotus based his figures cannot be simply ignored or dismissed. It is most likely to have been an official list of the *total* military forces available to Xerxes. The Persian bureaucracy would have needed such a list, and Herodotus could quite easily have obtained a copy.

The Persian Empire was an agricultural society, though several of the subject peoples followed a pastoral or even nomadic existence. In times of dire emergency all able-bodied adult men from such a society would turn out to fight. They would come with whatever lethal objects they had to hand, whether they were axes, knives, scythes or simple clubs. Such men could not be considered to be an army. They lacked training in even the simplest tactics and had no armour at all. More importantly, while the men were away from home the farms and livestock were not being tended. If all the men were away fighting for more than a few days there could be serious consequences for the farming populations, and unpaid taxes for the government.

There can be no doubt that the King of Kings would occasionally muster all the men of an area, but this would be for a short time only and for a specific purpose – either to repel a raid or perhaps to undertake construction work.

For such an army as invaded Greece, a ruler needed men who could afford to be away from home for months on end and who could spare the time to train for the battles ahead. Different agricultural societies have organised this in different ways, and the Persian Empire seems to have used a variety of methods with the various subject nations. Relatively uncivilised pastoral peoples, such as the Mysians, were simply given a number for the men they had to supply for long-term service and left to get on with it. Each man was expected to bring his own clothing and weapons as well as, most likely, food for a set period of time. Elsewhere the system was more sophisticated. The city of Babylon and its surrounding area was not asked to provide any soldiers at all. Instead it paid a heavy tax, which was then used to equip and supply more reliable troops from among the Medes and Persians themselves.

Whatever method was used, most agricultural societies can spare about one in ten of their young, fit men for lengthy service away from home. Assuming that Herodotus took his information from a genuine Persian document, it would be most likely that it was recording the total number of men that the Empire could call on for just this sort of service. In other words, it was telling Xerxes how many men he could rely on for useful armed service.

Of course, not all these men would have been available for the invasion of Greece. The Empire was surrounded by violent and hostile neighbours who would have enthusiastically crossed unguarded borders to loot and pillage. To the north, around the Black Sea, were the famously ruthless Scythians, nomads who had been unsuccessfully invaded by the Persians in 512BC. To the east lay the kingdoms of India, all of them equipped with effective armies. The Arabs to the south were more than willing to serve Xerxes in return for Persian gold, but were just as likely to raid the lands of the King of Kings if they thought they could get away with it. All these borders needed to be guarded and patrolled in sufficient strength to deter invasion.

Nor was it only against external threats that Xerxes had to guard. In 486BC the Egyptians had risen in revolt. This wealthy country had been conquered by the Persians in 525 but had never happily accepted foreign rule. The rebellion was a concerted attempt to drive out the Persians and re-establish a native dynasty of pharaohs. It had taken Xerxes two years to defeat the revolt, after which he put his own brother Achaimenes in place to rule the country. Then Babylon itself erupted in violent protest at heavy taxation.

Xerxes needed to leave troops and reliable commanders across his empire to ensure that taxes were paid, tribute collected and that no rebellions broke out. Nor could local troops be used in case they were in sympathy with any rebellious movement. Each province needed to be garrisoned by troops from elsewhere.

Quite how many of the 1.85 million men recorded by Herodotus were needed for garrison duties across the empire is unknown. Most likely it was the majority of men available for armed service. All armies suffer from natural wastage, in the form of sickness, death and desertion. The Persian army would have been no different. Added to that was the need to allow for units to be in transit, repairing fortifications and other tasks.

All told, Xerxes would have been lucky if he could have counted on a third of his army's nominal strength being available to march with him into Greece. This would have given a total of around 600,000 men. However, there were other limits imposed on Xerxes; and we have sources apart from the imposing list of figures given by Herodotus.

On the route from Sardis to Greece, the Persian army marched up what is now known as the Gallipoli peninsula. The British World War I commander, Major-General Sir Frederick Barton Maurice (1871-1951) had occasion to study the water supply of the Gallipoli peninsula. He estimated that in spring and summer, the season when Xerxes marched through, the area could provide enough water to supply an army of 210,000 men, together with the pack animals and horses needed to move their supplies.

This brings us back to the famous statement, often dismissed as a legend, that the Persian army drank the rivers dry as they advanced. In the summer months the rivers of Thrace, Macedonia and northern Greece are often little more than streams as the rainfall declines. We know that Xerxes sent an advance guard of labourers and engineers forward to prepare the route for his invasion. Thrace was already within the empire, but King Alexander II of Macedonia was compelled to assist and supply these workmen as a sign of his friendship to the Persian Empire.

While it is not recorded exactly what these men did, it is clear that they were undertaking construction work that would aid the army. Mending and improving roads would be an obvious task to be tackled, but so too would the preparation of food and water supplies. If streams were dammed to create reservoirs of water, it could be quite literally true that the advancing army ensured that the riverbeds were dry where they entered the sea. And it must be remembered that the swift Greek galleys would have been taking every opportunity to scout out the Persian army from off the coast. From their ships, the Greeks would have seen the empty rivers and taken note.

By preparing water supplies in this way, Xerxes would have been able to move an army considerably larger than the 210,000 men that General

Maurice thought the land could support. Even so, it is unlikely that the increase could have been more than around 50%, say a total of 300,000 to 350,000.

There are two other pieces of evidence that give a clue to the size of the Persian army. The first is the fact that Xerxes divided his army into six main groupings or corps, each under the command of a trusted member of his own family. However, once past the Dardenelles and into Europe, only three of these corps are mentioned in any source. It is possible, therefore, that the other three corps were left behind in Asia. This would make military sense. The Greeks could well have decided to launch a pre-emptive strike by transporting a raiding force over the sea to strike at Persian supply lines. During the Ionian revolt, Dionysius of Phocaea had done just this. With only six ships he had cruised the coast of Phoenicia capturing dozens of merchant ships and looting coastal villages. And Xerxes may have been aware of potential trouble at home of which we are unaware.

If Xerxes did, in fact, divide his army like this it might have reduced the total force going into Greece by half. Taking the estimate given above of a mobile field army of around 600,000 men, this would cut down the army invading Greece to around 300,000. This is close to the estimated number of men that an improved water supply could have supported.

The final clue comes from the opening stages of the battle of Thermopylae itself. The Greeks took up their position before the Persians arrived. From Thermopylae they watched the Persian army move in and make camp on the open land between the rivers Spercheius and Asopus. It took the Persians four days to arrive, marching south along the road from Lamia.

Assuming that the Persian army was as well organised as it appears to have been, Xerxes might have been able to move 40,000 or 50,000 men, plus their supplies and transport, past a point on a road in any given day's marching. If the army took four days to arrive, then it would have been about 200,000 strong.

This matches fairly well with estimates already given. By the time Xerxes reached Thermopylae he would have needed to detach troops to occupy Thessaly, to overawe Epirus and to guard his supply lines. As we shall see, he also had strong bodies of cavalry riding out across northern Greece on a variety of duties. These detachments, together with sickness, may have cumulatively accounted for between 50,000 and 100,000 men.

As can be seen there is no real need to discount either Herodotus's fabulous total, nor tales of rivers running dry, as pure nonsense. They are both consistent with a Persian army of around 300,000 men crossing into Europe. This also matches approximately with the statement made by Herodotus's contemporary Plato, in an aside on another subject, that Xerxes led 360,000 men to Greece.

It is not mere numbers that make an army effective. The quality of the men and their equipment, their training and morale are critical. Just how good were the Persian soldiers and their weapons? And how effective were they in combat?

Of the various peoples that sent contingents to Xerxes, only a few are specifically mentioned as being in combat in Greece. To say the least they were a mixed bunch. Among the cavalry the Guards, Persians, Medes, Cissians, Bactrians and Indians are recorded. Of the infantry the Immortals, Persians and Medes are mentioned often, with the Indians, Arians, Armenians, Phrygians, Lydians, Mysians and Thracians being mentioned less frequently. Undoubtedly other troops were present, but did not make it into the written record.

The most important troops in Xerxes's army were the Immortals, his personal guard. This unit gained its name because it was always at its full strength of 10,000 men. As soon as a soldier died or retired, his place was taken by a soldier promoted from other units. It is worth noting, in passing, the emphasis that the ancient sources place on this fact. Clearly all other units were not kept at full strength and were usually well below their nominal numbers.

Only Persians or Medes were eligible to serve as Immortals, as these two peoples were the historic base from which the empire had been formed. Competition to join the unit must have been fierce for these were the only full-time, professional soldiers in the Persian Empire. They were paid handsomely and provided with glamorous uniforms as well as comfortable quarters and plentiful food. They were even allowed to take their wives and children with them on campaign.

When on duty at home, or attending ceremonial occasions, the Immortals were a gorgeous sight. Each man was dressed in a full length tunic, reaching almost to the ankles, loosely cut and gathered at the waist by a cloth belt. The sleeves were wide and pleated. There was no uniform colour nor pattern to the tunic, each man choosing his own brightly coloured cloth and embroidery. In chilly weather, a tighter tunic with long, narrow sleeves was worn as underwear. The hair and full beard were elaborately coiffured, and topped by a turban-like headdress. On campaign, however, the Immortals were dressed and equipped much as were the ordinary infantry drawn from the Persians and Medes.

Together with the Cissians and Hyrkanians, who were similarly equipped, the Persians and Medes were the most useful and effective troops in the imperial army. It is likely that Xerxes took the bulk of these men with him into Greece. Although raised by levy, as were all troops in the army, it seems that these men were specially favoured. It is thought that they were paid and supplied from the imperial treasury and there is some indication that their equipment was likewise provided for them. These were the men who had won the empire in the first instance and, in the last resort, the power of Xerxes rested on their fighting abilities.

A Persian in his finest dress. He carries a heavy spear, wears light armour beneath his colourful robe and has a composite bow slung over his shoulder, together with a quiver of arrows. It is not clear from the ancient sources if the Persians wore this elaborate outfit on campaign, but it is likely that they adopted the more practical Median outfit most of the time and retained their distinctive national dress for parades and other occasions.

A Mede infantryman in campaign equipment. This man wears a long tunic over tight trousers, practical gear for long marches through difficult terrain. His head is covered by a cloth to provide protection from the sun. His spear is relatively short and light, while the shield would have been made of wicker covered with painted leather or fabric. The bow, carried over the shoulder, was of composite construction but was relatively weak compared to later weapons.

A Mysian soldier. These men were typical of the large numbers of more primitive tribesmen liable for service in the Persian army. He carries two spears with small heads, a small round, wooden shield and wears a conical helmet. His clothes are of wool and he has no armour. These men were of little use in battle, but helped to provide manual labour for road construction, bridge building and other tasks usual to an army on campaign.

A Thracian peltast. These lightly equipped men took their name from the curious, crescent-shaped shield that was called a pelta. The pelta was made of lightweight wooden construction, overlaid with colourful fabric. This man wears typical Thracian costume with a short tunic, long cloak and soft hat. He carries a number of short, throwing javelins with which he would harry enemy troops to disrupt their formation before the main clash of battle occurred. At this date the Thracians served with the Persian army, but would later act as mercenaries for most of the nations in the eastern Mediterranean.

On campaign the men wore a thigh-length tunic over trousers. The outer tunic shown on carvings was of a thin, lightweight material. Underneath the men wore armour of varying types. Most common was a tunic on to which were sewn small iron scales that overlapped to provide flexible protection. The head was covered by a padded cloth hood known as the tiara. The shield was a lightweight affair made of woven wickerwork, over which was fixed a leather covering. It was held at the centre by the left hand gripping a wooden bar. A domed metal boss covered the hand.

The main offensive weaponry consisted of a lightweight, recurved bow from which were shot short arrows tipped with iron arrowheads. For close combat, these men carried a heavy spear about six feet long. The broad bladed spearhead was some nine inches long and five inches broad, socketed on to the shaft. The butt end was equipped with a heavy metal globe, the shape traditionally based on the pomegranate. Immortals were distinguished by having a silver pomegranate, while officers had gold pomegranates. If the spear broke, each man had a dagger with a foot-long blade to use when at very close quarters.

In battle these core troops were rarely used until others, men less valued by the Persian monarch, had softened up the enemy first. When they did move, it was according to a pre-arranged plan. First they advanced to within bow range of the enemy formation. Here they halted and lay down their shields and spears. The bows were then used to shower the enemy with a dense flight of arrows. The Persians were famed for their high rate of shooting, rather than for their accuracy. By sending forward around 20 arrows per man in perhaps as little as three minutes, the Persians hoped to inflict casualties on the enemy that would cause them to lose formation.

Then it was time for the key blow. Snatching up their shields and spears, the men charged forward in a dense mass. If all went to plan, the Persians would reach the enemy before he had time to reform his ranks and formation after the damage inflicted by the arrows. Often the sheer impact of several thousand men charging at full run with levelled spears would be enough to break the enemy and put him to flight. If not, the spears were used for thrusting and stabbing, while the shields parried blows. Only in an emergency was the dagger used in combat.

Although the Persians, Medes and others similarly equipped fought to a plan and in formation, they effectively operated individually. Each man thrust as he saw the opportunity, and parried when he needed to do so. Good vision and hearing were essential to this style of fighting. Each man needed to be able to see the enemy around him, to hear orders shouted from behind and to be aware if a comrade fell so that he could react accordingly. This, in turn, meant that any helmet had to be open and non-restrictive. In practice, no helmet was worn and the only head defence was the padded tiara.

Of the other units we know to have followed Xerxes to Greece, the most useful would have been the Thracians. Living just to the north of Greece, the

Thracians would have been familiar with Greek weapons and tactics. They wore no armour, preferring to remain unencumbered by anything other than their distinctive crescent-shaped shield. The shield was known as the *pelta*, so these men were sometimes referred to as peltasts. Equally distinctive was the long cloak, which was worn hitched up over a belt in action.

Thracian weaponry was restricted to a handful of light javelins and a short, stout dagger. These were not men to stand and fight in a pitched battle. They preferred to raid, skirmish and ambush. They were not, however, without their uses in a battle. They could be sent forward to hurl their light javelins at the enemy. Not only did these inflict casualties, but they would also penetrate and stick in shields made of leather or wicker. A shield with the added weight of a javelin would be cumbersome to use, while it would be all too easy inadvertently to hit a comrade while wielding the shield in self-defence. Any man who found himself with a shield holding a javelin would have to take it off his arm and pull the javelin out. Not only did this leave him vulnerable, but would also serve to disrupt the formation in which he stood.

Also equipped with javelins were the Phrygians and Armenians. These two groups also carried a small, round wooden shield and a thrusting spear. These men wore helmets which were most probably made from woven ropes of boiled leather. They were dressed in a tunic worn over trousers and were noted for the quality of their knee-high boots. Although the preferred tactics of these fighters are not recorded, their equipment indicates how they would have fought. They would have followed a similar battle plan to the Persians and Medes, throwing their javelins to disorder an enemy before charging forward with spear and shield.

The Arians wore calf-length boots and baggy trousers with a knee-length tunic of patterned cloth. They carried a heavy spear, but no shield, so their use at close quarters is open to question. The most useful weapon of these people was a composite bow which was habitually carried in a case slung from the belt which held the tunic closed. With this weapon, the Arians could outrange most other bows then in use and provided useful distance hitting power.

The Indians seem to have come to war equipped only with a bow made from a single stave and of moderate power. Contemporary Indian armies are known to have included heavier infantry, but if the Persians raised such men from their Indian provinces, they did not take them to Greece in 480BC.

The Mysians were a pastoral people who herded goats and sheep through the highlands of what is now western Turkey. Their only weapons were light javelins that often lacked a metal tip. The wood was simply sharpened to a point and hardened in a campfire. These men also carried small wooden shields and wore simple conical helmets, which may also have been made from wood.

Interestingly, these poorly equipped Mysians were brigaded together with the Lydians. The Lydians were equipped with heavy armour, similar to that of the Greeks, so it may have been that the otherwise poorly armed Mysians were intended to provide missile weaponry. On the other hand, they may have been taken along as manual labour. Every army needs men to dig latrines, carry water and gather firewood. If this were not the case, it is difficult to see how Xerxes expected these men to be useful to him in the campaign.

It is interesting to note that all the infantry that we know Xerxes took with him to Greece were equipped with missile weapons of one sort or another. The infantry who lacked such weapons, such as the Milyae, armed only with a thrusting spear, or even the famed Assyrians with heavy shield and spear, are not mentioned. Perhaps they remained with that part of the army left in Asia.

Undoubtedly this arrangement was on the advice of his commanders who had fought, and lost, at Marathon. They would have been able to advise Xerxes that the armoured Greek infantry could defeat equal numbers of Persian or Mede infantry in close combat. The Greeks were, however, famously lacking in missile weaponry. They typically had a few slingers accompanying their armies, and sometimes hired mercenary archers from Crete. It may be that Xerxes hoped to use his bowmen and javelin throwers to slaughter the Greeks from a distance. That would certainly negate the Greek advantage at close quarters revealed at Marathon. Failing that, Xerxes could always rely on vastly superior numbers simply to overwhelm any Greeks who dared to oppose his invasion.

Xerxes had one other key weapon to deploy in the land battles that would give him a decided advantage: cavalry. Xerxes would have known that the Greeks delayed the battle at Marathon for several days, attacking only after the Persian cavalry had left the camp on the raid towards Athens. The lesson was clear: The Greeks wanted to avoid cavalry, which must mean that they were frightened of it.

The steeply mountainous land of Greece was not good country for horses. The few pockets of flat land were more productively used growing olives, grain and other human foods than being put down to grass to feed horses. In most Greek states, only the richest men could afford to own a horse. These were used for religious and ceremonial parades, but had no place in warfare.

The Persian cavalry would, therefore, have had the field almost to themselves. Xerxes sent all the way to his Indian provinces for their cavalry, so it must be assumed that he had a particular role in mind for them. The Indian cavalry came equipped with a bow of moderate power and a sheaf of light arrows. It can be assumed that they were used to scout and reconnoitre enemy territory. It may be that their presence is another example of Xerxes choosing exotic fighters deliberately to impress the Greeks with the far flung nature of his empire. Certainly, the Indian cavalry do not feature in any accounts of pitched battles.

Xerxes will have had more faith on the battlefield in his units of Guard, Persian and Mede cavalry. The Guards were brigaded with the Immortals and probably shared their privileges, though they would have been equipped in similar fashion to the Persian and Mede horsemen. They rode to battle dressed and equipped as their infantry colleagues. Each had a bow and a stout thrusting spear. There is some doubt as to whether they carried a shield into battle. It is shown on carvings, but is absent from written accounts. A shield may have been useful in combat, but would have been cumbersome in fast manoeuvring. Perhaps a shield was carried, but was frequently discarded in action. Also present in the invasion army were Bactrian horsemen. These men carried bows, and these were the principal weapon, although the Bactrians were also equipped with thrusting spears.

As with all cavalry of this date, Xerxes' horsemen lacked either stirrups or complex saddles. Most men would have sat on a blanket or padded leather seat secured to the horse by a simple girth. This would have inevitably given the rider a more precarious seat than the modern rider. On the other hand, the bridle was modern in all but detail and would have given the rider firm control over his mount.

There has been much debate as to how effective horsemen were in battle at this date. Skilled horsemen could shoot arrows accurately from a moving horse, and less experienced men from a stationary horse. The effectiveness of the spear is debatable.

With the added height advantage of sitting on a horse, the cavalry could presumably thrust over the shield of a man on foot and inflict damaging downward wounds. They also had the advantage of speed, being able to gallop up to attack a weak point in the enemy's formation before it could be reinforced, or to ride off to safety if danger threatened. But to be truly effective in battle, horsemen need to be able to use the momentum of the horse moving at speed. The impact of horse and rider is capable of simply crashing through infantry formations and trampling enemies underfoot. It is generally thought that riders of the time did not have a secure enough seat on their mounts to perform this sort of attack. Although sources relating to the Thermopylae campaign are unclear on the point, cavalry do seem to have carried out charges in other campaigns around this time. It may be that co-ordinated charges were performed with some degree of success, albeit not as effectively as would be the case later in history.

Such was the avalanche of humanity that Xerxes was preparing to march toward Greece. Clearly he had thought carefully about the types of troops to take with him, ensuring he had men equipped in a fashion that would be useful against the Greeks. He was also bringing as many men as he could, given the constraints put upon him.

Before the army marched there was an ugly scene which reveals much about both Xerxes and the nature of his system of rule. Among the many prominent men who had been forced to send their sons to join the army, as much as hostages as soldiers, was Pythius of Lydia. This Greek merchant and landowner of legendary wealth had remained loyal to Persia during the rebellion of the Greek cities. He had later sought to prove his loyalty by giving Darius a vine for his garden. The gift became legendary, being made of solid gold, with jewels as grapes.

When Xerxes sent to Pythius asking for support for the coming invasion of Greece, Pythius responded by offering his entire treasury of cash. This huge sum amounted to bullion equivalent to 3,993,000 of the new gold coins, known as darics, which Darius had introduced only a short while before. Xerxes turned down the gift, sending Pythius 7,000 darics to bring his treasury up to the round four million.

Now, Pythius felt secure enough in the King of Kings's favour to ask a favour. At a banquet the evening before the army marched, he obtained permission to approach Xerxes and asked, humbly, that one of his sons be allowed to stay behind to help him with his business dealings rather than march with the army.

Xerxes exploded in fury. Perhaps suspecting treachery, or at least impertinence he turned on Pythius. "When I, in person, am marching to war with my sons and brothers and friends – you, my slave, whose duty it is to march with me with every member of your house. You dare to mention your son to me." Pythius was thrown out, but worse was to follow. Xerxes sent the royal executioners to find the eldest son of Pythius. The young man was killed immediately. His body was then sliced in two, one half being tied to a wooden stake on either side of the main road out of Sardis.

As the army marched out, it passed between the bloody, butchered halves of the son of loyal Pythius. Nobody could be in any doubt of the determination and terrible anger of the Great King. But if this appalling act was designed to forestall desertion or treachery, it may have been performed in the wrong place. The loyalty of the army was not in doubt. Very different was the state of the fleet which was mustering, at the command of Xerxes, at Cyme on the coast of Lydia.

As with the army, Herodotus provides a detailed breakdown of the numbers of ships and where they came from. Unlike the information about the army, there is every reason to believe the figures that Herodotus gives. It is far easier to count a few hundred ships in port, than to number tens of thousands of moving men. In addition we have independent corroboration of the numbers of ships that countries could send to war that are very similar to those given by Herodotus, but for different conflicts.

The fleet that gathered at Cyme was made up of both warships and merchant ships. The latter were to carry supplies for both fleet and army, as well as carrying troops on any amphibious operations that Xerxes might order. At this date, merchant ships came in a variety of shapes and sizes, but a typical craft would have been around 13 metres in length, four metres in the beam and drawn about two metres of draft. These ships were short, stumpy vessels, which carried a single large mast on which was rigged a single spar carrying a rectangular sail. Some of the more advanced designs may have also had a second mast, projecting forward from the bows, which carried a second, much smaller sail. We know that there were larger vessels, up to 25 metres long, but these seem to have been rare.

The smaller merchant ships could carry about 50 tonnes of merchandise. Dry goods, such as grain, were packed into sacks but oil, wine and other wet goods were stored in pottery amphorae, carefully stacked to ensure they remained upright and did not move about in even the roughest weather. Herodotus says that 3,000 merchant ships set out on the invasion of Greece, but admits that this is really only an estimate. Given the quantities of supplies to be shifted, however, this is not a ridiculous figure and the maritime provinces of the Persian Empire could have supplied such a fleet.

Unlike the warships, merchant ships stayed in the water all the time. They were not hauled on shore for the winter, nor to escape summer storms. They were built to cope with rough weather and could ride out seas that would swamp the more delicate warships. They were not, however, unsinkable and most merchant commanders were wary of putting to sea if bad weather threatened, hastening to the nearest port if caught in a blow. During the campaign that followed, Xerxes more than once demanded his ships sail when the captains were reluctant to do so. He did not understand the sea, and his merchant ships suffered for his mistakes.

When entering or leaving port, the captains could not rely on their sails. To get in and out of harbour a captain would have his ship towed by local tugs, powered by oarsmen, who hired themselves out for the purpose. This too proved to be a problem in the campaign. On an average day no more than a few ships would enter or leave even the busiest harbour, so a couple of tugs were all that was required. But when the Great King's fleet came in sight, hundreds of ships would want to be towed at the same time. Congestion, confusion and delay were the inevitable results.

The warships were not quite so threatened by bad weather when close enough to shore as they could be hauled up on to any convenient beach to avoid a storm. But as we will see when we look at the construction and tactics of warships in the Greek fleet, warships had their own problems. Far from home, the Persian fleet would have more difficulties than the Greeks, operating in their home waters.

The great war fleet gathering on Xerxes command numbered 1,207 ships. Of these, some would be useful for various purposes. The ships from Egypt were heavier ships carrying more soldiers than was normal and even the rowers were armed. It is reasonable to presume that these ships specialised in boarding tactics. The Cilicians also had armed crews and probably fought in similar fashion. The Phoenician ships were lighter, faster vessels which were used most often for ramming. They were generally reckoned to be the best in the Persian fleet.

Although the Persians came from an inland plateau and had no experience of the sea, Xerxes put Persians in command of the fleet. He must have known that the loyalty of many of his ships' captains and crews was in doubt. The Greeks of Ionia, Doria, Aeolia, the Cycladic Islands and the Hellespont might desert to join their fellow Greeks if they felt able to do so. Moreover, Egypt had rebelled only a few years before and the Egyptians might not be too keen to fight for Xerxes.

To command the Egyptians, Xerxes appointed his brother Achaemenes, who was also commander in chief of the fleet as a whole. To command the squadrons of Ionians and Carians, Xerxes put his half-brother Ariabignes. The rest of the fleet was divided between Prexaspes and Megabazus, both senior Persian noblemen. None of these men had any previous experience of commanding fleets and, in practice, must have relied upon advice from more seasoned men in their flotillas. Clearly Xerxes preferred loyalty in his fleet commanders to skill. It is an understandable choice, but one that would cost him dear.

This mighty fleet was not as threatening as it may have looked. Many of the ships brought to Cyme were old, battered and quite unfit for use in battle. But then Xerxes had no intention of sending these older ships to fight the Greek warships. He had quite another purpose for them.

The Persian fleet at sea. The large square sails shown here were of use only if the wind was favourable.

The Persian Army according to Herodotus

Unit	Strength
Infantry	
Immortals	10,000
Persians	60,000
Medes	60,000
Cissians	60,000
Hyrkanians	60,000
Assyrians & Chaldaeans	60,000
Bactrians & Sakae	60,000
Indians & East Ethiopians	60,000
Arians	60,000
Parthians & Chorasmians	60,000
Sogdians	60,000
Bandarians & Dadicae	60,000
Caspians	60,000
Sarangae	60,000
Pactyes	60,000
Utians & Mycians	60,000
Phricanians	60,000
Arabians & Ethiopians	60,000
Libyans	60,000
Paphlagonians & Matieni	60,000
Mariandeni, Ligyes & Syrians	60,000
Armenians & Phrygians	60,000
Lydians & Mysians	60,000
Thracians	60,000
Pisidians, Cabelees & Milyae	60,000
Moschi & Tibareni	60,000
Macrones & Mossynoeci	60,000
Mares & Colchians	60,000
Alarodians & Saspires	60,000
Exiles	60,000
TOTAL	1,750,000

Cavalry

Guards	1,000
Guards	1,000
Persians & Sagartians	18,000
Medes	10,000
Cissians	10,000
Bactrians & Sakae	10,000
Indians	10,000
Caspians	10,000
Paricanians	10,000
Arabs (mounted on camels)	20,000
TOTAL	100,000

The Persian Fleet according to Herodotus

Unit	Strength
Phoenicia	300
Egypt	200
Cyprus	150
Cilicia	100
Pamphylia	30
Lycia	50
Caria	70
Ionia	100
Dorians	30
Aeolians	60
Hellespontines	100
Cycladic Islands	17
TOTAL	1,207

CHAPTER 3

The Greek League

A Greek javelin head. The weapon was designed for lightness so that it could be thrown with accuracy over a fair distance. The haft was socketed into the head and held in place by glue.

A Greek spear head. The broader blade and heavier construction shows that this was used for thrusting.

A Greek sword. The weapon is short, but heavy and could be used to thrust as easily as to cut.

As the mighty Persian host set out from Sardis, the Greeks were meeting once again at the Isthmus of Corinth to decide what to do. It was probably late in April when the meeting took place, and it lasted several days. By this date it was clear to all the Greek states that Xerxes meant business and that he was bringing the mightiest army and largest navy that anyone had ever heard of. Quite obviously the time for debate was over, it was time to take decisions.

Some Greek states had already made their decisions. They had opted to accept the deal on offer from Xerxes and failed to turn up to the meeting. Others were playing for time, coming to the meeting but not making any firm commitment.

By the time of this meeting, too, the Greeks had other information that they had not possessed the previous autumn. They had the reports of the spies they had sent to Sardis, so they knew the vast size of the army that was marching against them. They also had the answers brought by the various envoys sent out the previous autumn. And they also had the pronouncements of the Oracle at Delphi - which were to prove crucial both to this meeting and to the subsequent campaign.

The Delphic Oracle and its sayings are perhaps the most misunderstood feature of the entire Thermopylae campaign. And yet they were crucial to what happened. In view of the great importance of the oracle at this decisive time, it is as well to be clear about what the oracle was and what it was not.

There are two common modern misapprehensions about the oracle. The first is that the oracle produced prophecies or predictions of the future. Although some of the oracle's pronouncements did, indeed, take the form of prophecies, this was not what the oracle was about.

According to legend, the oracle at Delphi originated when Apollo, god of the sun and the arts, fought and killed a gigantic serpent named Python. To commemorate the act he set up an altar to himself, but could find no mortals nearby to act as priests. He forced a passing ship from Crete to come ashore and care for the temple of Delphi. In return for their devotion, Apollo established the oracle through which he would speak to them and tell them the plans of the gods.

This is what the oracle actually was: Apollo acting as an intermediary passing on divine information – and information about the divine – to mortals. Given the capricious, squabbling and selfish nature of the Greek gods, it was as much gossip column as it was a source of prophecy. Those who received a message from the Delphic Oracle had to bear in mind that the gods might change their minds, that they did not always make themselves very clear and that Apollo might have misunderstood what another god had told him.

In the author's opinion, the second misconception about the oracle at Delphi is that it was, quite simply, a con. It is all too easy in this secular age to assume that the ancient priests at Delphi did not believe in Apollo any more than we do today. The priests at Delphi have been accused of always issuing ambiguous prophecies so that whatever happened, they could claim to have been right. The most famous statement of this kind was given to King Croesus of Lydia in 549BC when he asked the oracle if he should go to war against the Persian Empire. The oracle replied that if he began a war by invading the Persian province of Cappadocia he would destroy a great kingdom. Assuming the oracle meant Persia, Croesus duly attacked Cappadocia. In the event it was Lydia that was destroyed.

However, as we shall see, some of the utterances of the Delphic Oracle were simple and direct. The priests did not always hedge their bets.

In the same vein, many contend that the sayings of the oracle were nothing more than the considered opinions of the priests. Effectively, they were giving advice couched in divine terms. Men from all over the Greek world came to Delphi to ask the oracle questions. This would give the priests an opportunity to probe for information from the supplicant's home city. They could, therefore, be in possession of facts that meant they could give sensible advice. There is no way to disprove this thesis, though it does depend entirely on the assumption that the priests were charlatans who no more believed in Apollo than do modern scholars. Others are even less charitable to the priests. They claim that the oracle would give whatever message it was paid to give. Under this thesis it is assumed that kings or nobles simply paid cash to get the prediction they wanted. This would then be used to persuade others that they were aided by the gods.

The counter-argument is that Delphi retained its reputation for centuries. Although, as related later, there was one instance of a false utterance gained for cash, this cannot have been usual. If it had been, then word would eventually have leaked out as to what was going on. The messages of the Delphic Oracle would have been given all the credence we reserve for newspaper horoscopes. Since this was clearly not the case, bribery cannot have been a usual activity at Delphi.

The way in which the oracle was consulted seems to indicate that everyone concerned believed absolutely that it was the god Apollo who spoke. Those wanting to consult the oracle arrived at Delphi after a stiff climb up the sacred mountain. There they washed themselves in the sacred waters of the Castalia spring. They were then welcomed into the sacred precinct through a gate by the priests. They were led up the Sacred Road, a path flanked by temples and monuments, to the front of the Temple of Apollo. Inside this large and imposing building was the dark and gloomy room of the adyton, where the oracles were given. The priestess, known as the Pythia, sat on a three-legged stool over a bottomless crevice in the rock from which issued noxious gas. By breathing in this gas, the priestess fell into a trance, which allowed her to talk with Apollo.

Those seeking advice from the oracle were led forward by the priests to read out to the Pythia their question. The Pythia would then respond. Sometimes the message was quite clear, but at other times the priestess spouted random words or even apparent gibberish. If the questioner could not catch what was said, the priests would interpret the ramblings of the Pythia.

Thus did Apollo speak to mankind. For the Greeks this was a serious business. They believed that the gods took a close interest in the affairs of humans, even going so far as to take on the form of mortals to influence events. The gods could cause earthquakes, blow up storms or make men mad. To get an inside knowledge of what the deities were up to and what they planned was valuable indeed. The messages given by the Delphic oracle to the Greek states that consulted it were taken most seriously. We do not know everything that the Pythia told the messengers on the eve of the Persian invasion, but some of the enunciations have been preserved.

When the envoys from the conference held at Corinth came to the powerful city of Argos, for instance, they were given the exact message Apollo had sent to Argos by way of Delphi. It was this:

"Loathed by your neighbours, loved by the gods
Hold your spear within and sit upon your guard.
Guard the head well, and the head will save the body."

This oracle had been interpreted as an exhortation to the Argives to stand on the defensive and guard their borders against all comers. In other words, they should be neutral in the coming war. Nevertheless, the Argives said, they were willing to join the war against Persia on two conditions. The first was that they should be granted a sacred 30-year truce by their old rival Sparta, and secondly that they should have joint command of the army.

One of the envoys was from Sparta. He declared that he could not grant a 30-year truce on his own, but would carry the message to his kings for them to decide. As to command of the army, he offered to put the Argive commander on an equal footing with the Spartan kings. The Argives realised this meant they would be outvoted by two to one on most issues and rejected the offer. The envoys were told to leave Argos by nightfall or risk instant death. They left.

Unknown to the other Greeks at the time, Argos had already received a messenger from Xerxes. The message he carried began by repeating the old legend that the Persians took their name from Perses, a son of Perseus, the mythical first King of Argos. Having thus invoked a mythical connection between the two peoples, Xerxes continued "You should therefore take no part in the war. If I am as successful as I expect, there is no people I shall hold in greater esteem than you."

It is likely that the Argives had already decided on neutrality on the basis of the oracle and of Xerxes's message. The conditions they demanded from the envoys were put in the expectation they would be refused. Thus Argos stayed out of the war while being able to claim that they had been willing to join.

Crete too received an oracle from Delphi. This ran:

"Foolish men, do you not still resent all the tears which Minos in his anger caused you to weep after you helped Menelaus? Was he not angry because the Greeks did not help you to avenge his death at Camicus, whereas you did help them to avenge the rape by a foreign prince of a woman from Sparta?"

This was a reference to the Trojan war. According to legend, that war had begun when Helen, wife of King Menelaus of Sparta, had been seduced and abducted by Paris, prince of Troy. The Cretans had joined the war on the side of the Greeks but had been badly let down by their allies. The Cretans took this reminder as an instruction to remain neutral, which they then did.

It is not recorded if the Corcyrians consulted Delphi or not, though it would be surprising if they did not. Whatever answer they got, they welcomed the envoys from Corinth and at once promised to send their entire fleet to join the anti-Persian alliance.

The answer from Gelon of Syracuse was less welcome. As ruler of much of Sicily, Gelon could put into the field an impressive army of 20,000 hoplites supported by 2,000 archers, 2,000 slingers plus 2,000 heavy and 2,000 light cavalry. He also had 200 triremes in his fleet. However, Gelon had troubles of his own. He expected the spring to bring an invasion of Sicily by the Carthaginians and knew he would need all his resources to defeat it.

Hoping to keep his options open, Gelon offered to take his entire armed might to Greece but only on condition that he was given sole command of the allied forces. The condition was unacceptable, as Gelon must have known it would be. Professing friendship, Gelon sent the Greek envoys on their way. It is possible that Gelon intended to join the Greeks if the Carthaginian invasion did not take place. In the event the Carthaginians did attack and Gelon stayed in Sicily. It has been suggested that the

Carthaginians were acting in alliance with Xerxes. This may have been so, but it is just as likely that they simply decided to take advantage of the Persian attack to strike at Gelon.

When the Greeks met again at Corinth, probably in late April, the news was not particularly good. No help could be expected from Sicily, Argos or Crete. Thebes and the cities of Boeotia were refusing to commit themselves. And although Corcyra had offered help it had yet to materialise.

Events in the core states already determined to fight the Persians were more promising. The powerful Spartan army was ready to march, as were their Peloponnesian allies. Corinth was ready with men and a fleet, while several of the smaller states north of Athens were declaring for resistance to Persia.

Athens itself had experienced a difficult winter. Work to get as many ships as possible into fighting condition had been going on apace, and by the spring the city was able to send to sea the largest war fleet she had ever possessed. The problems had been political.

Arthimius, who lived in Athens with his family, had originally come from Zeleia, a town on the eastern coast of the Aegean Sea that then lay within the Persian Empire. He was caught with far more gold than he had any right to possess. It was assumed that the gold belonged to Xerxes and that Arthimius was busily using it to bribe influential people in Athens to give in to Persia. The populist politician Themistocles had the man and his entire family banished from Athens on pain of death.

The news of a Persian agent active inside Athens cannot have come as a surprise. Although the stated objective of the Persian invasion was the utter destruction of Sparta and Athens, things were not that simple. Whatever the justifications Xerxes gave for the war, his main aim was to add the states of Greece to his empire. If this could be achieved with little or no fighting, so much the better. And there were plenty of men in Athens who might have been open to Persian persuasions. Faced by the overwhelming might of the Persian Empire, there must have been many men who genuinely believed that it would be best for Athens to try to negotiate a surrender rather than to fight.

If Athens fought and lost, the Persians were going to kill the adult men and sell the women and children into slavery. The temples of the gods would be destroyed, the entire city levelled and all the lands of Attica divided up among foreigners. Athens and the Athenians would, quite simply, be brutally wiped from the face of the earth. It was an appalling prospect.

There might not be much of a deal on the table from Xerxes, but for men who believed that resistance was useless there was a prospective way out. Hipparchus, the exiled brother-in-law of the former dictator Hippias, was living at the Persian court as a guest of Xerxes. He was not alone, for several members of the wealthy Alcmaeonid family were likewise in exile for various reasons and had congregated in Persia. It was well known that several of the richer, more aristocratic families opposed the new-fangled democracy of Athens and preferred the old days when only noblemen were eligible for public office. There was a continuing fear that such men might prefer to rule as placemen of Xerxes than remain free but out of office.

Even among those who wholeheartedly favoured war, there were disagreements. For most of the previous decade Themistocles and his supporters had retained a firm grip on power in Athens. They favoured the naval policy as a means of defending their city. Others, however, preferred to put their trust in the army. It had been the army, after all, which had won the Battle of Marathon ten years earlier. Relying on the army was a tried and tested policy which had obvious attractions, though it took little account of the massively larger invasion force now being mustered by the Persians.

In February the internal tensions at Athens threatened to come to a head in the annual elections of the generals. Themistocles was, of course, the candidate of those who were determined to fight Persia, and to do so by sea. He was opposed by Epicydes, a nobleman who was famous as one of the greatest orators in Greece. Epicydes made a series of speeches which managed to appeal to those who favoured the army, and to those who opposed war altogether. Quite what his own views might have been he carefully avoided stating.

As the election approached, Themistocles began to get worried. More and more citizens seemed to be won over by Epicydes. Desperate to keep the naval policy intact for the coming war, Themistocles decided on a bold step. He went to see Epicydes and offered him a large cash bribe in silver coin if he withdrew from the election. Epicydes took the money, pulled out of the election and retired from public life. Thus it was that Themistocles was elected unopposed and led the Athenian delegation to the reconvened meeting at Corinth. He was aware, however, that there were many in Athens who did not fully approve of his policies.

We know as little as ever of the internal affairs of Sparta during the winter of 491- 490 following the autumn meeting in Corinth, but the fact that Sparta sent to Delphi for advice from the oracle is well known. The pronouncement of the oracle was not particularly cheering.

> "Hear your fate, O dwellers in Sparta of the wide spaces;
> Either your famed, great town must be sacked by Perseus's sons,
> Or, if that not happen, the whole land of Lacedaemon
> Shall mourn the death of a king of the house of Heracles,
> For not the strength of lions or of bulls shall hold him,
> Strength against strength; for he has the power of Zeus,
> And will not be checked till one of these two he has consumed."

There were two things about this pronouncement that must have shocked the Spartans who heard it. The first was that the Persians were said to have the power of Zeus. Given that Apollo, who spoke through the oracle, could be relied upon to know the minds of his fellow gods, this meant that the chief god of the Greeks was on the side of the Persians. To a religious people such as the Spartans, this must have been deeply unnerving.

Second, the oracle described the Persians as "Perseus's sons". This, as explained earlier, referred to the mythical links between Persia and Sparta's old enemy of Argos. Again, not good news for the Spartans that Apollo was thinking along these lines. And depressing that Apollo seemed to be taking the Persian claims at face value.

That apart, the message was clear. The royal families of Sparta claimed descent from the mythical hero Heracles, so the oracle was saying that either a king of Sparta must die or that Sparta would be destroyed. It was not exactly an appealing choice, particularly for the kings concerned. The question was, of course, which king?

Sparta was ruled by two kings, one drawn from each of two branches of the royal family. Uniquely in Spartan history, however, there was a third king: Demaratus. A few years earlier a scandal had enveloped the Spartan thrones. King Demaratus had been born less than eight months after his parents were married. At the time it was assumed he had been born prematurely, but after he inherited his father's throne, Demaratus fell out with his fellow king, Cleomenes.

Cleomenes got his friends to revive the old worries about the paternity of Demaratus. The doubts about Demaratus became so widespread that something had to be done. Cleomenes persuaded the leading citizens to send a delegation to Delphi to ask advice. Cleomenes had, meanwhile, paid a massive bribe to the priest Cobon at Delphi to ensure that an answer was given that undermined Demaratus. Cobon in turn persuaded the priestesss Perialla to deliver the pronouncement Cleomenes wanted.

When the answer came back from Delphi, the Spartans deposed Demaratus and put his brother Leotychides on the vacant throne. Demaratus then left Sparta to seek a new life elsewhere. As a Spartan he could expect to find employment as a mercenary commander almost any-where, but as a former Spartan king he could command a particularly high price. And nobody was willing to pay more than Darius, King of Kings. Darius appointed Demaratus to be governor of Pergamum. When Xerxes became ruler of the Persian Empire, he confirmed Demaratus as governor, and frequently consulted him on military matters. When he mustered his army to invade Greece, Xerxes summoned Demaratus to join him at Sardis to act as advisor.

The chronology of what followed in Sparta is confused. Some time after Demaratus left, the Spartans discovered that Cleomenes had been behind the gossip and was the source of the trouble. When it was discovered that he had bribed Delphi, the scandal was overwhelming. Cobon and Perialla were stripped of office and exiled from Delphi. (The story is related in book six of Herodotus' *Histories*.) Cleomenes, too, was deposed and fled into exile. His successor was his half brother Leonidas.

In exile, Cleomenes began plotting his return. He tried to recruit other cities for a war against Sparta to reinstate him. The moves came to nothing and he was handed over to the Spartans, who locked him up on the probably spurious grounds that he had gone mad.

Soon afterwards Cleomenes was found dead of multiple stab wounds. The official story put out by the government was that Cleomenes had persuaded a servant to bring him a knife, and had then committed suicide. It was widely believed, however, that he had been murdered on the orders of powerful men in Sparta. Herodotus himself says "My own opinion is that he came to grief as retribution for what he did to Demaratus."

It was bad enough to have one king, Leotychides, on a throne that everyone knew should rightfully belong to the former king in exile in Persia. Having a second king, Leonidas, sitting on a throne previously occupied by a man in prison had been too destabilising with a major war approaching. Cleomenes had had to go. Sparta was not a happy kingdom.

There was, however, some unexpected good news for the meeting at Corinth from Thessaly. The city of Pharsalus had sent a representative, supported by leading citizens from other Thessalian cities, to pledge support for what was now clearly a League determined to fight Persia. The alliance of Thessalian notables seems to have achieved a temporary ascendancy over the pro-Persian Aleuadae, for the message they delivered was this:

"Fellow countrymen, in order to save Thessaly and the whole of Greece, it is necessary to defend the passage past Mount Olympos. We are ready to assist you in the defence of this vital pass, and you, for your part, must send a strong force. If you do not do so, we give you fair warning that we shall come to terms with Persia. We are in an exposed position, and cannot be expected, alone and unassisted, to give our lives merely to save the rest of you. If you are unwilling to send us aid, you cannot compel us to fight your battle for you. For sheer inability is stronger than any compulsion. We shall try to devise some means of saving ourselves."

The message came at a critical moment in the discussions. Debate was focussing on what strategy to use to defeat the Persian invasion. There were, essentially, two ideas being floated at the conference from those determined to fight: A land strategy and a sea strategy.

Those supporting a land strategy pointed to the fact that the previous Persian attack, that of 490BC, had been defeated on land at Marathon. They argued that the Greek hoplites could defeat the Persian army so long as they fought on ground that favoured the Greeks. There was some disagreement as to where the battle should be fought. Obviously it would need to be somewhere with secure flanks and firm, relatively level ground. But political considerations soon became embroiled with military necessity. Every state wanted the battle fought to the north of their own territory so that they would be spared Persian occupation.

The Peloponnesian states argued that the battle should be fought on the Isthmus of Corinth. This was, indeed, a magnificent defensive position, but it would mean abandoning all territory to the north – including Athens – to the enemy. Others wanted to hold the enemy at Thermopylae, which would save Attica and Boeotia. Others argued for Thaumaki even further north.

Those who preferred a sea strategy pointed out that the Persian army lumbering towards Greece was at least ten times larger than that defeated ten years earlier. And with a powerful Persian fleet in attendance, there was nothing to stop the Persians transporting a large body of troops by sea to outflank any position held by a Greek army. The Persians had actually tried this trick in 490 and had been defeated only by fast marching by the Athenians.

This argument, put forward forcefully by Themistocles of Athens, envisaged the key engagement being fought at sea. Once the Persian war fleet was defeated, the Greek galleys could destroy the Persian supply fleet and so leave the army short of food and supplies. This would leave the Persian army vulnerable and open to attack.

Neither side was convincing the other, most obviously because neither idea was able to guarantee victory in the face of the overwhelming might of the advancing Persian forces. The intervention of the Thessalians was probably more than welcome. A new argument now began.

It is not entirely clear how well informed the men meeting at Corinth were about conditions in Thessaly. They must have known that the ruling elite of the region was divided on the merits of fighting or capitulating to the Persians. The men who arrived at Corinth showed that those favouring resistance were currently in the ascendant. But how strong was this faction? Would the Thessalians change their minds once the vast host of Xerxes actually arrived on their borders?

The question was of critical importance. Any action fought north of Thessaly would rely heavily on supplies from Thessaly, on troops drawn from Thessaly and on local information.

On the other hand, the option of fighting in northern Thessaly had some obvious attractions. The area was wealthy and productive. Having the Thessalian states on the side of the League would be a major boost in terms of money and manpower. It also helped solve the dispute between the sea and land strategists. The coastline of Thessaly is rocky and inhospitable with only a few small beaches where ships can land. The Persians would have been quite unable to land a powerful outflanking force behind a defensive force in the north. This situation solved the strategic argument and allowed all the delegates at the conference to agree.

There was, however, a serious weakness and it is not at all clear that the men taking the decision knew about it. The pass that flanks Mount Olympos, the Tempe Pass, is not the only route into Thessaly from Macedon. There is a second over the Volustana and Petra passes to Oloosson, and thence into Thessaly by way of the Meluna Pass.

Whether or not the Greeks at Corinth were aware of the problems of holding a defensive line north of Thessaly, they decided to send an army north to do just that. Command was given to a Spartan general named Euanetos and orders sent out to muster an army. The decision was taken. The war would begin at Tempe.

Ancient Corinth, the site of the conference of the Greek states in the face of the Persian threat. Corinth itself remained loyal to the League, providing both men and ships.

CHAPTER 4

The Opening Moves

The Hellespont just to the west of where the bridge of boats was constructed. The narrowness of the strait is clear in this photograph.

The preparations that Xerxes made for his invasion had not been limited to gathering a vast army and immense fleet. Unlike the Greeks, the Persians had experience of handling and moving large forces and knew the importance of logistics. Herodotus and other Greeks were prone to portraying Xerxes' preparations as being inspired by pride. On the whole, however, they were nothing more than sensible military preparations that would be second nature to any modern staff officer.

Thrace was already part of the Persian Empire, so making preparations in this area posed no particular problems. Large stocks of grain were gathered together in guarded stores at intervals along the route. The Persians and Medes, in particular, had a fondness for meat so Xerxes gave orders that herds of livestock were to be bought and, when the time came, herded down ready for slaughter beside the route to be taken by the army. White Cape in Thrace, Tyrodiza, Doriscus and Eion were the places at which the major food dumps were built up, but smaller collections were made all along Xerxes' intended route. Water was of critical importance in this arid land during spring. As we have already noted, the Persian engineers were busy damming rivers and preparing reservoirs to cope with the vast thirst of the enormous army.

The roads also received attention from the Persian workers. Roads in ancient times were often of course rudimentary. Where the ground was firm and drainage reliable they were nothing more than routes across open ground. Marshy areas were often improved by having rocks or bundles of sticks thrown into them to give firmer footing. In mountainous regions, boulders were rolled out of the way and embankments used to widen a track to allow carts to pass. Bridges were not usual, fords being much cheaper to maintain and usually more reliable.

All this was good enough for local traffic and farm carts, but hopelessly inadequate for the vast army and its supply train that would shortly be moving on Greece. A full three years before the invasion was due to take place, engineers were at work. They organised massed labour forces to produce huge quantities of stone chippings that were spread over the roadway. The chips were then pounded down to give a firm, well drained layer that would withstand the tramping of thousands of feet and pummelling of thousands of wheels. The roads were built with such care and skill that even 50 years later they were still reckoned to be the best roads in Thrace.

Where rivers had to be crossed, the engineers broke down banks and dumped large quantities of stone to improve the fords. Where fording would not be possible, they built bridges. At the River Strymon the bridges were probably pontoon constructions, though this is not certain. What is known is that the engineers sacrificed a team of white horses before they began their work. More gruesomely, they finished their work by sacrificing nine local boys and nine girls, burying their bodies under the roadway. This marks the engineers out as definitely not Persian. As a religion Zoroastrianism has no place for human sacrifice. Almost certainly the bridge builders were Phoenicians, for such ritual killing was commonplace in their culture.

Xerxes certainly made use of Phoenician workmen in the preparations taking place in Thrace. They were most prominent in the construction of the Athos Canal. In 492, a Persian fleet had been hit by a storm while rounding the headland at Mount Athos, where sea currents are particularly treacherous. Large numbers of ships were wrecked and hundreds of men killed. With the Persian fleet accompanying the invasion of 480 being several times larger, and also journeying with a huge merchant fleet, Xerxes wanted to take no chances. Rather than risk his ships rounding the cape, he decided to have a canal dug right across the headland.

The work was entrusted to a cousin named Atachaees. This man was famous as being the tallest man in the entire empire, reputedly an astounding 2.48 metres (eight feet). He was also possessed of the loudest voice in the world, which must have been useful when supervising gangs of workmen many hundreds strong.

The canal that Atachaees was to dig proved to be a magnificent feat of engineering. It was wide enough for two triremes to pass each other, or to move along it side by side. Breakwaters were erected at either end to protect the canal from storms and turn it into a gigantic safe anchorage in bad weather. Most impressive of all, the canal did its job. Not a single Persian ship was lost in these waters.

A small war fleet was stationed at Elaeus to guard against a pre-emptive Greek strike, and work began in the spring of 483BC. Teams of workmen had been brought in from various areas of the empire, serving out their military obligations as labourers on the great project. Atachaees began by laying tapes across the narrowest part of the isthmus linking Mount Athos to the mainland. He then divided the route of the canal between the various nationalities present. This made sense, for a massive engineering project of this type is complex enough without language difficulties between foremen and workers.

All the teams set to work, but the Phoenicians won general contempt by starting to dig their section of canal twice as wide as Atachaees had decreed. It was not long before the other teams stopped laughing at the Phoenicians and began copying them. The soft soil collapsed after the teams had dug to a certain depth, except in the Phoenician section where the walls of the canal were sloped.

Finally the canal was finished. It is sad to relate that Atachaees died a few weeks later. He was buried at Acanthus, close by the canal, and a small shrine built over his grave.

It may have been this foresight on the part of the Phoenicians that persuaded Xerxes to employ them on the greatest feat undertaken in preparation of the invasion: the building of bridges over the sea. Between Sardis and Greece were hundreds of kilometres of road, but the most difficult obstacle was clearly going to be the Hellespont, the stretch of salt water that links the Black Sea to the Mediterranean. At Abydos, its narrowest point, the Hellespont is about 1.2 km wide, and a strong current flows toward the southwest. Xerxes had a choice between using ferries or building a bridge to get his army across. He chose to build a bridge.

The decision was rational. It is much quicker to march an army over a bridge than to use ferries shuttling back and forth. The process of marshalling troops to march over a bridge is vastly simpler than dividing them into batches, scrambling into boats and then getting them out again on the far side. And that is if all goes well. If a ferry sinks or capsizes the problems are far worse.

The great difficulty was that the waters were far too deep for piles to be put down, while the distance to be bridged was unprecedented. Xerxes sent for his engineers and told them to solve the problems. Their answer was to build a pontoon bridge. Hundreds of old and decrepit ships were pressed into service as the pontoons and fresh gangs of labourers put to work. The task was handled by teams from Phoenicia and Egypt.

There were, in fact, two bridges. The northern bridge had 360 ships, while that to the south had 314. The Phoenicians lashed their ships together with cables made of flax, while the Egyptians used papyrus. Two cables were strung the length of each bridge, the ships being lashed to them by smaller ropes. Anchors were dropped either side of the growing lines of ships to stop them from drifting before the bridge was complete. Most ingenious of all, ships at intervals of a third of the distance along each bridge were lashed only loosely to the linking cables. These ships were kept manned so that if a through travelling vessel wanted to pass the bridges these semi-loose ships could be untied and rowed out of the way. The passing vessel could then lower its mast and slip under the cables.

Unfortunately for all involved, a terrific storm blew up as the bridges were being secured. The cables parted and the ships were scattered widely across the Hellespont. Xerxes was furious. He began by ordering the execution of the men who had designed the bridges, then turned his rage on the Hellespont itself. It was a potentially humiliating moment for Xerxes,

King of Kings. One of his personal ideas was failing right at the start of the campaign. Drastic action was needed and Xerxes took it. He sent out a number of small boats on which were men armed with long whips. While a host of priests on the shore called out curses and reprimands to the gods of ocean and wind, the men whipped the sea surface and the air as if flogging the gods themselves.

"You salt and bitter stream", the men shouted as they whipped, "your master lays this punishment upon you for injuring him, who never injured you. But Xerxes the King will cross you, with or without your consent. No man sacrifices to you and you deserve the neglect by your acid and muddy waters."

As a devout Zoroastrian, Xerxes did not believe in these pagan gods and so had no fear of annoying them. His audience, however, was very different. The army and navy was made up largely of non-Persians. These men believed firmly in the gods that Xerxes was subjecting to such a public flogging. No doubt they were hugely impressed that their mighty monarch, the King of Kings, could treat gods with such arrogance and impunity. It was a magnificent piece of propaganda theatre and it worked brilliantly. The humiliation of the broken bridge was forgotten and the morale of the army restored.

The bridges were quickly reassembled, the ships put back in place and the cables reattached. This time, each bridge had mixed cables of papyrus and flax to increase strength and rigidity. Then the cables were pulled taut by means of massive wooden windlasses on shore.

Next the roadway was constructed. Planks were laid horizontally between the two cables to form a solid wooden path. These were then covered over with brushwood and soil, that was stamped down to give a firm but yielding surface on which animal hooves could get a good grip. Finally wooden fences were built along both sides of the road so that horses, mules and other animals could not see that they were crossing a bridge at all.

Beyond the Hellespont, instructions were sent to allies and neighbouring states about supplying the army. It was made clear that the King of Kings expected and demanded the support of his friends in the very practical form of food for his men. King Alexander of Macedonia was ordered to prepare a vast supply dump at Therme, and told it was his responsibility to feed the army while it was in Macedonia.

The scale of the cost of supplying the Persian army was recorded at Thasos. This Greek island was free, but remained so only at the behest of the Persian Emperor. A few years previously, Darius had ordered them to dismantle their city walls and the island was obliged to use the port of Abdera on the mainland for their war fleet. Thasos was enormously wealthy due to its gold mines, and kept detailed financial records.

Xerxes informed Thasos that it would be responsible for feeding the army as it passed along the shoreline opposite Thasos. Messengers came from Persia frequently, detailing exactly how much of what types of food would be required. Poultry had to be raised in coops and waterfowl on ponds. Cattle were put to grass and grain ground down for flour. Not only that, but other messengers came giving detailed instructions about the tableware to be provided for the King of Kings and his Persian nobility. Drinking cups were to be of gold and silver, plates of the finest pottery and the tables of quality wood. Even the tent to be made in which Xerxes was to sleep had to be provided exactly to specification.

Antipater, the treasurer of Thasos whose task it was to organise everything for the arrival of the army, estimated that the preparations cost 400 talents. This at a time when the proverbially rich gold mines were producing 300 talents a year. What made the situation so much worse was that after the army had moved on, Antipater found that Xerxes had taken with him the tent, gold cups and silver tableware. Not even the wooden tables were left behind.

The city of Abdera was ordered to feed the army for a single day. The cost of this has not been recorded, but the words of the city's leading citizen Megacreon have. After surveying the damage done to the city's food stores by the passing army, Megacreon called the citizens together and led them to the temples to give thanks to the gods that Xerxes ate only one dinner each day.

As planned, everything was ready by the spring of 480BC. The army was gathered, the route prepared and diplomacy concluded. At the end of March, the campaign began as Xerxes led his army out of Sardis, heading northwest towards Abydos and the bridges to Europe.

While his army toiled forward, Xerxes had a piece of propaganda to enact. He rode to Troy and had the local people show him the sights. Xerxes would have known that this was sacred soil for the Greeks. Their greatest historic epic concerned a joint expedition of all the Greek cities led by Sparta that invaded Asia to besiege and conquer the enormously rich city of Troy. The Greeks had captured Troy, destroyed it and stolen its fabulous wealth.

As at Sardis, Xerxes was making the point that it had been the Greeks who had attacked Asia. His invasion of Greece was justified by the Greek action and was a matter of revenge, not aggression. The point was well made, but Xerxes went further. He now organised a massive and ostentatious sacrifice of 1,000 oxen to the goddess Athene at her shrine at Troy. Again, Xerxes cannot have believed Athene to be a goddess for his own religion did not allow this. The act was pure propagandist theatricals.

Athene was, of course, the patron goddess of the city of Athens. And Xerxes was marching to destroy Athens. But Athene had also been the patron of Perseus, whose son Perses was said to have founded the Persian kingdom. Xerxes was making the point that even the patron goddess of his chief enemy would have divided loyalties in the coming war. And by getting in first with a sacrifice on a monumental scale he was doing his best to buy the favours of the goddess. At least, that is what he hoped the

Greeks would think. Anything that undermined the enemy's morale was a good ploy at this stage.

From Troy, Xerxes led his army to Abydos. Before crossing the Hellespont, Xerxes organised rowing contests between his finest warships in front of his assembled army. Sitting on his white throne, transported for his use on campaign, Xerxes surveyed the awesome military might at his command and declared himself a happy man. Then he burst into tears. One of the few men who dared to speak to Xerxes at such a time was his uncle, Artabanus. Now this grizzled old warrior asked what was causing the Great King to weep so soon after declaring that he was a happy man.

"I was thinking," Xerxes replied, "and it came to my mind how pitifully short human life is. Of all these thousands of men, not one will be alive in a hundred years time."

It was a momentary weakness. Later that day a Persian officer approached Xerxes, hoping to gain favour from his king and commander. He offered Xerxes a dish of fresh figs from Attica, the land around Athens. Xerxes laughed ostentatiously and waved the dish aside. "We will be able to eat all the Athenian figs we want when we get there," he declared. Victory was not a matter of if, but when.

It was at this point that Artabanus, who had previously tried to persuade Xerxes not to invade Greece, tried once more to talk some sense into his nephew. Without actually telling the Great King to call off the campaign, Artabanus did warn him that the two mightiest powers in the world were ranged against the Persian force. When Xerxes scoffed, indicating his vast army and fleet, Artabanus replied "I will tell you what they are: the land and the sea."

To drive his point home, Artabanus continued. "So far as I know there is not a harbour anywhere big enough to receive this fleet of ours and give it protection in the event of storms. There is not a single one on our route . . . And the land itself will become more and more hostile to you the further you advance. The mere distance will starve us. The best man, in my belief, is he who lays his plans warily and then, when the time comes, acts boldly."

Xerxes agreed with his old uncle, but pointed out with some justification that he had taken every precaution that could be taken. Perhaps tiring of the advice he received from Artabanus, Xerxes sent him back to Susa to manage the empire in the absence of the emperor.

The preliminaries over, the army crossed the bridges into Europe and headed for Doriscus. Here the army was halted to take advantage of the plentiful food and water that had been prepared in advance. The fleet of warships was hauled out of the water on to the beach so that last minute repairs and maintenance could be carried out. Messengers were sent hurrying westward to announce the coming of the Great King and to ensure that everything was ready.

Meanwhile, the Greek force ordered to Tempe had been taking shape. Although the command had been given to the Spartans, it is clear that they did not provide many soldiers. They and the other Peloponnesians had been in favour of holding the strong defensive line at the Isthmus of Corinth and were probably unconvinced by the idea of fighting in Thessaly.

For whatever reason, the Spartans did not send many men nor did they send one of their kings to take command. Instead the nobleman Euainetos was given command. This was a respectable choice for Euainetos was a seasoned commander, but there was no disguising the fact that Sparta was not making a major effort. The other Peloponnesian states promptly followed suit and sent only token forces, if any. Although Thebes was still nominally a member of the League, she did not send any troops at all. The other cities of Boeotia, as expected, followed the Theban lead and kept their men at home.

The bulk of the hoplites to be sent to Thessaly came from Athens. These men were commanded by Themistocles, who had all along favoured the naval strategy. He had, however, also advocated fighting the Persians as soon as possible if only as a delaying action. It was probably in this light that he looked on the expedition to Tempe.

In all there were some 10,000 hoplites assembled in Piraeus, the port of Athens, by mid-April. There would have been a number of lightly armed troops as well, perhaps another 10,000 men. This was a good sized army by Greek standards, though it was dwarfed by the forces of Xerxes. The men were loaded into Athenian ships and transported north to Halus on the shores of the Gulf of Pagasae. There they received an ecstatic reception and set off on the road north to Tempe. They arrived early in May.

Euainetos found himself in a magnificent defensive position and can have had little doubts that he could hold out almost indefinitely. To the north was the large massif of Mount Olympos, almost 3,000 metres tall and to the south that of Mount Ossa almost 2,000 metres tall. The Tempe Gorge had been carved between the two by the River Peneius. The gorge was over 7km long and, in places, only 100 metres wide. In dry weather the river bed could be used by pack animals and men, though wagons had to use the road. In May the meltwater of the winter snows was abating, but still present. The area to be defended would have been narrower still.

It was true that there was a narrow path over the southern shoulder of Olympus, near Gonnus, but this could be negotiated only by men or goats and was barely a metre wide. It could easily be blocked or made impassable. Tempe was a magnificent place to defend.

But Euainetos was not to remain confident for long. If he did not already know about the other route from Macedon to Thessaly, he must have soon found out about it from the locals. In theory this route was to be guarded by the Thessalians, but it was not so easy to defend as was the Tempe Gorge and the loyalty of the Thessalians was in doubt. Just how precarious that loyalty was, Euainetos and Themistocles could judge for themselves. They would have found many locals avoiding them and finding excuses not to serve.

It was at this point that King Alexander of Macedon intervened. He sent a message to Euainetos that drastically altered the situation. Alexander laid bare the extent of agreement and correspondence between the Thessalians and Xerxes. These messages would have had to pass through Macedon, and Alexander was too cunning a ruler not to acquaint himself with what they said. Quite obviously the rulers of the various states of Thessaly were going to defect to the Persians as soon as the Great King's army arrived on their borders. If Euainetos and Themistocles stayed at Tempe they would be caught between two hostile armies and destroyed.

There has been some debate as to why Alexander risked angering Xerxes by betraying his plans to Euainetos. After all, Xerxes had already demonstrated how brutal his anger could be by the execution of the son of Pythius and Macedon would be quite helpless in the face of the vast Persian army. When the war was over, Alexander made out that he had been on the side of the Greeks all along and only helped Xerxes because he was forced to do so. His actions, however, are ambiguous.

The reason for his action probably had more to do with geography than anything else. If the Greeks stayed in the pass at Tempe, they would have been able to delay the Persian army for days, perhaps weeks. This would have kept the vast Persian hordes in Macedonia and Xerxes had already made it clear to Alexander that Macedon was responsible for supplying the army so long as it remained on Macedonian territory. It was to safeguard is own stores of food and money that Alexander wanted the Persian army off Macedonian soil as quickly as possible.

Alexander probably believed that he was taking a reasonable risk. It was unlikely that Euainetos or Themistocles would tell the Persians that he was sending them confidential information. Nor was the information detrimental to the League. So far as Alexander could see, everybody won from his action. The Persians avoided a potentially costly and time-consuming battle. The League avoided losing an army through betrayal at Tempe. And Macedon avoided bankruptcy and possible famine by having to feed the army of Xerxes.

Whatever Alexander's motives may have been, his message had an electrifying effect on Euainetos. He ordered the League army to abandon Tempe and march south the way they had come. The army was re-embarked on to the Athenian ships at Halus and shipped back to Athens. The League had to think again.

Around 10 June at Doriscus, Xerxes summoned Demaratus, the exiled former King of Sparta to his tent. Demaratus was his main adviser on Greek military matters, and it was to the Spartan that Xerxes turned for information. The question asked by Xerxes was simple "Will the Greeks dare to lift a hand against me?"

Demaratus said that he could not speak for all the Greek states, only for Sparta, then continued "Firstly, they will not under any circumstances accept terms from you which would mean slavery for Greece. Secondly they will fight you even if all the rest of Greece surrenders. There is no use in asking if their numbers are up to the task. Suppose that only a thousand of them take the field, then that thousand will fight you and all your army."

Xerxes asked if Demaratus thought the Spartans some sort of super humans. Demaratus replied "Fighting singly the Spartans are only as good as any others, but fighting together they are the best soldiers in the world. They are free, yes, but not entirely free for they have a master, and that master is Law, which they fear much more than your subjects fear you. Whatever this master commands, they do. And his command never varies: it is never to retreat in battle, however great the odds, but always to remain in formation and to conquer or die."

At this point Xerxes laughed, but he would have done well to have listened to Demaratus. His words were a fair summing up of Spartan attitudes.

The role of Demaratus in the campaign is an interesting one. He was kept close by Xerxes throughout and his opinion was frequently asked, though more often ignored than acted upon. What is interesting is that none of the contemporary Greeks who wrote about Demaratus condemned him for his actions. Other Greeks serving Xerxes were treated as traitors and collaborators, but not Demaratus. Perhaps it was recognised that having been unjustly driven off his throne, the Spartan was simply earning as honest a living as he could.

Soon after this encounter, the precise date is unknown, the Persian army set off to march from Doriscus to Therme. It was on this stretch of the march that they feasted at Thasos and Abdera. With such magnificent local sources of supply, the army did not need to draw on the supplies of the merchant ships. The fleet travelled independently to Therme by way of the Athos Canal. By the end of July both army and fleet were safely arrived at Therme.

This was the last major outpost of friendly territory where a large supply dump had been prepared by command of Xerxes – King Alexander of Macedon being the unlucky host on this occasion. At Therme, Xerxes was expecting to meet the envoys of those Greek states who had decided to come to terms rather than to fight. They would bring with them the symbolic gifts of earth and water. He would also be meeting his agents and spies who had been scouting out the possible routes for the army and navy.

But before business, Xerxes decided on pleasure. The Persians had a fine tradition of appreciating natural beauty and Xerxes had heard many stories about the dramatic scenery of the Tempe Gorge. From Therme he could see the peaks of Olympos and Ossa, so he decided to go to Tempe. Summoning his royal galley, an especially fast vessel probably from Sidon or Tyre, he set off.

The scene he saw from his galley offshore was dramatic. "It was a great marvel to him" records Herodotus. Xerxes asked if there was any other route for the River Peneius to take from Thessaly to the sea. On being told that the gorge was the only route through the mountains, he mused "Nothing more is needed than by damming this gorge, and so forcing the river from its present channel, to put all Thessaly under water". Herodotus, as usual, presents this as an example of the megalomania of Xerxes, but it could have simply been a statement of geological curiosity.

Whatever else Xerxes thought of the Tempe Gorge, he did not think it suitable as a main route for his army. The roadway was narrow and winding, which would make it unsuitable for his wagons, and the towering heights above invited ambush. Even without a Greek defence force, it was no place through which to march a large army.

Returning to Therme, Xerxes found the welcome news that all of Thessaly had sent representatives carrying earth and water. The great, rich plain was his without having to strike a blow in anger. He also received news that Thebes and the smaller Boeotian states would defect to the Persian cause as soon as it was safe to do so – only Thespiae and Plataea refused to do so. It is likely that his spies brought back news of the dire pronouncements of the Delphic Oracle, and almost certainly he knew about the attitudes of Argos and Crete. He hoped that other states would join him as had the Thessalians as his army advanced.

Confident of ultimate success with minimal effort, Xerxes ordered his engineers into the forested hills that led up to the passes for Volustana and Petra. The road would need improving before the wagon train could lumber safely into Thessaly. Then the Persians could march south to victory.

Ironically, it was this decision to improve the passes that finally goaded the League into action against Xerxes.

This solid-wheel cart was photographed at the beginning of the 20th century on the Plain of Thessaly. The carts of Xerxes' army would have been little different. Thessaly surrendered to the King of Kings, the "ruler of heroes" (a probable rough translation of Xerxes), without a fight.

CHAPTER 5

Hoplites

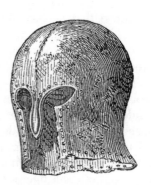

A Corinthian helmet. This example lacks the ornate crests that were worn into battle to make the wearer appear more impressive.

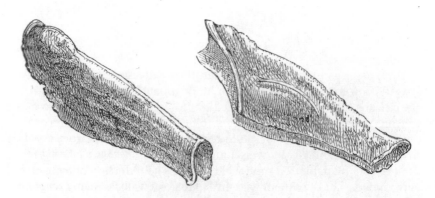

A pair of hoplite greaves. The armour was held in place around the shin by the springiness of the metal, not by straps or laces.

The soldiers on whom the Greeks put their trust to halt the advancing tide of the Persian Empire were the citizen soldiers of the various states who rallied to the cause. Every citizen of a state had a duty, at least in theory, to turn out to defend the state in times of war. The armies fielded by the vast majority of the Greek states to face the Persian invasion were part-time citizen armies. The exception was Sparta, which is dealt with in the next chapter. But whatever city the men came from, nearly all of them fought as hoplites, with the distinctive weaponry and tactics that this implied.

Like the Persian Empire, the various states of Greece were essentially agricultural societies, though some cities had a higher proportion of specialist craftsmen and merchants. Unlike most other cultures, however, the Greeks chose to mobilise their entire adult male population for war. Of course, they were constrained by the need to tend the fields as were others, so the Greeks mobilised for short periods of time only. In many cases the men would go to war for only three days.

The key to understanding the hoplite is the interlocking social, military and political lives of a Greek man. Although each of the 300 or so Greek states had its own constitution, it was rare indeed for the citizens not to be consulted on key issues. In some, all the citizens would meet in an open space to vote on each new law or motion. Elsewhere the citizens elected officials who took these decisions. Many states operated a blend of the two with officials taking day to day decisions and the citizens meeting to decide major issues.

No issue was more important than those affecting war and peace. It was the citizens who decided to fight, negotiate or surrender and it was the citizens who went to fight. The right to vote meant the duty to march to war. None of the citizens wanted to be away from their farms or businesses for very long, so they preferred to vote for short, sharp wars. This, in turn, affected how wars were fought.

Sieges are by definition protracted affairs. The reduction of a Greek city, surrounded as most of them were by stout stone walls, was no exception. It might take weeks to batter down a wall, or months to starve a city into surrender. No Greek army was prepared to be away from home long enough, so siege warfare was effectively unknown among the Greeks. In theory an army could simply retire behind the city walls and wait for the enemy to go home. In practice this rarely happened. The invading army would burn farms, destroy crops and slaughter livestock. The defenders either had to endure the destruction of their wealth, or sally out to fight. They would want a decisive battle to take place every bit as quickly as did the invaders.

Just as sieges were rare, so was any form of guerrilla warfare or sneak raids. Fast moving, lightly armed troops trained to ambush the enemy were also rare in Greek warfare, but not unknown. Light troops always have their uses.

In a typical war between Greek states, the issue was decided in a single battle fought between the massed citizens of each side. In such a situation, the most effective troops are those that are heavily armoured for defence, heavily equipped for attack and trained to perform battlefield moves en masse. Thus was the hoplite born.

The process that led to this state of affairs came quite quickly to Greece, probably in the space of a generation, some time before 700BC. By the time of the Persian invasion of 480BC, hoplite equipment was fairly standard-ised, as was training and tactics.

The arms and armour of a hoplite are generally known as the panoply. Each citizen was expected to bring his own panoply to war, and some states restricted voting rights to those able to do so. The equipment was not cheap. At its most basic it consisted of helmet, spear and shield. We know that in Athens this cost the equivalent of a month's wages for a skilled crafts-men, and so about three months pay for an unskilled labourer. If the man equipped himself with a cuirass and sword as well, the cost rose to about double. It is no wonder that arms and armour were handed down from father to son, nor that they were the most prized booty on the battlefield.

The key distinctive feature of the hoplite that dictated both the style of fighting and appearance was the shield, or aspis. This was a composite construction of wood and metal that was perfectly round, measuring about 90 cm across. The main part of the shield was domed forward and covered in a much thinner layer of bronze, in some cases less than 1 mm thick. The rim was flat, about 5 cm wide and sheathed in a thick layer of bronze. This rim was made of several pieces of wood, the joints cut at varying angles to the inner dome. This held the shield together and gave it the ability to spring back into shape after bending to absorb the power of a blow.

The shields were proof against spear thrusts or sword blows, but not against the more concentrated penetrating power of javelins or arrows. Not that these weapons could smash a shield. Instead they pierced the bronze to stick in the wood. This made the shield heavier and clumsier in combat.

The shield weighed about 6 kg, not a negligible weight to carry on one arm. When not in action the shield could be supported on the shoulder by the inner edge of the dome. In the centre of the shield was a metal arm band through which the forearm was slipped. The hand gripped a second

A Greek hoplite of 480BC. He wears a Corinthian
helmet with a single crest, marking him out as a
volunteer footsoldier. Officers wore a transverse
crest while senior commanders wore a double or
triple crest. His shield is decorated with the head
of Medusa, a common design of the period. He
wears metal greaves that reach above his knees,
so may have been one of the veterans in the front
rank of the phalanx. Greaves helped protect the
lower legs of the front rank from arrows, slingshot
and other missiles. Men in the rear ranks were
protected by the shields of those in front of them
and so did not need greaves. This man carries
a sword slung to his right side, which made it
easier to draw in the cramped, packed conditions
of a phalanx. The cuirass is of layered linen with
metal scales overlaying the more vulnerable areas.

A Greek slinger of the Thermopylae period.
He carries a small shield, but is otherwise
unarmoured. These men relied on being able to
run away from serious danger for their safety
and preferred to go into battle unencumbered by
armour. The pouch holding his sling shot is at
his left hip, suspended by a strap from his right
shoulder. Most slingers preferred purpose- made
shot of lead, often engraved with suitably martial
sentiments such as "take that" or "strike hard",
but in an emergency pebbles and stones might be
used.

band close to the rim. Some shields had the second grip also made of metal, others had a band of linen looped around the rim. This linen band could be adjusted in length to become a shoulder strap for carrying the shield when the owner was not in combat.

The face of the shield was decorated with whatever design its owner preferred. Most opted for martial designs such as lions, bulls or eagles, but others preferred the symbols of particular gods or goddesses. A few opted for the symbol of their state, often the initial letter of the state name. In later years this latter became the preferred option with all the hoplites of a state carrying the same design on their shields.

The second key defensive element in the panoply was the helmet. Ideally this was in the style known as the Corinthian helmet, as it had first been developed in Corinth. This consisted of a single sheet of bronze beaten methodically into a deep bowl shape to cover the crown of the head. At the rear a neck guard swept down and out, while at the front the entire face was enclosed by cheek pieces which came down to below the chin and closed in toward the mouth. A T-shaped opening was left for the mouth and eyes, often with a nasal guard running down to protect the nose.

On top of the helmet were lugs to which could be fitted a variety of crests to make the wearer look taller and more imposing. These crests were often used to indicate rank. Older helmets had an upright metal prong, bending forward at the top, to which was attached a fringe of stiff horsehairs. By 480BC, more modern crests ran flush along the top of the helmet, rather like a mohican haircut, with a dense brush of upright horsehair and often a trailing tail behind.

In the Spartan army at least, officers were distinguished by having crests that ran from side to side across the helmet while senior commanders had a double or even a triple crest. On some helmets a number of exceptionally long feathers were attached to the crest for a similar purpose.

Inside the helmet was an integral padded cap of leather or linen. This made the helmet more comfortable to wear for extended periods of time and helped to cushion blows so that the wearer was not concussed. It also enabled the wearer to push the helmet back so that it rested on the top of the head, with the face left open.

This type of helmet took several days for an experienced craftsman to produce and was correspondingly expensive. Cheaper versions could be made by using several different pieces of metal, which were then fixed together. Needless to say, such helmets were considerably less effective in combat.

The Corinthian helmet provided good, all round protection to the wearer but had the unfortunate effect of restricting vision somewhat and reducing hearing drastically. The constant movement of hair and skin against the inside of the helmet produced a sound rather like that of a shell held to the ear and has been likened to the sound of waves breaking on a pebble beach. Once having donned his helmet, the typical hoplite was aware only of what was going on in front of him.

Wealthier men, or those lucky enough to be left such equipment by their fathers, would also have worn greaves. These were sheets of bronze beaten into shape so that they covered the leg from ankle to knee. Typically they were shaped to resemble the leg beneath, complete with muscles, bones and sinews. They were held in place simply by the springiness of the metal, being pulled apart to be slipped on and snapping shut around the leg when worn.

The greaves were designed to protect the legs below the shield. They were proof against arrows or javelins and could ward off any slashing blow from a sword once close combat had been joined.

The final item of armour in the full panoply was the cuirass, which protected the body. In its earlier form this was made of sheet bronze, one sheet for the front and another for the back. The two parts were attached at the shoulders and the sides by clips. The bronze was made thick enough to deflect spear thrusts and sword blows directed down over the top of the shield. The bottom of the cuirass flared outward to provide some cover from downward thrusts and falling arrows to the otherwise unprotected groin and thigh areas. The distinctive flare has given this piece of kit its modern name: the bell cuirass.

The all-metal cuirass was expensive and many found it rather heavy and cumbersome. For less wealthy citizens an alternative was on offer in the shape of the linothorax. This was a cuirass made of linen. This may not seem a terribly effective material for armour, but the finished item was adequate for its purpose.

The linothorax was constructed from a number of panels, each made by glueing together between nine and 14 sheets of linen using bone glue. Typically, there was a front panel, a back panel, two side panels and two shoulder panels, all joined together by laces or buckles. A number of flaps hung down from the waist to give protection to the groin and backside. In its raw state, this layered linen is extremely stiff, so getting into the cuirass could take the combined efforts of two men. However, after a short period of wear the combined effects of body warmth and sweat made the material relatively flexible.

Clearly the linothorax was not as effective as the bronze cuirass at stopping incoming weapon blows, and arrows in particular, but it was better than might be expected. It had the great advantage of being much lighter to wear. Those who wore it did not become tired simply to standing around and were able to move more quickly in combat. By 480BC, the bell cuirass was becoming old fashioned. Most hoplites were adopting the linothorax, even those who could afford the more expensive equipment. Some sewed small metal plates to the linen to make the material more effective as armour. In time this would lead to the entire garment being covered in metal scales, or even being made of metal sheets, but such was not the practice in 480BC.

The main offensive weapon was the spear, or dory. As with all hoplite equipment, this was variable in terms of shape and size as all men provided their own gear. Typically, however, it was between 2.2 and 2.8 metres long and tapered from around 5 cm thick at the butt end to 3 cm at the head. Ideally the spear was made of ash, bundles of rods being regularly imported for the purpose by most states from Macedon or Epirus. Ash combines light weight with a formidable strength in compression, as experienced when thrusting. It was also much less prone to 'wobble' than other woods. Spear shafts were manufactured in all states in great numbers, which would indicate that they broke regularly in combat.

The head of the dory had an iron spear point. This tended to be around 15 cm long and fairly broad. It had a central spine, inside which was a socket that fitted over the spear shaft and was secured in place with pitch or glue. At the butt end of the spear was the sauroter, or "lizard-sticker". This was shorter and stouter than the spear-head, being square in profile.

The sauroter had three functions. The first was to act as a counterweight, and for this purpose it was often given a lead collar. The aim was to ensure that the spear balanced in the hand about three quarters of the way along its length from the spear point. This meant that it projected some 1.8 metres forward from the shield, but less than 80 cm backward. Such a balance was crucial in the dense formation fighting the hoplites practised. The second function was to stick the spear into the ground, keeping it conveniently upright when the hoplite was resting or in camp, making it much easier to snatch up in a hurry if the enemy appeared.

The third function of the sauroter is more controversial. Some helmets have been found that have been pierced by the distinctive square cross section of the sauroter. Clearly this means that the butt end of the spear was used as a weapon, presumably if the shaft broke and the spear point was lost. What is not known is if this was an expected part of hoplite warfare or simply a desperate ruse of men who had lost their main weapon.

More usual as a secondary weapon was the sword. During the Persian invasion, most men carried the sword known as the *xiphos*. This weapon had a fairly straight blade, tapering slightly to the point and a conventional cross-shaped hilt. It could be used to cut or thrust, and was drawn if the spear broke. It could be used to poke over the top of the shield, seeking a weakness in the opponent's guard. Less subtly it could be swung overarm in a chopping motion to bludgeon through the enemy's helmet or cuirass. Interestingly, tuition in sword fighting was an added extra that was not included in standard military training. Perhaps it was not considered to be essential.

In battle the standard formation for the hoplite soldiers was the phalanx. This dense formation was taken up only once the army was in position. Until then the men advanced in single files of twenty or more men. This made it easier and quicker for them to thread through olive groves, over broken ground or between crops.

Details of phalanx formation varied from state to state with, as might be expected, Sparta thinking up a number of unique features. It is thought that the preferred form for the phalanx was to line the men up eight ranks deep, with each man covering about 80 cm of frontage. It was not always possible to form up in this way. Sometimes a phalanx was only four men deep so that it covered a wider frontage to avoid being outflanked by a more numerous enemy. On other occasions a commander might double the depth to sixteen ranks if his men were inexperienced or low in morale. Other states used different numbers of ranks, and written sources from this early period are rare.

At this point, the men would have their shields resting on the ground and spears stuck upright beside them. When the order to advance was given, the men lifted their shields so that the inside of the rim rested on the shoulder. This kept the shield on their left side and relieved the weight on the arm so that it remained fresh for combat. The spears were held upright, close to the right side.

As the phalanx advanced the officers sought repeatedly to keep it in formation. The men needed to open out as they marched around trees or bushes, then close ranks again on the far side. Inexperienced men found that even small obstacles could disorder the formation, allowing one section to push ahead or causing ranks to become mixed. Even the most skilled at formation marching would need to halt after crossing a wall or ditch to get back into phalanx.

As they marched forward, the men would begin to sing. The most traditional song for hoplites was the paean, a hymn praising Enyalios, god of battles, and invoking his aid. There were many regional variations of the paean, and each state had its own songs commemorating past victories and local heroes. No doubt the singing did much to raise morale and to enforce the bonds of loyalty between the men pressed so closely together as death approached.

This stage of the battle was crucial. The two forces would have been within sight of each other and able to hear each other's singing and chanting. Morale affected the volume and enthusiasm of the singing, which was self-perpetuating. At a football match, the supporters whose team is in the lead are more vocal than those of the losing team.

As the forces closed, the opposing commanders would be weighing up the situation. Men who were eager for the fight would be singing lustily and gazing forward with determination. Those who were not would be mumbling their chants and looking around to make sure that the way of retreat lay open. It is recorded that in 422BC before the battle of Amphipolis the Spartan commander Brasidas studied the approaching Athenian phalanx carefully. "Look at them," Brasidas said. "Those men will not stand up to us. You can see it by the way they move. Men who act like that will never await the charge of their opponents." He was right.

When about 200 metres from the enemy phalanx, a final dressing of lines would take place. Shields were taken off the shoulder and brought forward to face the enemy. With a shield being 90 cm across, but each man occupying only 80 cm of frontage there was overlap. The shield of each man projected sideways to protect the man on his left. It was essential in the battle to come that each man could hold his shield rigidly still, no matter what was happening to him or to those around him. Spears were lifted up and held overarm. Then the advance would recommence.

At some point, the phalanx would be ordered to charge at a run for the final impact. On receiving the order to charge, the men stopped singing and instead let rip a terrifying yell or scream of ferocity. This was a critical moment in the battle. A good display could destroy an enemy's nerve. In 368BC, the Spartans won what they called the Tearless Battle against a league of Arcadian cities. The moment the Spartans yelled and surged forward, the entire Arcadian army turned and fled.

It was well known that launching the charge first gave an army an advantage in terms of morale and momentum, but deciding when to charge was a difficult decision for any commander. Keeping formation when advancing at a walk was difficult enough, doing so at a run was exceptionally tricky. Inexperienced men might be kept at a walking pace almost to the point of combat so that they retained formation, but that was to give away the advantage of impact.

If a commander ordered the charge too soon, he might find that by the time his phalanx reached the enemy it had lost formation; or that his men were out of breath and unable to sustain the fight. If he left it too late, the commander might find that the enemy charged first, and that his own men would not break into the charge. Or if they did charge that they had not reached top speed before the moment of impact.

Once the charge began, it was virtually impossible to stop. The sheer momentum of eight ranks of running men, all moving as a block was formidable. If a man at the front did try to stop, he would have been simply pushed over and trampled by those behind. The only choice was to keep running with shield held out in front and spear held aloft, pointing downward over the shield.

The crash of opposing phalanxes of hoplites running into each other was frightful. At the last moment the men in the front ranks tried to aim their spears at a gap in the enemy shields, while ensuring that their own shields were firmly locked together. Some spears hit the opposing shields and snapped, others slipped through to plunge into flesh, or to spear harmlessly into empty air.

The men in the front ranks were often winded by the impact. Their own shields crashed solidly into those of the hoplites coming the other way at a run. This brought the men to a shuddering halt. A split second later their own second rank crashed into them from behind, then the third rank made impact, jamming the men together even further. Men found themselves lifted off their feet by the pressure, jostled sideways or backwards, or forward and trampled under foot.

If neither side gave way in the immediate aftermath of impact, the real fighting began. In the front rank, many men would be left holding broken spears. They might reverse their spear and begin stabbing with the sauroter, or they might draw their swords and begin hacking at the enemy heads and shoulders. They were jammed tightly together, close enough to smell each other's sweat and feel each other's breath. Hacking, thrusting and stabbing, the men tried to reach the enemy, while always keeping their shields locked to those of their comrades in a solid wall. So dense was the press that the wounded could not fall, nor the fit stand up once down.

The men of the second and third ranks were meanwhile getting busy with their own dory spears. Able to reach almost two metres forward, these men could easily contact the enemy. While the front rank stabbed with swords and sauroter, those behind them thrust forward with their spears to seek an opening or unguarded victim. It was now that the importance of having a carefully balanced weapon of fine ash became clear. A spear must not wobble when being aimed, nor break if it hit helmet or cuirass. Add to this bloody scrimmage if you wish the blinding light and dusty heat of a Greek summer's day.

Meanwhile, the rear ranks were playing their part. It was usual to put the older and more experienced men at the back. They pushed forward with their shields, rather like the back row of a rugby scrum. They kept the line steady, shoving with co-ordinated surges in an attempt to drive the phalanx forward and push the enemy back. If a momentum could be got going, the enemy would begin to fall away. Their rear ranks would trip and stumble as they stepped about blindly. In turn this would reduce their pushing power, increasing the speed of their backward movement.

Meanwhile the younger men in the front continued their deadly duel of thrust and slash. The older men at the back would keep an eye on how things were going. They could surge forward to replace losses or push others into line. But if things looked like they were going badly, they might start to step back.

Whatever began the backward movement, it could last only so long. Then the phalanx would collapse. Often the breakdown of formation came quickly. It would start in one place, then spread rapidly. The rear ranks would go first, the move to turn and flee running along the line like a ripple. As the men in front felt the pressure behind them go, they too would turn and flee. Suddenly what had been army was simply a disorganised mass of retreating men.

The victorious phalanx could move forward again. The wounded enemy were quickly dispatched as the phalanx rolled forward. More disciplined units could now advance at the trot to try to catch the fugitives, increasing the death toll. Less disciplined forces might race forward individually, losing their own formation as they ran. This undoubtedly led to even more enemy dead, but also gave the fugitives the chance to turn and spear their pursuers. And it was possible that the fleeing enemy might have a reserve in place, for just this outcome. If so, a disorganised pursuit could turn into defeat in its turn.

The commander of the victorious army would at some point halt the pursuit. There would then follow a systematic looting of the dead. Any jewellery was taken, as were the costly weapons and armour of the fallen. Generally the loot was collected together. A proportion was dedicated to the gods, at least one captured panoply would be nailed to a nearby tree as a symbol of victory, and another set was taken home to be displayed to the public. The rest was sold off and the money raised distributed among the army.

It is impossible to be certain because the records are scant, but there are some clues as to how deadly hoplite warfare could be. In the instances from which figures survive, it would seem that about 5% of the victorious army was killed in the fighting, while up to 15% of the defeated would not survive the day.

This was carnage indeed for a battle that might have lasted only an hour or two from start to finish. The dense formations and close quarter fighting meant that casualties would inevitably be high. But given that most wars were settled in a single day, the death toll was socially, politically and economically sustainable. There were rarely long-drawn out campaigns in which battle followed battle and which led to civilian starvation and epidemic disease. Hoplite warfare ensured that campaigns were short, brutal and decisive.

The herald of the defeated city would then appear, usually later that same day, to arrange a truce and ask for the bodies of the dead for burial. Once this was agreed, the business of peace negotiations would begin. Most of the wars in ancient Greece were fought over disputed patches of border territory. The loser would hand over the disputed region, and both armies would go home to return to their usual jobs as potters, farmers or fishermen.

On rare occasions the outcome of a war was more serious. The victor might impose tribute on the defeated, or even declare the defeated state to be absorbed into that of the victor. Sometimes the defeated were treated as little better than slaves, at other times they negotiated free status for themselves or even equal voting rights as citizens of the amalgamated state.

Hoplites were not the only troops to fight of course. Every state had a few men rich enough to own horses, and much larger numbers of men too poor to afford a full hoplite panoply. The richer men often marched with their fellow citizens, but sometimes rode to war as scouts and messengers.

Termed *psiloi*, peltasts and other designations, the poorer, lightly armed infantry came with a variety of weapons. Most were armed with either slings or javelins. Most, if not all, of these men carried light shields made of woven reeds or wicker. These were proof against javelins and sling stones, but useless in pitched battle. Mainland Greeks were never very proficient with bow and arrow, but the Cretans made it a speciality. Archers from Crete were hired as mercenaries by most Greek states at one time or another.

However they were armed, the light troops were used in the same way. They ran ahead of the hoplites to pelt the opposing army with missiles while it was forming up. Of course, the enemy's light troops were doing much the same, so in practice the slingers and javelin throwers tended to fight each other more often than not. In any case, the light missile weaponry was unable to do much other then cause a nuisance to the heavily armoured hoplites. Light troops had their uses, but the battle was decided by the hoplites.

As can be seen, fighting as a hoplite demanded a fair degree of skill in handling weapons and even more proficiency in formation marching: square bashing. Obviously, this meant that the citizens had to train for war. But time for such training was limited by the more pressing needs of sowing, harvesting and other work. Remarkably little information has survived about hoplite training, though it must have taken place. As we shall see the regime in Sparta was described in great detail by other Greeks, but only because it was unique and quite unlike that elsewhere. From the few records that survive it would seem that young men underwent an intensive period of military training before being accepted as citizens by the state. Thereafter, there were periodic weapon inspections to make sure each citizen had his panoply ready for use. It can only be surmised that the weapon inspections also included refresher courses in formation marching and phalanx drill.

The training of youths in Athens at a later period was carefully recorded, and gives a clue as to the earlier regime typical outside of Sparta. The process began once the harvest had been collected, when the young men were no longer needed on their family fields. All boys who had reached their eighteenth birthday since the previous harvest were taken to the Temple of Aglauros, a nymph who had a daughter by Ares, the god of war and was later involved in a quarrel with Poseidon. There they took an oath to protect the soil of Athens and to obey the law and the orders of those lawfully in authority. Most especially the young man swore never to abandon his comrades in battle. The oath was sworn to a number of gods, but noticeably to the war god Ares and to the patron goddess of Athens, Athena herself.

During their first year these ephebes, as the trainee citizens were known, spent their time in athletic training. They were put together in groups that would remain fixed as units throughout their military lives to ensure solidarity and loyalty. They also acquired their panoply and became accustomed to wearing it for long periods of time.

In their second year the ephebes became more formally trainee hoplites. They moved away from home to live together in barracks. There they were trained in weapons drill and formation marching. They were also used as permanent guards on the state's borders and outside the temples or civic buildings. In most states these young men were the only full-time soldiers to hand, so they learned the business of guard duty and discipline on the job.

Each ephebe came under the guidance of an older man. How close this guidance was varied greatly. Some took a real interest in the younger men, others merely checked their weaponry and skills from time to time. After all, the trainees were being given their instruction by a full-time instructor. The pairing of an older man, who would have stood in the rear ranks in battle, and a younger man, who would have stood in front of him in battle, was often termed "lovers". This has given rise to a great degree of speculation as to the prevalence of homosexuality in the military systems of ancient Greece. In truth it is difficult to tell from the sources whether the word is used in the sense of physical, carnal love or of a tight, brotherly love between men who depend on each other in battle.

At the end of the second year of training, the ephebes became full citizens of the state. They were entitled to vote at elections and required to fight when occasion demanded. The event was celebrated by a parade of the ephebes in a theatre, no doubt watched by their proud parents and siblings. It was with such men, weapons and tactics that the states of Greece prepared to meet the Persian horde. But none of the states was really prepared to risk its citizens in a battle against the vast army of Xerxes until one state in particular mustered its hoplites to war. Everyone waited for Sparta, for Sparta was a very special state.

A Greek hoplite of about 450BC. The helmet is of a later pattern.

In these illustrations we have assumed a subunit of 16 men, which seems to have been common at this time. Some states preferred a decimal system, while others opted for units of 12. Our sources are often vague and unclear on the detail of organisation at the period of the Persian invasion. Detailed information comes from about 80 years later, by which time the phalanx had changed somewhat to meet changing battle conditions.

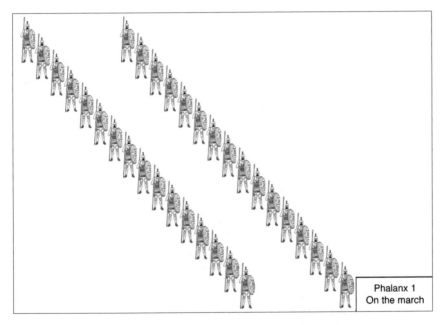

Phalanx 1
On the march

1) On the march the unit formed up in single file. On a road two or more files might march side by side. When the army entered the presence of the enemy, the files would form up about two or three metres apart and march in parallel until it was time to form the phalanx. This gave the men space to step around trees, rocks and other obstacles without getting in each other's way, but kept them close enough that they could form phalanx at short notice.

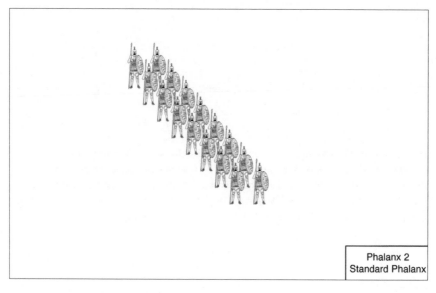

Phalanx 2
Standard Phalanx

2) In a standard phalanx formation the men formed up in eight ranks. The younger men were at the front where the fighting would be most intense, while the older men were at the rear where they could steady the formation and watch for problems or opportunities.

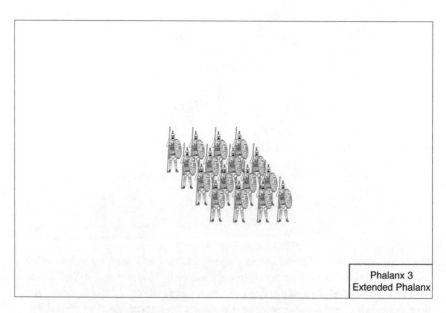

Phalanx 3
Extended Phalanx

3) In an extended phalanx, the depth of the formation was reduced to four men so that a wide frontage could be covered without compromising the density of men in the front rank and their ability to protect each other with overlapping shields.

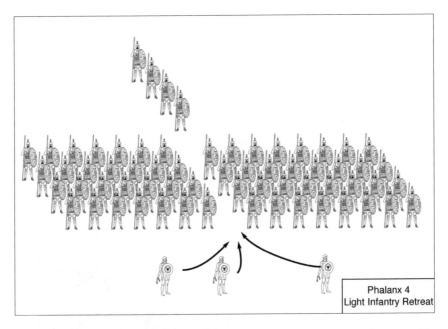

4) *The phalanx needed to open to allow light troops to withdraw, one file of men would march back out of line to open up a gap. When the light troops had withdrawn, the men would retake their positions to reform the phalanx.*

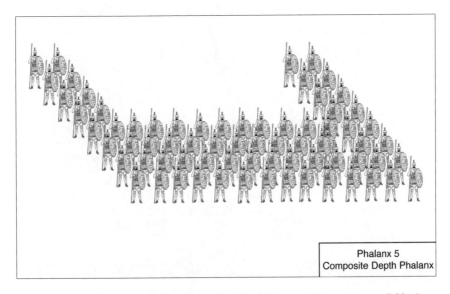

5) *The flanks were usually the weakest point of a phalanx so, if men were available, it would be here that a full depth of men would be maintained.*

CHAPTER 6
Sparta

Thermopylae photographed in the 1900s, viewed from the west. The building or shrine in the centre of the picture is gone.

The Spartans were the most feared warriors in the ancient world. They routinely outfought armies three times the size of their own. And they did so with a steady courage and discipline that amazed all who saw them. When it came to fighting, everybody wanted to have the Spartans on their side.

Even their contemporaries in ancient Greece, however, recognised that they were a strange people. Writers went out of their way to comment on Spartan customs, Spartan dress, Spartan food and how odd it all was. For one thing, the Spartans gave their girls an education every bit as good as that they gave their boys. And, for an ancient Greek, you don't get much odder than that!

An event at the Olympic Games some years after the Persian invasion shows quite clearly an attitude among other Greeks to the Spartans. An old man was trying to find a place to sit down, limping and stumbling as he did so. He walked haltingly along the front of the grassy banks where the spectators sat, looking for a spare patch of ground, but there was none and nobody was prepared to give up his seat. Then the old man reached the section reserved for Spartiates. At once, every single man stood up to offer the old man his place. The rest of the audience broke out into applause for the Spartiate's behaviour. The old man looked around and called out. "I see what this means. All Greeks know what is right – but only the Spartiates do it."

To understand Sparta and the Spartans, it is necessary to understand that theirs was a society geared for war. The state had been born in war, formed by war and existed solely for war. The entire society was dedicated to winning wars.

The early history of Sparta is shrouded in myth and legend. Although these stories are usually dismissed by historians, they were very real to the Spartans themselves. Two brothers descended from the mighty Heracles (Hercules) brought the Spartans to the broad valley of the Eurotas Valley in the region of Laconia. They are said to have arrived about 80 years after the Trojan War. These two brothers divided up the valley between them and founded two royal lines: the Eurypontidae and the Agidae. After innumerable quarrels between the two families, it was decided that they would rule jointly. Then, about a date traditionally given as 776BC, Sparta came under the control of Lycurgus who was uncle to the infant King Charilaus of the Europontidae line. At the time, Sparta was engaged in a ferocious war against the neighbouring state of Messenia. Lycurgus set about a total reform of the state and its constitution. Later Spartans gave the credit for all laws, constitutional offices and state regulations to Lycurgus.

What seems to lie behind these tales is an influx of Dorian Greeks about the year 1100BC to what was already a settled agricultural society in the valley of the Eurotas. These Dorians founded a number of small city states. Sparta itself was composed of five villages standing close together near the confluence of the Eurotas with the Oenous. These villages joined together before 900BC, under the leadership of the two royal families. Perhaps these were originally the rulers of two of the villages.

The five villages of Sparta very quickly conquered or formed alliances with all the other Dorian states in the valley. In this new state the citizens of Sparta were known as the Spartiates, and kept control of foreign affairs and the joint army firmly in their hands. The other cities, known collectively as Lacedaemonians, enjoyed self-government but were under the dominion of the Spartiates.

Together the new Spartan state then conquered the non-Dorian peoples of Laconia. These people were known as Helots, from their largest city, Helos. The Helots were treated very much as second-class citizens, though they were not reduced to the status of slaves. They were forced to work largely for the benefit of the Spartans as waged *serviles*, though the exact terms of such work is unclear.

It was this amorphous state that Lycurgus reformed to cope with the pressures of the war against Messenia. By about 730BC, Messenia had been conquered and its peoples reduced to the status of the Helots. The state that emerged from this turmoil was, indeed, strange. The arts were ignored, the gods worshipped with great fervour, fine architecture scorned and courage in battle hailed as the main virtue of men. It was a society formed by and for the Spartiates and, to a lesser extent, the Lacedaemonians. When it came to war, it was the Spartiates who were the most important fighters, though the Lacedaemonians also marched as hoplites and the Helots as servants and skirmishers. At the time of the Persian invasion there are thought to have been about 7,000 adult male Spartiates, and perhaps 20,000 Lacedaemonians.

The Lacedaemonians earned their livings as did the citizens of most Greek states. When they mustered for combat, they were equipped identically to the hoplites and, like them, preferred short wars so that they could return home. It was widely recognised, however, that they were better trained and more effective in combat than those of other states due to the fact that the Spartan state demanded regular training and drill from them.

It was the Spartiates who ruled supreme on the battlefield. This was because they were full-time soldiers, the only such people in ancient

Greece. Their status was made possible by the fact that the state owned all the land captured from the Helots and Messenians. These estates were parcelled out to the Spartiates, who lived off the rents but took no part in running the farms.

The training of a Spartiate was famously tough and arduous, but was carefully designed to produce the finest fighting hoplite possible. The process began just a few days after birth when the baby boy was shown naked to a government official. If the boy was crippled in any way, he was taken to a nearby hillside and left to die. Only boys able to grow into able-bodied men were wanted.

At the age of five the boy left home to live in barracks, with each group of boys eating, sleeping and learning together. Known as *paidion*, these boys learned to read and write, to carry scaled down weaponry for hours on end and to know by heart the marching songs of the Spartiates. Most of these were credited to the poet Tyrtaios, a typical example running:

"Standing foot to foot,
Shield pressed on shield
Crest to crest and helmet to helmet,
Chest to chest,
Engage your man
Use your sword, strike with your spear".

As the Messenian War reached its crisis, the Spartans asked the oracle at Delphi for advice, and were instructed to ask Athens for a leader for their army. The Athenians, wanting neither to help the Spartans nor to defy the oracle, sent Tyrtaios. They no doubt thought they were being clever for the poet was not only known for his love songs, but was also severely disabled. Nevertheless he wrote a series of marching songs that so inspired the Spartans in battle that they credited him with victory and ever after sang his compositions.

At the age of 13 the Spartan boy became a youth, or *meirakion*. Now the training really began. He had his hair cut short, to show he was not a man, and was given a single cloak which was all he was allowed to wear. He had to go barefoot to toughen his feet, and spent hours every day in athletic exercise. Food was kept to a minimum at barracks, and the youths were encouraged to steal food to supplement their diet. The penalties for being caught stealing food were severe, but the punishment was for being caught. Thus the trainee warriors learned both to work on an empty stomach and how to forage for food on campaign. Needless to say, weapons training and formation marching were daily experiences.

At the age of 18 the youth became a man. His first duty was to act as a trainer for the boys and youths below him. At the end of this year he was ready to become a full citizen-soldier of Sparta. First he had to undergo a brutal religious rite. Cheeses were piled on the altar of a shrine at Limaion dedicated to Artemis Orthia, a version of the hunting goddess closely connected to woodland and the wilds. The priests and their helpers stood around the altar armed with long whips. The youths then had to fight their way past the priests to grab a piece of cheese and escape from the shrine. It was a violent ceremony in which death among the youths was not unknown. But the Spartans were famously devout and assiduous in carrying out rituals to please the gods.

After this ceremony, the youth moved to the adult messes. These messes were the key to much of the famous Spartan discipline. The men of each mess fought together in the phalanx. It is thought there may have been sixteen men to a mess, meaning they could form two files in a standard Spartan phalanx eight men deep.

All Spartiates had to be a member of a mess, even the two kings. The food served at these messes was healthy and wholesome, but almost as unappetising as that served to the youths. The main meal consisted of barley bread and broth, followed by figs and cheese with a limited amount of wine. To be asked to dine at a mess was a sign of great honour, but it was not always appreciated. One Greek visiting from another state dined at a mess during his stay in Sparta and was asked about the experience on his return home. "Now I understand why the Spartans do not fear death," he replied.

At some point in this first ten years in a mess, a Spartiate might be removed to spend two years in the *krypteia*, meaning "hidden ones", a sort of secret service. One role of these men was to keep an eye on the Helots and Messenians for signs of rebellion, but they had other duties as well. What these were is unknown; they were a secret service after all.

Each mess was made up of men of all ages, the 19-year-old newcomers joining whichever mess had a gap created by death or old age. Throughout their adult lives the Spartiates ate in their mess, exercised daily with their messmates and practised weaponry with their colleagues. At some point, probably at the age of 30, the Spartiate was allowed to marry and sleep at home. Even then he had to dine and train daily at his mess. It is not entirely clear for how long a Spartiate remained liable to serve in war. It is most likely that a man would march with his messmates for as long as he was physically able to do so.

Two anecdotes point to this. One concerns a Spartiate named Hippodamus who was killed in battle at the age of 80. He had been fit enough to march with his comrades, and to keep up with the army as it advanced. Similarly, Androkleidas mustered with his panoply to march to war despite having a severe limp caused by an earlier wound. When told he could not go to war, he responded "I don't need to be fit enough to run away, only fit enough to stand alongside my comrades and fight".

The purpose of this emphasis on keeping the mess together is clear. The men who were going to fight together had to know and trust each other completely. This is important in any army, but for hoplites it was doubly so. Encased in a helmet the men could see little except what was directly in front of them. They needed to be able to trust their colleagues on either side and behind them to fight resolutely and to hold their ground whatever happened. Only then could a man give his full concentration to the grim business of killing. As was to be proved time and again, this trust between Spartiates was total – and incredibly effective in battle.

The constant training and drilling had other advantages. Not only was the Spartan phalanx able to move faster and with more cohesion than any other, it could also perform manoeuvres that no other body of men could even attempt. These moves are generally described in amazed wonder by onlookers who recorded them, but only three have been described in sufficient detail for us to understand what was going on.

The first was the outflanking manoeuvre. This was performed by detaching a force from the flank of the advancing phalanx. The detached force was formed in column. It advanced parallel to the phalanx, but moving outside the flank of the enemy phalanx. Once they reached the correct position, the men in the column were ordered to turn inward, creating a mini-phalanx. This then charged in the normal manner into the flank of the enemy formation.

Phalanxes were notoriously vulnerable on their right flank, where the men would have difficulty turning to get their shields into position. However, for the move to succeed called for fast marching and precise positioning. If the outflanking column moved too early the opposing commander could simply extend his formation to meet it head on. If the move was left too late, the battle might be over before contact was made. There was also the risk that an alert opposing commander with reliable troops might strike at the weak link between the phalanx and the flanking force, which could spell disaster for the attackers.

The second battlefield manoeuvre which gave the Spartans the victory on more than one occasion was the feigned retreat. This can be a difficult proposition for any army. Once troops have begun to pull back it can be a hard job to stop them. In the context of a phalanx, it is even more tricky to march back without breaking formation than to advance.

The ancient sources are not particularly clear on how this manoeuvre was performed in battle, but it does seem to have been a phased operation. This might mean that the rear rank, usually composed of the older and more experienced men, would break off from the phalanx and pull back to a previously arranged position. There they would form up again in a single line. This would form an effective brake on the main body of the phalanx when it retreated, giving the men a clear position on which to form.

Whether the main phalanx then fell back as one, or in two more phases is unknown. Given that the idea was to give the impression of a panic-stricken rout, it is likely that the main body fell back in two stages. First the middle ranks would go, falling back to form up on the rear rank. This would greatly ease the pressure supporting the front two ranks, which would then naturally be pushed back by the opposing phalanx. When these two ranks then suddenly gave way and ran, it would have seemed to the men in the enemy army to have been a quite natural collapse of the Spartan formation. If the Spartans gave a good impression of panic-stricken flight, this would add to the illusion.

The men in the opposing phalanx would, quite understandably, be thrilled and delighted at having defeated the legendary Spartans. The chances of the commander being able to restrain them from pursuit would be negligible. Forwards would go the phalanx, no doubt breaking up into some disorder as the men surged on over the wounded and dead to try to get at the fleeing hoplites.

But it was a trap. Once the Spartans had formed up again, the pursuing phalanx would be close. The leading pursuers would no doubt come to a halt at the sight of levelled Spartan spears, but those to the rear would be unable to see clearly and would push on, further disordering the ranks. Then the Spartans charged. This time they struck a disordered and con-fused opponent. Assuming the feigned retreat was conducted properly, it never failed to deliver victory. (A far simpler example of the feigned retreat can be found in the memoirs of Charles Sazarin, a French army surgeon in the Franco-Prussian War of 1870-71: "In order to dislodge the Bavarians from a wood . . . the General ordered the Zouaves to advance upon them, to brave their fire and, at 100 metres from the edge of the wood, to turn and run away . . . then to turn again and charge them with the bayonet. This manoeuvre, impossible for any other regiment than the 1st Zouaves, was completely successful.")

The third manoeuvre recorded by the Spartans' contemporaries is one that has been performed by most formations of soldiers engaged in square bash-ing over the centuries, and is still a favourite with marching bands today. To the ancient Greeks it was known as the Spartan countermarch. This was performed by troops in open order, with gaps between the files of men. Presumably alternate files dropped back to fall into line behind its neighbour to achieve this. Each file leader then turned about and marched down the gap between the lines, followed in turn by each man in his line. Eventually the men of each file ended up facing the opposite direction, but in the same order as they had begun. The alternate files then closed up again to reform the phalanx. An about turn of this type kept the phalanx in its strict formation, but enabled it suddenly to face the opposite direction. This was, presumably, of some use in the preliminary stages of a battle when the opposing phalanxes were jockey-ing for position. The Spartans may have wished to feint in one direction with part of their force, to lure the enemy forward, then pull back again. It also has the benefit of looking very impressive and so would have helped get the mes-sage across to an enemy that they were rank amateurs in comparison to the Spartans they faced, a useful contribution to the pre-combat psy-ops.

Although the Spartans were such famous fighters, it is almost certain that there was little special about their equipment. They carried shields and wore helmets indistinguishable from those of other states and their spears were much the same. The only weapon that was at all different was the sword. This was a shorter and heavier weapon than was usual among other Greeks. Moreover the blade bulged towards the tip, making the end of the weapon heavier.

The design of the sword would have encouraged stabbing, rather than slashing, in combat. Perhaps the Spartans jabbed over the tops of their shields at their enemies, or upward from beneath the shield edge, in the hope of inflicting wounds. This demands rather more practice than slashing over arm, but the Spartans had plenty of time to practice with their weapons.

That the Helots were subordinate in the Spartan state is well known. There was a strict night curfew on the Helots, enforced in brutal manner. Men serving in the *krypteia* were sent to roam the countryside, sleeping by day and patrolling at night. They were free to kill any Helot they found outside his house during darkness. This did not stop the Helots from playing a role in Spartan society, nor in Spartan warfare.

It is clear that each Spartan hoplite took with him one Helot as a personal servant. The man's duties included carrying the hoplite panoply when on the march, cooking meals and collecting firewood. He also helped his master to arm himself for battle and, it is thought, sought to retrieve the hoplite if he fell, whether for medical treatment or funerary rights.

It is thought that when retrieving the wounded or dead, the Helot would place the body on to the fallen man's shield, placed face down on the ground. He would then drag the man clear, with the shield sliding over the ground like a sled. Thus it seems to have become traditional to tell a departing Spartan soldier to "return carrying your shield or on it": in other words to come back dead, wounded or still standing and fully equipped to fight. Only those who fled threw away their shields in order to run faster. To return home fit and healthy, but without a shield was the height of disgrace.

Other Helots marched to war as soldiers. They were not equipped as hoplites, this privilege being reserved for Spartiates and Lacedaemonians, but as *psiloi* or light infantry. They carried a set of javelins to throw at the enemy before the phalanxes clashed and may have had daggers as well for despatching enemy wounded. On occasion the Spartans included large numbers of Helots in their armies, sometimes seven times as many as there were hoplites. It is likely that these large numbers of light infantry were deployed to protect the army's camp when the hoplites were fighting a battle, or protect passes and bridges and other ancillary duties. None of this is certain, however, as most written attention is given to the hoplites.

The Spartans did not neglect religion when on campaign. The devotion which the Spartans paid to the gods was proverbial and, being Spartan, most of the rituals were connected to war. Greek religion was not based on concepts of moral behaviour approved of by an all-seeing deity. Instead it revolved around the need to please, mollify and even bribe the gods. Ceremonies had to be carried out exactly as prescribed by tradition, rituals needed to be performed on time and with the correct dress and participants. To do otherwise would be to anger the gods, and divine retribution could be swift and terrible.

More than once the Greeks, and others in the ancient world, behaved in ways that seem frankly bizarre to modern eyes. Urgent actions were put off in deference to a religious festival. Actions were hurried to please the gods. To a Greek this made sense. There was no point, say, caulking split seams in a ship if that meant missing a ceremony at the temple of Poseidon. The anger of the sea god was far more likely to sink a ship than was a missing bit of tar.

This was how the Spartans viewed war and their religion. They were late for the Battle of Marathon in 490BC simply because their king was needed in Sparta for a ritual, and the army could not march without a king to command it. To modern historians the need for the Spartan soldiers at Marathon was urgent and paramount. To the Spartans it was secondary to the ritual. If the army had marched without the ritual being properly performed, the gods would have ensured it was defeated. Better to appease the gods and arrive late than to arrive on time, but to anger the immortals.

Before the Spartan army was allowed to march, the ephors would make a sacrifice and inspect the portents. These ephors were annually elected government officials who supervised public finances and ensured the kings obeyed the law in carrying out their duties. If the indications were good, a torch would be lit from the sacred fire on the altar. An ephor would carry this torch ahead of the king and army as it marched through Spartan territory. At the border, the ephor would step aside so that the army marched past the sacred fire as they left their homeland. Even before battle was joined, the Spartans remembered their gods. Before ordering the phalanx to advance, the king had to sacrifice a she-goat to Artemis. The entrails were inspected. If it appeared that Artemis was unhappy, the Spartans would not attack.

Something must be said about the appearance of the Spartans. While their military equipment was similar to that used in the rest of Greece, their overall appearance was distinctive and instantly recognisable. Most famously, the Spartan hoplites wore cloaks and tunics of a particular shade of red. It is impossible to be certain, but this was probably close to crimson. More than one writer spoke of the red cloaks marching to war when speaking of the Spartan army.

This cloak was of the style called *himation*. It was a large oblong of woollen cloth that was worn wrapped around the body. It could be worn over the shoulders and pulled down to envelop the body for warmth. Alternatively, it could be doubled over and worn like a long skirt on warm days when only modesty was needed. On campaign the himation, as well as being a cloak, doubled up as a sleeping blanket for use on chilly nights. Rather more practical for fighting was the tunic, or *chiton*. This was also red, though it was often embroidered with patterns or decorative motifs. It was often made of linen for summer use, or wool for the winter. In shape it was a pair of oblongs, attached to each other at the shoulder and under the upper arm, then gathered in at the waist with a belt. The fabrics may have been distinctive and bright, but tailoring was never really a Greek art.

Unlike the citizens of any other Greek state, the Spartiates wore their hair long and with great pride. Most of the hair was drawn backward to fall down from the rear of the helmet, but two or more braids were often brought forward to dangle over the front of the shoulders. The beard was, likewise, kept long though the moustache was shaved off. It is often forgotten just how much hard work long hair was to care for before the days of modern soaps and shampoos. To keep long locks tangle-free and to ensure that the natural oils were evenly distributed took as much as an hour of brushing each day. And hair in its natural state is much stickier than hair washed by modern chemicals, so it was far more prone to pick up dust and bits of vegetation etc. As a result, long hair was totally impractical for men who worked in fields or workshops. In ancient Greece, long hair was the mark of a king or aristocrat. Since the Spartiates considered themselves the aristocrats of war, they all wore their hair long.

The final word on the Spartans belongs to King Agesilaus who was leading an army of allied states in war against Athens some 40 years after the Persian invasion. The leaders of the allied states complained at one council of war that it was always the Spartan king who gave the orders, when the other states between them supplied much larger numbers of men. Agesilaus had the entire allied army drawn up as if for review, then told them all to sit down. He then sent out the Spartan herald to call out for all the farmers to stand up. Large numbers of the allied soldiers did so. Then the potters were told to stand, then carpenters and so on until all the professions had been called. Then Agesilaus showed his fellow commanders the scene. Almost every allied hoplite was standing, but not a single Spartan had moved.

"You see, my friends," said the Spartan king. "You send more men, we send more soldiers".

A Spartan sword. The blade has the distinctive bulge to add weight to the weapon.

Spartan Flanking Manoeuvre

The flanking manoeuvre performed by the Spartans called for fast marching and precision positioning of the highest order. Only the superbly trained Spartans were able to carry it out in battlefield conditions.

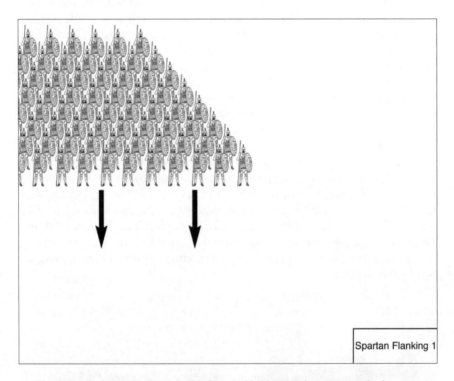

Spartan Flanking 1

1) The Spartan phalanx is drawn up 8 deep and begins to advance towards the enemy phalanx. The enemy commander, naturally draws up his phalanx so that it is as wide as that of the Spartans. This will allow all men to meet the enemy head on in approved hoplite fashion. We see only the far left wing of the Spartan phalanx here.

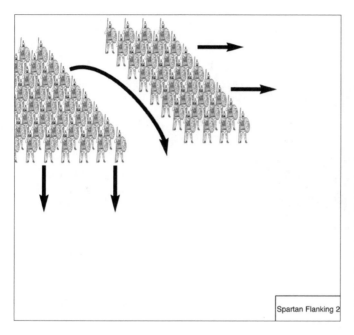

2) *As the phalanx advances, a section of the left wing turns to form a column facing to the left and marches off in that direction.*

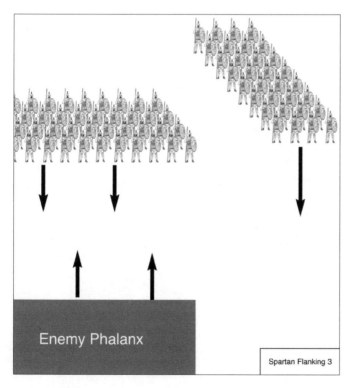

3) *The files on the left of the remaining phalanx redeploy to be only four men deep, maintaining the original frontage of the phalanx. The flanking force now turns and advances at double speed to overtake the phalanx.*

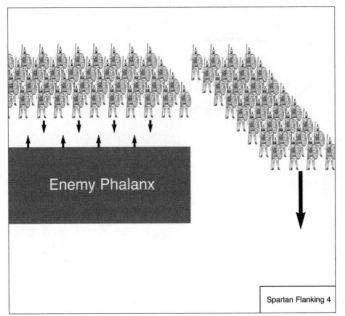

Spartan Flanking 4

4) Contact is made with the enemy phalanx. The flanking force is now ahead of the main phalanx and will turn to face the flank of the opposing formation.

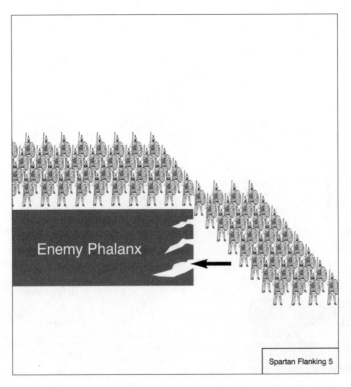

Spartan Flanking 5

5) The flanking force charges into the vulnerable, shieldless side of the men in the enemy army. The enemy flank quickly disintegrates, the collapse spreading rapidly until the entire enemy force is fleeing.

1. The sacred olive tree on the Acropolis in Athens. Branches from the predecessor to this tree were probably offered to the gods by the Athenians in the hope of appeasing their wrath.

2. The statue of Leonidas which tops the modern monument at Thermopylae. The words engraved beneath the figure are those spoken by Leonidas when asked to surrender his weapons: "Come and get them".

Opposite

3. *Above:* The Middle Gate seen from the west. This was the view the Persians would have had as they advanced.

4. *Below:* The Vale of Tempe, the "river of dreams" between Mounts Olympos and Ossa. Xerxes found enough time for some sightseeing and visited the famously beautiful gorge. "It was a great marvel to him" records Herodotus. It was also useless as a route through the mountains for his mighty army.

5. A strange picture to include here perhaps; but an effective reminder that despite the great passage of time since the events of the Thermopylae campaign, what is being described is no Greek myth. The silver mines at Laurium that paid for the Greek fleet (see page 4) were still productive in the 20th century (but mainly worked for lead, manganese and cadmium). Did any of the miners about to start their shift here in the 1900s know what effect their place of work had had on their country's history? And indeed, on the history of the World?

6. The temple of Apollo at Didyma, now in southern Turkey and then in the Persian Empire. Although this was the second most important temple dedicated to Apollo at the time of the campaign, the priests here received no word from the god, unlike those at Delphi.

7. A view of the Athenian Acropolis from the north, with the ruins of the Agora in the foreground. The Agora was the main commercial heart of the ancient city. It was looted thoroughly by the Persians, then destroyed. Most of the ruins seen here today date from after the Thermopylae campaign.

8. The Library in the Greek city of Ephesus. As a self-governing city within the Persian Empire, Ephesus was forced to contribute ships and men to fight against her fellow Greeks.

9. The Harbour Road at Ephesus, a Greek city within the Persian Empire. The harbour is now silted up, but originally lay at the end of this columned road. It was from here that the Ephesian ships left to take part in the Thermopylae campaign.

10. The Parthenon, or temple of Athena, on the Athenian Acropolis. This magnificent building was erected to replace the temple destroyed by the Persians.

11. The Temple of Hephaestus in Athens. This temple dates to after the Persian attack, but it was completed in the Doric style giving a good idea of the appearance of the temples and public buildings destroyed by the Persians.

12. Looking across the Euripus to the island of Euboea from the mainland, near the modern town of Kamena Vourla. It was up this channel that the Persian fleet hoped to move to trap the Greek fleet.

13. The inscription on the modern monument to the Spartans at Thermopylae. The words translate as "Come and get them", the famous answer given by Leonidas when asked to surrender his weapons.

14. A stone carving of a lion devouring a bull. This panel was discovered among buried rubble on the Acropolis and almost certainly comes from the pediment of the temple of Athena destroyed by the Persians.

15. The foundations of the temple of Athena that was destroyed by the Persians. The famous Parthenon was built after the war to replace the structure.

16. The North Wall of the Acropolis. It was at more or less this spot that the Persian soldiers climbed up under cover at night to gain access to the fortress.

17. A group of hoplite re-enactors form up as the front line of an advancing phalanx with shields held forward and spears in the overhead position. In reality there would have been another seven or more ranks of men in close order. *(With thanks to the Hoplite Association.)*

18. A re-enactor dressed as a Scythian foot archer looses an arrow at advancing hoplites. Even at such close quarters the lighter arrows used in the Persian army made little impression on hoplite armour. *(With thanks to the Hoplite Association.)*

19. A re-enactor demonstrates the defensive position adopted by hoplites when under attack by arrows, javelins or other missile weapons. The shield and helmet cover the entire man and protect him from injury. *(With thanks to the Hoplite Association.)*

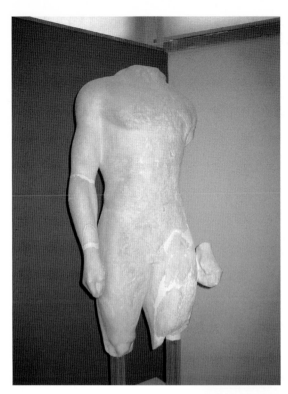

20. A kore, or nude male statue, found buried on the Athenian Acropolis. Its style dates it to around 550bc, making it some 60 years old at the time of the Persian attack. The statue appears to have been deliberately smashed and buried, while scorch marks from an intense fire are visible on the torso. The damage was almost certainly inflicted during the capture of the Acropolis.

21. A modern re-enactor shows off the detail of a hoplite's armour. Note the grips on the inside of the shield and the deeply dished shape of the shield. This man wears scale armour on his body of a type that was new during the Thermopylae campaign. His helmet is of the Corinthian style that was favoured by the Greeks from the Peloponnese, including the Spartans. (*With thanks to the Hoplite Association*)

22. A junior officer, recognisable by the crest running sideways over his helmet. Most Greek cities employed full time professional junior officers to oversee training and to check the equipment of their citizens. His stout wooden stick is both a staff of rank and a useful tool for pushing recruits into position or for dishing out punishment to defaulters. (*With thanks to the Hoplite Association*)

23. A typical scene in a camp of hoplites. The tents and wooden weapon stands are taken from contemporary depictions on vases and reliefs. Note that the spears are stuck upright in the ground while the shields are leaning against the armour stands. The Greek camp at Thermopylae would have looked very much like this. (*With thanks to the Hoplite Association*)

24. Aristeides and the peasant, an engraving from a 19th century painting. The incident, in which Aristeides helped the peasant vote against Aristeides himself, displayed the sense of honour for which the Athenian statesman was famous (see page 99).

25. A fanciful depiction of the victorious fleet returning to an indeterminate Greek city by J. W. Appleton. The battle at Artemisium had not been decisive. But at Salamis a month later, the divided Persian fleet would lose 200 ships, which meant the end of any plans for a sea-borne invasion of the Peloponnese.

Spartan Feigned Retreat

This manoeuvre called for iron discipline and high morale if it were not to end in catastrophic defeat for the army that attempted it. In ancient Greece only the Spartans had the combination of abilities to be able to perform this subterfuge on the battlefield.

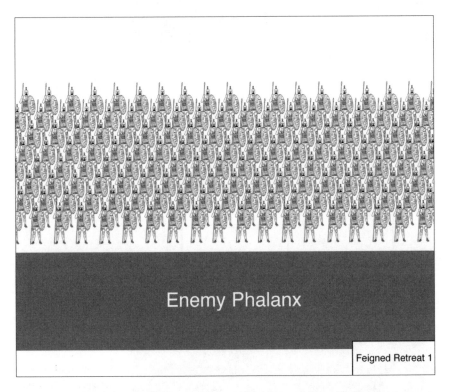

Feigned Retreat 1

1) *The Spartan phalanx is drawn up 8 deep and in close combat with the enemy phalanx, both sides having charged into action.*

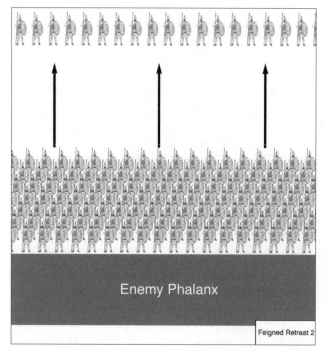

Feigned Retreat 2

2) *The rear rank of the Spartans withdraws to a previously agreed position, which may have been marked on the ground by piles of clothing or other temporary marks. In reality the position may have been as much as 200 metres behind the phalanx to allow space for the enemy to become disordered as it advanced.*

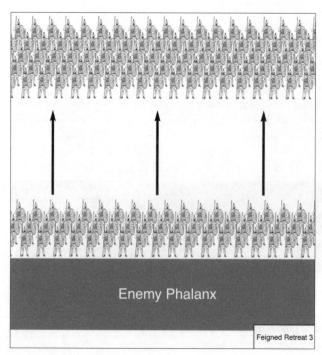

Feigned Retreat 3

3) *The main body of the Spartan phalanx pulls back to form up on the rear rank.*

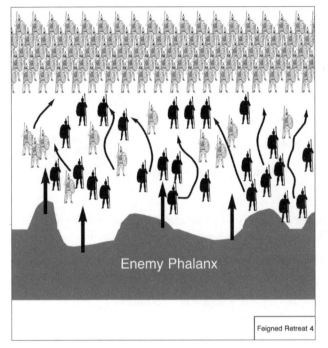

Feigned Retreat 4

4) Deprived of the support of the central and rear ranks, the front three ranks of the Spartan phalanx would naturally break down and crumble. The men in these ranks behave in this fashion, simulating panic and disorder as they appear to flee before the enemy. Men shown as silhouette are running away from the viewer. As the enemy phalanx rushes forward it becomes disordered.

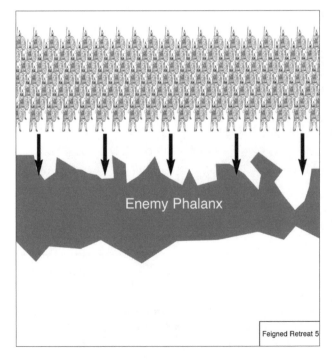

Feigned Retreat 5

5) Now thoroughly out of formation, the enemy troops are faced by the reformed Spartan phalanx. When the Spartans charge, they smash the enemy formation to pieces to win a complete and overwhelming victory.

Spartan Countermarch

This manoeuvre was used to enable the phalanx to reverse direction while keeping formation and, crucially, ensuring that the front ranks remained at the front and the rear ranks at the rear.

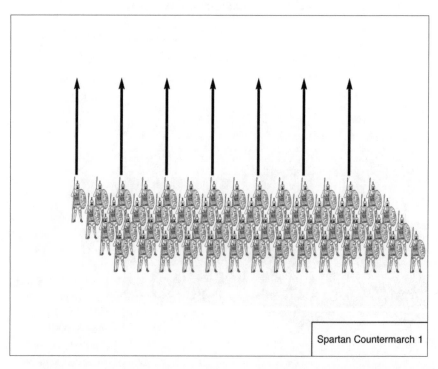

Spartan Countermarch 1

1) *The Spartan phalanx is shown drawn up 4 deep for clarity, but the manoeuvre could be performed 8 or 12 ranks deep. Alternate files drop back to take up position behind what were previously their neighbouring files.*

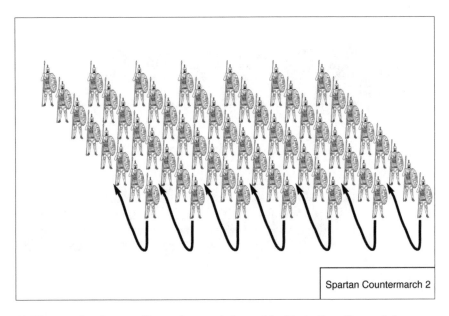

Spartan Countermarch 2

2) *The move by alternate files produces a phalanx of double depth, with gaps between each file the width of a file. The leader of each new double file turns about and marches up the gap beside his file, to be followed by all members of his file.*

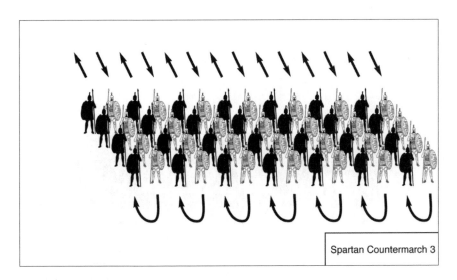

Spartan Countermarch 3

3) *Half way through the countermarch, the phalanx has reformed in general shape, but alternate files are now marching in opposite directions as the men follow the leader through the manoeuvre. Note: A black silhouette indicates a man marching away from the viewer.*

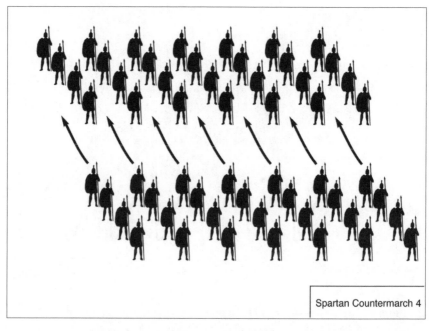

Spartan Countermarch 4

4) *As the turnabout is completed, the phalanx is still formed up in files of double-depth, but facing in the opposite direction from that in step 2. The rear half of each double file now moves forward through the gap between the files to fill it and reform the phalanx.*

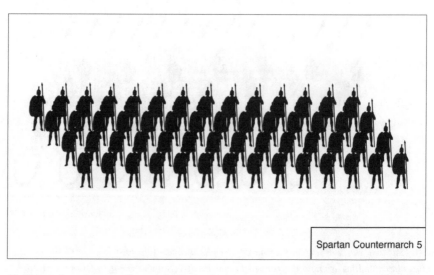

Spartan Countermarch 5

5) *The phalanx is now reformed facing in the opposite direction from that in step 1, but with the same men as previously being front rankers and rear rankers.*

CHAPTER 7

The Warships

A Greek warship, as depicted on a contemporary vase. The twin steering oars and boarding ladder can be clearly seen to the rear of the vessel, while the ram projects at water level from the bow.

While the Greek army was preparing to meet the invader, the Greek fleet was also mustering for war. The exact size of the fleet that met at this point in the campaign is open to some debate. Smaller states were still deciding whether or not to fight the Persians. Some sent their fleets, others supplied only a token ship or two to show willing while still keeping their options open. Notoriously, the commander of the 60 modern and powerful ships coming from Corfu used every excuse possible to put into port en route to the scene of action. The ships arrived when the campaign was over.

Eventually more than 500 ships would serve with the Greek fleet, though they were never all present at the same time. Of these the largest number came from Athens, which provided 200 new triremes plus another 60 or so older ships. The Corinthians sent 40 ships, and the Aeginetans 30. The other states sent smaller numbers, but even military Sparta managed to supply sixteen.

The ability of a state to put a war fleet to sea depended on two key elements: men and money. Each trireme, the dominant type of warship, required a crew of around 200 men. A force of a thousand men, therefore, would crew only five ships. Many would argue that such manpower would be better used in land warfare, but that is to ignore an important economic element.

The men who marched to war were expected to supply their own weapons and equipment. As we described earlier the full panoply of a hoplite was not cheap and only a minority of citizens in any Greek state could afford it. Most men, therefore, marched as light infantry or served as garrison troops. Useful as such men were, they were not the decisive factor in a pitched battle.

Sailors, however, needed nothing except their muscle power to be useful at sea. Nor did they need to be rich enough to provide for their families while they were away fighting, for it was normal to pay naval seamen. At the time of the Thermopylae campaign the going rate was three bronze coins, known as obols, per day. This was not far off the wage a skilled labourer could expect. With six obols to the silver drachma that put the cost of a crew at around 3,000 drachma per month. In addition to this, it was generally thought that during a season's fighting a trireme would need to have around 3,000 drachma spent on repairs, refitting and new equipment. It was, for instance, assumed that at least half the oars would be broken even if no combat took place. Thus the running cost of a trireme for six months of fighting was around 21,000 drachma.

Compared to the running costs, the initial construction of a trireme was a surprisingly modest 6,000 drachma. The process of construction took about two months, but all states had only limited numbers of skilled workmen. Even at full stretch the Athenian shipyards could produce only 50 triremes per year, and this led to many complaints that merchant shipping was suffering from the diversion of labour.

Given the costs of building, maintaining and crewing a warship, the Greek states had every incentive to keep their ships out of action for as long as possible. To this end every port had a number of ship sheds built along the shore into which the warships could be dragged for storage. Here they were protected from the sun, rain and wind. Just as important they were out of the water, ensuring that no weeds grew on the hull and no boring animals drilled into the timbers to weaken them. Only when they were needed, were the poorer citizens hired as oarsmen, the ships launched and sent off to war. Not only did this provide a useful summer income for thousands of men, but some states also earned a tidy sum by renting out ships, complete with crew, to other states. A fee of around 5,000 drachma per month was considered reasonable, which represents a mark-up of about a third, a decent profit. Of course in the emergency of the Persian invasion, every ship was needed. There was no time for money-making ventures.

The fleet was to play a crucial role in the Thermopylae campaign, so it is as well to know something about the ships that served in it and the tactics that the commanders employed in action. Both would have a crucial effect on how the campaign was conducted.

The basic Greek warship was the *pentekonter*, which translates as "50 oars", though by this date it was becoming obsolete. As the name suggests, this ship was powered by 50 men, 25 per side, each pulling on a single oar. A mast and sail was carried for use when the wind was in the right direction, but for combat this was left ashore and the ship relied on oars alone. A typical pentekonter was about 34 metres long, four metres wide and drew less than a metre of water. This made it very long and thin, meaning that it was unable to cope with rough seas. If bad weather threatened a pentekonter had to be pulled up a beach, out of the reach of the waves. Typically, these ships were useful for only about half the year in Greek waters as bad weather was too frequent in the winter to allow them to achieve very much.

The construction of the pentekonter and of the other types that evolved from it, dictated the way in which it was used in battle. Modern wooden craft are built by laying down the keel and ribs first, to which the planking is then attached. Ancient shipwrights worked the other way around. The planking was put together first, each plank being attached to the next by tightly fitting mortice and tenon joints. Only when the planking was complete were the ribs fitted at about one-metre intervals. The top of each rib was then linked to its opposite number on the other side of the ship by a timber. This framing kept the planks in shape, but the main strength came from three main timbers that ran the entire length of the ship.

The first of these was the keel, itself constructed in two parts. Inside the hull the keel was a stout timber of hard wood, such as oak, which provided the main strength. The outer keel was made of a cheaper wood and was designed to take the battering of being hauled over sand and pebbles whenever the ship was beached. This outer keel was usually replaced annually. The two other main timbers, the zosteres, ran along the top of the side planking, attached to the ribs that projected upwards another metre or so.

At the rear of the ship the three main timbers were turned upward and gathered together before bending forwards to form a characteristic shape often likened to a scorpion's tail. It was here that the commander stood on a small platform. He was accompanied by the flute player who played a tune to which the rowers kept time. The faster the tune, the quicker the ship moved. Behind the commander stood the helmsman, who steered the ship by means of two broad-bladed oars which pointed backward over the stern.

At the bows, the zosteres swept down to join the keel at or below water level. The three timbers projected forward from the ship to form a ram, which was encased in bronze. This ram was the key weapon in pentekonter warfare, though each ship also carried armed men to act as a boarding party. Ships also carried one or two archers, whose job was to pick off men in opposing ships. To guard against incoming arrows, the upper parts of the projecting ribs were covered with screens of leather.

By around 700BC the pentekonter was joined in naval warfare by the bireme, meaning two banks (of oars). The bireme was essentially a pentekonter with a second bank of rowing benches set above and behind the first set. This made the ship slightly taller, but doubled the number of oars and so the motive power. This gave the bireme the edge in terms of speed, essential in combat.

Sometime around 550BC, the date is not recorded, a new type of warship appeared. This was the trireme, which was to dominate the naval conflict during the Thermopylae campaign. Essentially this was an enlarged bireme on both sides of which was built a light wooden outrigger construction. This projected half a metre outside the hull and stood two metres or more tall. In it sat a third rank of oarsmen, their oars projecting out beyond those wielded by the two lower ranks of rowers.

The trireme had a few other improvements, as well as increased power. The ram was made shorter, but stronger, so that it was less likely to break off in combat. Above the ram was an upright timber that stopped the ship penetrating too far into any vessel that it rammed so that it would not become stuck and sink along with its victim.

There was also more room for soldiers; a complement of four archers and ten hoplites was to become standard. However, many ships went into battle with far fewer soldiers on board, sometimes none at all, if ramming was intended to be the main route to victory. Others preferred to board the enemy in order to defeat him. These ships may have carried 40 or more soldiers.

Although some of the older ships used in the campaign may have been biremes, and several pentekonters were used as fast scout and messenger ships, it was the trireme that was the most numerous and effective warship. Herodotus says that the Persian war fleet was entirely composed of triremes, though in reality there were probably small numbers of other types of ship.

It is therefore important to understand the abilities of the trireme. On long voyages, the sail would be hoisted whenever the wind was in the right direction. Under sail, a trireme could make around three knots, covering some 50 km in a good day's sailing. When the wind was not favourable, a trireme would revert to oars and adopt the slow cruise pace. This involved each bank of oarsmen rowing for an hour, then resting for two hours while the others rowed. In this way a constant speed of some three knots could be achieved. If all the oarsmen rowed at a slow pace, a cruising speed of some five knots could be achieved, but this could be maintained for only four hours or so before a rest would be needed. In combat, a ship would adopt the cruising speed for most of the action. However, when ramming another ship, or attempting to evade such an attack, a trireme's crew would row at maximum power to achieve a speed of around nine knots. This was an exhausting pace that could be maintained for no more than twenty minutes, and usually for far less.

A key feature of the trireme, and other oared ships, was their great manoeuvrability. A stationary ship could spin around on the spot by rowing forward with one side of oarsmen and backward with the other. At fast cruise, the turning circle would have been about 80 metres, making these remarkably handy craft in confined spaces. By combining oars and steering a much tighter turn could probably be achieved. Ships could move backward, simply by rowing backward, though the speed achieved was probably only half that of forward motion.

The ability of a ship to perform such manoeuvres, so crucial in combat, was entirely reliant on the skill of the crew. An average trireme carried 170 oarsmen, together with fourteen soldiers and twenty other men – the commander, flautist, helmsman and others. The 170 rowers needed to be able to row in time with each other, or their oars would clash. This was the basic skill demanded of a trireme crew, and it took some days to learn properly. It took several more days for even experienced oarsmen to learn to operate as a crew, able to perform the various manoeuvres demanded by a commander in combat. It is hardly surprising that experienced crews which had worked together before were highly prized, and effective in combat.

In addition to the manoeuvres of the individual craft, ships were expected to be able to work together as a fleet in combat so as to defeat the enemy. The Greeks tended to prefer ramming to boarding, and their fleet tactics were developed accordingly. By the time of Thermopylae there were a number of well known moves used by fleets in combat.

The basic naval tactic in open water was to form the fleet into a line abreast, each ship some 50 metres from the next. Each ship guarded the flank of those beside it. The fleet would row forward at cruising speed, seeking a weak spot in the enemy fleet which would be approaching in a similar line. If any ship fell off station, it would open up a gap into which an enemy could dart at maximum speed to attempt a ram.

A development of this formation was the tactic that became known as the *periplus*. Typically, this was used by fleets which had more ships than their enemy. The more experienced and expert crews would be given a position on one flank of the fleet. As the fleets approached each other, these ships would surge forward at high speed to get around the end of the enemy line. They could then attack from the beam to ram and sink those enemy ships closest to them. In theory this would inflict casualties without loss, after which the attacking ships would be joined by those closest to them in rolling up the enemy line.

A commander of a numerically inferior fleet could try a devastating tactic known as the *diekplus*. This relied upon the crews being highly trained and commanded by captains able to react quickly to the changing situation. It was most effective carried out against slower ships or less experienced crews. A diekplus involved forming up in line ahead, then breaking through the enemy line. The leading ships in the column would be those with the best crews and commanders. At first the attacking ships concentrated on smashing the oars of the enemy ships, thus temporarily crippling them. Once the enemy formation was disrupted, the business of ramming and sinking would begin.

A third formation seems to have been in its infancy at this time and was first used to any real effect in the Thermopylae campaign. This was the defensive *kyklos*. The ships of the fleet were arranged in a circle, with their prows facing outward. Within the circle a smaller number of ships were kept as a mobile reserve ready to plug gaps or exploit any successes. The commanders of the ships would watch the enemy for any openings, darting out to ram, then backing water to return to station. Like the diekplus, the kyklos called for a high degree of skill and was used most often by smaller fleets.

In reality, of course, sea battles rarely took place in open water. And the enemy was never considerate enough to wait while a fleet got itself into position to perform a manoeuvre. As with all battles, the naval commanders needed to be able to adapt their tactics and intentions to the rapidly changing situations as they arose. The commander who was able to think quickly and who had subordinates able to react to new orders or to take the initiative themselves, was likely to triumph.

Given the comparative strengths of the two fleets, the Greeks and Persians had very different tactical imperatives. With larger numbers of warships, the Persian commanders would want to engage the enemy in open water. They would be able to carry out periplus flanking attacks, wrapping their lines around the edges of the Greek fleet. The prospect of an annihilating triumph in which the enemy fleet was utterly destroyed was what spurred on the Persian high command. However, as described later, the numerical superiority of the Persian fleet in each individual encounter was not as great as is sometimes supposed. Nor was it the case that the Greeks were better at naval fighting. The Persian fleet included Phoenician ships, acknowledged to be the best fighting ships in the Mediterranean at this time, as well as several Greek contingents from states ruled by Xerxes.

The Greeks, on the other hand, needed to stay in confined waters where their flanks would be guarded by land. This would also give the Greeks the advantage of being in waters affected by currents and winds that would be familiar to at least some of their commanders, but not to the Persians. More than once the Greeks gained an advantage from some local factor.

From a strategic point of view, it is important to remember that there was no hold in the trireme. There was no space for stores of food or water. Because they were operating off friendly coasts, the Greeks could arrange for food supplies to be delivered to convenient beaches and for local guides to show them sources of fresh water. The ships would need to come to shore each evening to feed and water their crews. Except in emergencies, the crews preferred to land around noon as well to eat. As a consequence the Greek fleet was never far from shore and was usually tied to operating from an agreed base where supplies were gathered.

The Persians, by contrast, were operating off a hostile shore. It was for this reason that the warfleet was accompanied by so many merchant ships. These carried the food and water needed by the thousands of oarsmen. Although this freed them from the need to return each night to a supply base, it did bring its own problems. Most noticeably, the fleet needed to come to shore so that the supplies could be unloaded from the merchant ships. The naval crews then landed to eat and drink.

Therefore a suitable beach needed to be found each night. There was also the problem that the merchant ships could not sail into the wind. Thus the Persian warships could row only so far upwind on a mission, before needing to turn back to rejoin their supply ships.

Finally, the Persian supply system meant that at any given time a number of warships had to be used to protect the supply ships from attack. This reduced the number of warships that could be mustered into the main force to attack the Greek fleet. Without vulnerable merchant ships to protect, the Greeks were free to concentrate all their forces for decisive battles. Time and again, this was to give the Greeks an advantage when it came to combat.

In July the fleet that had by then mustered for action was divided in two. One force was kept back, in and around the Saronic Gulf, south of Athens. Its task was to guard against any attempt by the Persians to land soldiers in the Peloponnese or Attica. We know that 100 of the new Athenian ships and ten of their older vessels were in this force, but how many and which other ships were included has not been recorded.

We do know, however, the precise composition of the fleet that went north as an advance fighting force to meet the Persians as they came south along the coast. There were 100 new and 27 old ships from Athens, 40 from Corinth, twenty from Megara, eighteen from Aegina, twelve from Sicyon, ten from Sparta, eight from Epidauros, seven from Eretria, five from Troezen, two from Styra and two from Ceos. Plataea and Chalcis had no ships of their own, but each sent enough men to row twenty of the older Athenian vessels. In all there were 224 front line warships, plus 67 older ships. In addition there were nine pentekonters in the fleet, provided by Locris and Ceos; and there would seem to have been other small craft as well.

This was a significant force, and certainly represented the bulk of the available Greek ships. It drew on states from both north and south of the Isthmus of Corinth and so was a good representation of the states still in the League. Interestingly the commanders of the smaller contingents refused to serve under an Athenian commander. Eurybiades, the commander of the Spartan contingent, was chosen as admiral instead.

The Athenians later claimed that Eurybiades was a mere figurehead of a leader, and that their own commander, Themistocles, was in real control of the fleet. It is certain that Eurybiades held frequent conferences at which he asked the opinions of his subordinates. It is equally well known that Themistocles was one of the more vocal of these subordinates. The exact relationship between the two remains obscure, however, for we have only the Athenians' side of the story.

It is a shame that more is not known of Eurybiades. He is recorded as being the son of Eurycleides and to have come from a non-noble family. Otherwise he is unknown to history outside of his role as fleet commander at this crucial time. Clearly he had won his position as commander of the small Spartan fleet by merit rather than birth. This might indicate that he was rather more experienced than the Athenian sources would have us believe. His frequent conferences may have been a way to keep his fractious command together, more than a sign of his own indecision. Whoever commanded the Greek fleet as it set off northward, he would have known that the Persian fleet outnumbered his own. Just how great was the Persian superiority would not become clear until the fleets met. By all accounts, it came as something of a shock.

Model of a Greek warship. Obviously,
a trireme would be faster than a bireme
(though nowhere near one-third faster).
But it would also be more expensive
because rowing crews were paid on
campaign, so the slower design was not
immediately abandoned and was only
just being superseded at the time of the
battle of Thermopylae.

CHAPTER 8
The Choice of Thermopylae

Looking northeast to the Temple of Apollo and the most famous oracle, at Delphi. The oracle would hint at the death of Leonidas; but it would also imply that his death would not be in vain.

It is one of the frustrating aspects of the Thermopylae campaign that the key factor in determining the actions of the Athenians is clouded in mystery. Like other Greek states, Athens sent an embassy to Delphi to ask the Oracle for the advice of the god Apollo. The message given was of profound importance, so it is vexing that we have only the vaguest idea of when this event took place.

Herodotus places the Athenian embassy to Delphi in the early spring, but it is clear that the debate on the answer and vote on what action to take did not take place until after the expedition to Tempe, perhaps in late June or early July. But whenever the visit to Delphi took place, it was a dramatic one.

The Athenian envoys travelled to the sacred city, climbed the holy hill and washed themselves in the sacred spring. They were then admitted to the precincts of Apollo and escorted up the Sacred Way to the Temple of Apollo. So far everything had been carried out as prescribed by tradition and as expected. But when the envoys entered the room where the oracle priestess herself awaited them, they were in for a shock. They had not even had time to approach the priestess with their enquiry, when the oracle priestess shrieked at them in fury:

"Why sit you, doomed ones? Fly to the world's end leaving
Home and the heights your city circles like a wheel.
The head shall not remain in its place, nor the body,
Nor the feet beneath, nor the hands, nor the parts between:
But all is ruined, for fire and headlong god of war
Speeding in a Syrian chariot shall bring you low.
Many a tower will he destroy, not yours alone,
And give to pitiless fire many shrines of gods,
Which even now stand sweating, with fear quivering,
While over the roofs black blood runs streaming
In prophecy of woe that needs must come. But rise,
Haste from the sanctuary and bow your hearts to grief."

The Athenians were stunned, as well they might have been. This was one of the most dramatic, lengthy and most detailed utterances ever given by the Delphic Oracle – and it was all bad news for Athens. There could be no doubt that the city would be destroyed, its temples defiled and its people doomed.

What happened next is rather obscure. Herodotus describes how the Athenians returned to the oracle a second time, on this occasion carrying olive branches as a symbol of their supplication and devotion. The priestess was this time moved to give a different message from the god Apollo.

"Not wholly can Pallas win the heart of Olympian Zeus,
Though she prays to him with many prayers and all her subtlety.
Yet will I speak to you this other word, as firm as adamant:
Though all else shall be taken within the bound of Cecrops
And the fastness of the holy mountain of Cithaeron
Yet Zeus the all-seeing grants to Athene's prayer
That the wooden wall only shall not fall, but help you and your
    children.
But await not the host of horse and foot coming from Asia,
Nor be still, but turn your back and withdraw from the foe.
Truly a day will come when you will meet him face to face.
Divine Salamis, you will bring death to women's sons
When the corn is scattered, or the harvest gathered in."

This second divine message was not much more encouraging than the first; though it was to prompt the Athenians to change their plan for the war.

There are a couple of allusions within the prophecy which would have had a great impact. First, as in the message to the Spartans, Apollo makes it clear that Zeus is on the side of the Persians. Second, Athene is shown to be on the side of the Athenians – so Xerxes's sacrifice to the goddess at Troy had not worked. Pallas is a title of Athene, meaning "maiden".

There are also clues that some time had elapsed since the first prophecy. Herodotus implies, but does not state, that the two messages were given during the same visit to the oracle by the envoys of Athens. However, his insistence that it was the bringing of branches of olives to Apollo that caused the new message to be given hints at a delay.

High on the Acropolis in Athens, outside the temple of Athene, grew a sacred olive tree. The Athenians believed that the olive had been a special gift from the goddess Athene to her beloved city in the remote past. The sacred tree was the direct descendent of this original plant, tended by priests since the dawn of time. It would make sense for the Athenians to do something special to try to gain a change of heart from the gods. What better than to return to their city, arrange for their fellow citizens to pray to Athene and then take sprigs of the sacred olive to Apollo? The Oracle's statement that Athene was pleading with Zeus to spare Athens would imply that some such action had been taken. If this were the case, the journey to and fro would have taken some time. The interval between the two trips to Delphi may have coincided with the Tempe expedition.

Whatever the exact timing of the Athenian visits to the Delphic Oracle, the second message was delivered to the people at about the time that the army led by Themistocles got back from Tempe. As was usual, the message first went to the priests who gave their opinion on what the god Apollo meant. Then both the Oracle and its interpretation by the priests went before the Assembly for discussion. The debate would end with a vote on what action to take.

The debate at the Assembly was prolonged and bitter. Some of the divine message caused few problems. The references to Cecrops and Cithaeron were to geographical features that indicated that the message applied to all of Attica, not just the city of Athens. It was the rest of the message that was the subject of heated debate.

The "wooden wall" referred to caused particular problems as Athens was surrounded by stone walls. They were strong by Greek standards, but as events had already shown the Persians were masters of siege warfare and would have had no problems overcoming them. However, the Acropolis at the centre of the city did have a section of wooden palings which stood on top of the steep slope that gave access to the hilltop. The priests argued that Apollo was telling them to abandon most of the city, but to retreat to the summit of its central hill and gather in the holy temples and ancient palaces.

Themistocles and his supporters, on the other hand, suggested that the "wooden wall" referred to the fleet of wooden ships. If this were the case, Apollo was clearly telling the Athenians that their army could not stand up to the might of Persia, but that their fleet could. They should, therefore, take up a position where the fleet could protect them. This, Themistocles argued, accorded with the line "Nor be still, but turn your back and withdraw from the foe." The civilians and valuables should be evacuated to a place that could be defended by the fleet.

But Apollo was not telling the Athenians simply to run away, for the message went on to state that the two forces would meet face to face in a decisive battle at "Divine Salamis". As everyone in Athens knew, Salamis was a small island just off the coast a few kilometres west of the city. There was, however, nothing divine about the place – no special temples nor sacred places. Themistocles suggested that Apollo had used the word "divine" to indicate that if a battle were fought there it would be a victory for Athens. Otherwise, Themistocles said, Apollo would have said "Hateful Salamis" or some such phrase.

After hours of debate, argument and counter-argument, it was time for a vote. Themistocles put forward a motion that was passed overwhelmingly. Unusually for a motion from this date, a copy of it has survived.

When the war was over the Athenians were so proud of their achievement that they carved the motion on to a pillar and set it up at Troezen, a city in the Peloponnese that featured within it.

There have been attempts by some historians to discredit the inscription as a fallacy dreamed up long after the event. However, it was set up at a time when most of the men who had voted on the motion at Athens were still alive and would have been able to complain if it were wrong. Moreover, there are some obvious indications that the motion was passed before the meeting of the League that decided to fight at Thermopylae, for no mention of the place is made. Instead it talks about the Athenian fleet and its movements while giving the commander of that fleet – Themistocles – freedom to co-operate with the other Greek states. It is most likely that this is the genuine motion passed at Athens in response to the messages sent from Apollo via the Delphic Oracle.

Much of the motion was taken up with technical details of getting the full strength of the fleet into the water with complete crews. There then follows some details of the religious preparations and sacrifices to be made. Provisions are also made to ship all the women and children of Attica to the city of Troezen, which had offered them hospitality if the need came. The moveable valuables, state treasury and anything else that could be transported were to be loaded on to ships and taken to Salamis. There they were to be guarded by the men too old or infirm to man the ships. The fleet would then be divided into two. The first half was to row off to face the enemy in co-operation with the allies of Athens. The second half was to remain in the waters off Salamis to guard against a raid by the Persian fleet.

A touch of grim irony may be found in the section of the decree that reads that the people decide "to entrust the city to Athena, the Mistress of Athens, and to all the other Gods to guard and defend from the Barbarian for the sake of the land. The priests and priestesses are to remain on the Acropolis guarding the property of the gods." So those who had advocated trusting the wooden walls of the Acropolis were told to stand by their advice.

Another provision in the decree called on all Athenians not in the city to return home to join the war against the barbarian hordes. Some of these men were, no doubt, merchants or others on legitimate business abroad. Others, however, were men who had been sent into temporary exile by the Athenian Assembly for various reasons. There is no mention of how the message is to be sent to these men, nor how it might be enforced. Perhaps it was more wishful thinking than a practical measure.

Some of these exiles did, in fact, go back to Athens. The best known of these was an impoverished nobleman by the name of Aristeides. Known as "the Just" for the impartial manner in which he presided at trials and conducted state business, Aristeides was sent into exile in 494BC. It was thought that his absence would break the deadlock that was stopping the state from spending money on building the new fleet. Even in being exiled, Aristeides the Just gained new honour.

The process of exile, or ostracism, involved each citizen attending the Assembly writing the name of a person they wanted exiled on a piece of broken pottery. When the shards were collected anyone who had received the required number of votes was forced abroad, usually for ten years. While the voting was going on in 494 an illiterate peasant citizen from a rural village who was entitled to vote approached Aristeides holding out his shard of pottery. The peasant asked Aristeides to write the name "Aristeides" on the shard as he did not know how to do so himself.

"Why do you want this man exiled?" asked Aristeides. "Has he ever done you harm?"

"No," came the all too-human reply, "and I do not even know him. I'm just tired of hearing everybody call him 'the Just'." Aristeides duly wrote his name on the shard, enhancing his reputation for honesty.

Although he had been exiled, when he heard of the city's need, Aristeides hurried back to Athens. He helped crew one of the ships and fought bravely throughout the rest of the year. The following year he was given command of part of the Athenian army and his exile was ended.

Others were not so dutiful. Hipparchus, the nobleman in exile and now protected by Xerxes, still dreamed of returning to head a government of nobles in Athens. He was relying on Xerxes to install him in power as thanks for his marching into Greece with the Persians and serving as an advisor on Athenian affairs. The failure of Hipparchus to return as instructed led to his being stripped of his citizenship by the Athenian Assembly once the war was over. Moreover the bronze statue of Hipparchus, erected on the Acropolis in gratitude for his earlier service in government, was melted down. The metal was used to make a pillar on which were to be engraved the names of all future traitors to Athens.

Not all exiles were treated so harshly. Dicaeus, a supporter of Hipparchus, was likewise marching with the Persians. In later life, however, he was allowed to return in peace to Athens. Displaying more courage than tact he used to regale his fellow citizens with tales about his time with Xerxes.

All the preparations contained in the motion put forward by Themistocles would, of course, have taken some weeks to put into effect. The Persian army was advancing and, if the Delphic Oracle was correct, would march into Attica in the not too distant future. It must be assumed that as soon as the meeting broke up, the city and surrounding villages became a hive of activity as the ships were prepared, men made ready for war and civilians got ready to flee.

Meanwhile, Themistocles set off for Corinth to attend the meeting of the League that would decide what to do now that Thessaly had been abandoned to the Persians. It was by then early July. He found the various delegates deeply worried, but at last ready for united action. Or so it seemed. The news that Xerxes had sent his engineers and workmen to widen and improve the roads from Macedon to Thessaly seems to have shaken the delegates gathered at Corinth. Perhaps some of them realised for the first time that the King of Kings actually intended to invade and conquer all of Greece.

It was known that the Thessalians had defected to Persia, and there were real grounds to believe that the Boeotians, most obviously those at Thebes, would do the same. There was, therefore, much discussion on the wisdom of trying to help them at all. If the army were sent north of Boeotia they might ensure that the Boeotians remained loyal. On the other hand, the Boeotians might stab the army in the back and destroy it utterly.

Once again, there were those from the Peloponnese who argued that a defensive line should be built at the Isthmus of Corinth. As before, however, they had no real answer to the threat posed by the Persian fleet and its ability to land troops on the Peloponnese. They might suggest that the Greek fleet stop such a move, but the Greek fleet was outnumbered and clearly unable to guard such a long coastline. As before, the peoples from the area north of Corinth were just as determined to face the Persians north of Attica in an attempt to save their country.

It is not known who finally suggested that the stand should be made at Thermopylae, though Plutarch implies it was Themistocles. But whoever came up with the idea, it was a stroke of strategic genius. The true importance of the move was missed by both Plutarch and Herodotus, but it was obvious to King Leonidas of Sparta. As a trained military professional of many years experience, he was delighted at the choice.

The key to understanding why Thermopylae was chosen is to think logistically. As will become clear there were some very good tactical reasons to fight at this pass, but they were not paramount. It was logistics that determined the choice of ground.

Nor is it that there were no other routes by which Xerxes could have advanced to the south. North of the Gulf of Corinth the towering Parnassos Mountains form a barrier across Greece from the Aegean to the Ionian Seas. But it is not an impassable barrier. There were many tracks over the massif; one ran from Lamia direct to Delphi for example, but these were rugged and unsurfaced footpaths. Only infantry could negotiate these routes, and Xerxes needed a road able to carry cavalry and supply carts.

There were only three routes through the mountains where the roads were wide enough and the gradient gentle enough to allow carts and pack horses to move without difficulty. One was at Thermopylae on the east coast. The second was at Astakos on the west coast. The third was the pass through the mountains at Stratos. Both Astakos and Stratos lay more than a hundred kilometres to the west of the Persian line of advance, and reaching them would involve a lengthy detour over the rugged terrain of the Pindos Mountains.

Scouting parties and raiding forces might be sent this way, and probably were. But the westerly routes would have involved delays stretching into weeks. By the time Xerxes was in a position to use them, it would have been late summer. He could have opted for these routes, but this would have meant the campaign would not have been finished before winter.

Apart from time, there was a second and decisive factor counting against the western routes through the Parnassos Mountains: supply. Xerxes would be marching through Thessaly with all his vast army. There can be no doubt that among the various impositions he laid on the Thessalians in return for peace were those he had also imposed on Thasos, Abdera and Macedon. Namely, that they would have to supply the army as it marched south. The east coast of Thessaly is notoriously inhospitable. There were a few beaches where warships could be dragged ashore, but no ports large enough to handle even a fraction of the vast fleet of merchant ships loaded down with supplies for the army. The merchant fleet would not have been able to supply the army until it reached the Gulf of Pagasae in southern Thessaly. It was this same safe anchorage that had been used by the Greek ships moving their expeditionary force up to Tempe.

And when the Persian army had reached the Gulf of Pagasae the chances were that they would desperately have needed the supplies on board the ships. Thessaly was not a province of the Persian Empire, nor had it been an ally. As a consequence no messages from the King of Kings had been sent out in previous years to order the Thessalians to lay up stocks of food in preparation for the arrival of a vast army. The Persian host would have had to rely on pretty amateur provisioning.

Nor can it be supposed that the Thessalian farmers would have been any too willing to hand over their stocks to the Persians. Throughout history peasant farmers have been determined to hang on to their food. That current year might have been one of plenty, but if stock had been sold or handed over as taxes and the following harvest had been a bad one starvation might have followed. It must be supposed that the farmers would have buried large quantities of grain and driven their herds into mountains or thick forest. This would have left them with small stocks of food to show the men who came to requisition supplies for the passing army of the King of Kings. The Thessalian farmers would have pleaded poverty and handed over as little food as they could get away with.

No doubt the spears of the Persians would persuade the farmers to hand over more than they wanted to, but once the vast army had moved on the local Thessalian officials were unlikely to have wanted to extort further supplies from their own people. As elsewhere on the line of march, the army would have been supplied as it passed through, but with the bare minimum.

By the time the vast army reached the southern end of Thessaly, it would have been short of food. If Xerxes had then led his army over the Pindos Mountains to use the westerly passes over the Parnassos Mountains, he would have been marching them to destruction. The land here is inhospitable and bereft of villages or crops. There would have been nowhere near enough food to feed the army. The routes were impossible.

Xerxes might have hoped to continue to gain supplies as he marched into Boeotia. He knew the Thebans and their allies were just waiting for the chance to defect. No doubt supplies for the Persian army would again be a condition of peace.

The only route from Thessaly to Boeotia was through the Pass at Thermopylae. If that pass were to be blocked by the Greek army, Xerxes would face a difficult supply problem. If food in large quantities could not be obtained quickly, the vast Persian host would face starvation. The only alternative would be to break up the army and spread it over Thessaly in search of hidden stocks of food. Either way the army's advance would be over for the foreseeable future.

The obvious source of food at this point and the one that Xerxes clearly intended to use, was his supply fleet of over 2,000 merchant ships. For months before the invasion force set out, these merchant ships had been gathering in the ports of Asia Minor. There they had been loaded down with grain, oil and dried meats. The huge stores of food had not been needed while the army marched through Thrace or Macedonia, nor Thessaly. But they would be needed now.

It was at this weak spot that the Greeks intended to strike. The route into the Gulf of Pagasae passes through a narrow strait between the large island of Euboea and the Cape Sepias Peninsula. If this strait could be plugged by the Greek fleet, the supply ships could not get into the Gulf of Pagasae to feed the army. As Themistocles well knew there was at Artemisium on the north coast of Euboea a long sandy beach wide enough to accommodate the entire Greek fleet.

From Artemisium the Greeks could watch the straits from a secure position. Persian warships would be able to move at speed through the straits without much risk. In fact the Greeks could afford to let them do so. But the slow, lumbering merchant ships would be at the mercy of the winds and they would be easy prey for the Greek war galleys. Nor could the Persian war ships escort them effectively. In the narrow waters it would be difficult for the Persian galleys to guard the merchant ships and fight the Greek ships at the same time.

Xerxes would be trapped. As his uncle Artabanus had told him some months earlier, his most dangerous enemies were the land and sea. With a little help from the Greeks these two impersonal and implacable forces might yet defeat the Persian monarch. By putting an army at Thermopylae and a fleet at Artemisium, the Greeks would not actually need to defeat the vast army of Xerxes at all. After a week or two starvation would do the job for them.

If hunger did not defeat the Persian monarch, there was another deadly enemy, faster to strike, that would soon set to work. Before modern medicines got most common infectious diseases more or less under control, they were a constant threat to armies in the field. As late as 1915 a simple fungal infection was able to render 20% of the British army in France unfit for duty for weeks before a cure was found. For an army in 480BC the situation would have been far worse.

Given the primitive sanitary arrangements of an army on the march, diseases of the stomach and gut were spread easily by infected drinking water. The only effective ways for an army of this period to avoid such diseases was either to take advantage of sewers and drains of a local town or village or to keep on the move. A small force can use local civilian arrangements without much trouble, but a large force would overwhelm the system. And the Persian army was a very large force indeed. It had to stay on the move to remain healthy.

If brought to a halt in front of Thermopylae, the vast army would not be able to move. Again, a delay of as little as two weeks would be fatal. The Great King's army would melt away through sickness and hunger like the winter snows disappear in spring.

So the Greek League took the decision to make a stand at Thermopylae and Artemisium. But then, as so often in ancient Greece, religion took a hand. No sooner had the League meeting at Corinth agreed to make their stand than the Spartans raised a problem. It was now the beginning of August and the annual festival of Carneia was due to start on 11 August. This nine-day celebration was the most important in the Spartan calendar and was timed to end on the August full moon, which in 480BC fell on 20 August.

In origin the Carneia was a shepherd's festival sacred to Apollo Carneius – or Apollo the Ram. The details of the way the festival was celebrated in Sparta are sketchy at best, but one feature is known for certain as it was raised at the meeting in Corinth. The Spartans were forbidden to march to war during the Carneia festival. The other Peloponnesian states at once pointed to the fact that the Olympic Games were also about to start. They argued that they could not march to war while the sacred games were in progress; though it was clear that their real objection was to fighting without Spartan leadership.

All this talk of delay was to prove crucial. Clearly if the Spartans and Peloponnesians did not leave home until after 20 August it would be too late. Xerxes could be expected to reach Thermopylae any time after 10 September. The Athenians and other Greeks from north of the Isthmus of Corinth were furious. If Thermopylae were lost then all Greece north of Corinth would fall to Xerxes. The Athenians even suggested that they would abandon Greece altogether. Rather than move their population and valuables to Salamis and Troezen, they would take them to southern Italy to found a completely new city.

It was probably Leonidas, King of Sparta, who stepped in to solve the dispute. As a King of Sparta he had certain privileges. One of these was to have a personal bodyguard of 300 of the finest soldiers in Sparta on permanent standby and ready to march at a moment's notice. If he moved quickly he could get to Sparta, summon his bodyguard and march out of Lacedaemon before the Carneia Festival began.

This intervention proved to be a key moment in the entire campaign. The news that a Spartan king was marching to war galvanised Greece. The Peloponnesian states suddenly remembered that they too could send an advance guard despite the Olympic Games. Athens withdrew its threat. Corinth, Megara, Thespiae and many others ordered the mobilisation of their forces.

The scarlet cloaks of the Spartans were on the march.

The sanctuary at Delphi as it appeared in about 300BC. The temple of Apollo, where the oracle spoke, dominates the centre of the scene.

CHAPTER 9

The Routes to Thermopylae

The multi-towered wall at Mantinea, scene of a Theban victory over Sparta in 362BC. As discussed, the Greeks were unused to siege warfare and fortifications and this wall did not feature in the battle, one which weakened both sides enough to aid the Macedonian conquest of the central Greek city-states by Philip II, father of Alexander the Great.

About the time that Leonidas hurried away from Corinth, Xerxes was leaving his advanced base at Therme. The roads over the passes to Thessaly had been completed, messengers from those Greek states willing to accept Persian overlordship had returned and the spies were back. It was time to move.

The peaceful progress of the army through Thessaly was now assured. All the states had surrendered to the Persians. No doubt the King of Kings insisted that part of the price of peace was to feed his great army as it passed through. In any case there was no harbour on the coast able to cope with the merchant fleet. Xerxes repeated his arrangements for the journey to Therme. The army set off first as its journey would take longer, then the fleet left some days later. Thus the two forces would arrive at approximately the same time.

The rendezvous point was Halus on the western shores of the Gulf of Pagasae. A war galley might make the journey from Therme to Halos in two days. If they had a good following wind, the merchant ships might make it in four or five. The army, however, would need a good two weeks to make the march overland. Xerxes accordingly gave his fleet commanders instructions to get the merchant ships underway some ten days after he himself left Therme.

Achaemenes, brother to Xerxes, seems to have been the more senior of the four fleet commanders. He is certainly the only one of the four that Herodotus credits with any understanding of the sea. It may have been he who decided that it would make sense for most of the war ships to stay close to the merchant fleet to protect it from an attack by Greek ships, but it was also common sense to send a small force of warships on ahead. Indeed, a forward force would have some vital tasks to perform. The arrival of several thousand ships at Halos might overwhelm the facilities. Somebody would need to make sure the docks were cleared, workmen hired and everything made ready for the quick unloading of ships. Offshore some sort of system would be needed to ensure that captains unfamiliar with the place would know where to anchor safely and get themselves into position so that ships with the more urgent supplies could move up to the dock first. It was a major task of logistical organisation, and no sensible Persian was going to leave it to whatever passed for harbour control at a rural backwater such as Halus.

Achaemenes decided to send a force of ten fast warships ahead of his main fleet to sort things out. They were the fastest ships he had and so must have come from Phoenicia. They may have been under the command of Tetramnestus of Sidon or Matten of Tyre. Whoever the commander was, he was to have a very different voyage than the one he expected.

As for Xerxes and the army, there was no great need to rush through Thessaly. So far everything had gone exactly to plan. Even before his army had got within 200km of Tempe, the Athenian army blocking the pass had fled. As soon as his army appeared on the borders of Thessaly, the states of that area had hurried to capitulate. Already messages had come from Boeotia that Thebes and most of the other states there would surrender as soon as the King of Kings arrived. Argos in the Peloponnese had said as much as well. It must have seemed to Xerxes that as his vast forces rolled south through Greece there would be little or no fighting, just a succession of surrenders.

Perhaps it was for this reason that he chose to indulge in some leisure activities in Thessaly. At Larissa, races were organised between the fastest horses of Thessaly and the swiftest brought along in the Persian army. The horses of Thessaly were universally acknowledged to be the best in the Greek world, principally because of the wide pasture meadows to be found there. "The Greek mounts," Herodotus records, "were soundly beaten." Xerxes was jubilant at the superiority of his own steeds over those of Greece, though tactful jockey instructions on the part of the Thessalians may have had something to do with the result.

At some point in this journey, Xerxes was informed that there was a small Greek force at Thermopylae. He was not worried. A similar force of hoplites from the southern Greek states had assembled to block his path at Tempe, then disappeared. Xerxes must have thought that this new force would flee too. The conditions were, after all, very similar. At Tempe, Xerxes had promises to defect from the Thessalian states behind the Greek army. Now he had promises from the Boeotian states behind the new defensive position. The Greeks had run before, they would run again.

Xerxes then moved on to Halus. There was no sign of the fleet, but Xerxes does not seem to have been unduly worried. Perhaps he had arrived early, or the winds had been contrary for the fleet. For whatever reason, Xerxes dallied for a day or two before moving on without any apparent concerns.

At Halus, the Persian monarch enacted yet another piece of hearts-and-minds propaganda. Due to an ancient legend of fratricidal murder and mayhem that was typically Greek, the great god Zeus had laid a curse upon the people that first-born sons were forbidden to enter the precincts of the Council Chamber. Any who did so had to be crowned with a wreath, then led away in solemn procession to be sacrificed. Xerxes was himself the second son of Darius, but he ordered and let it be known that none of his men should enter the area just in case any of them were first-born sons. Xerxes wanted the message to get out that he would respect the traditions and religion of those who surrendered promptly to his forces. Halus had been at first inclined to join the League, welcoming with great warmth the expedition to Tempe when it passed through. Xerxes needed other Greek states to know that he bore no grudges for past attitudes or acts of defiance. He wanted the cities and states south of Thessaly to capitulate quickly, as Halus had done.

From Halus, Xerxes moved on along the coast towards Lamia. This city is still a major transportation centre, though the silting of the river has long since rendered it useless as a port. Perhaps Xerxes hoped his fleet would meet him here, instead of at Halus. Or perhaps he thought the overland journey from Halus to Lamia short enough for his carts and pack animals to transport supplies.

It was probably at Lamia that Xerxes learned that the campaign had taken a sudden turn for the worse. The Greek army at Thermopylae had not run. Instead they were digging in.

After leaving Corinth, Leonidas must have ridden home to Sparta at some speed. He got his bodyguard of 300 elite Spartiates mustered and ready to march. Each of the Spartiates would have taken with him at least one Helot to act as his servant and carry his weapons on the march. These Helots would have been armed with daggers and, perhaps, slings so that they could act as light infantry in battle. There were also some Lacedaemonian hoplites, perhaps as many as 500.

With this small force, Leonidas marched north from Sparta along the valley of the Eurotas. At the head of the valley, the Spartans marched up into the hills. At the borders of Laconia the column halted while the necessary religious rites were conducted. Sacrifices were made to Zeus and Athene and the priests inspected the results to see if the omens were good. Clearly they were, as Leonidas continued on, accompanied by a small herd of goats marked out as victims should further sacrifices be deemed necessary.

Just north of Laconia was Arcadia, a loosely allied number of cities. The Spartan column halted at Tegea, where 500 hoplites joined their force. They then moved on to Mantinea where another 500 armoured infantry joined the swelling army. The city of Orchomenus sent 120 men, Phlius 200 and the smaller towns of Arcadia between them sent 1,000 men to join the small column as it marched northward.

The column then swung over the hills to the valley of the Asopus to avoid the territory of hostile Argos. Risking the wrath of her neighbour, Mycenae sent 80 men to join Leonidas. At Corinth another 400 men joined the column. As Leonidas marched over the Isthmus of Corinth he marched at the head of close on 4,000 men.

This was a small fraction of the total army that the states of the Peloponnese could send to war. It was, however, the best that they could do given that the sacred Olympic Games were actually in progress at the time. This was not just an athletic competition, but an extremely serious religious rite to be carried out precisely if offence was not to be given to Zeus, in whose honour the games were celebrated. Given that the god Apollo, speaking through the Delphic Oracle, had already announced that Zeus favoured the Persians it was probably thought a wise move to do everything possible to placate this enormously powerful god. The games went ahead as usual.

Across the Isthmus of Corinth, Leonidas was marching into potentially hostile, or at best indifferent, territory. The cities of Boeotia had long since shown themselves to be prepared to reach an accommodation with the Persians. Only Thespiae and Plataea had not sent messages to Xerxes, though it is likely that Leonidas was unaware of this.

He will have been aware that the receptions he received as he advanced were very different. The Thespians welcomed him with open arms, adding another 700 men to his army while the Locrians sent every man they had and the Phocians a thousand. Unsurprisingly, the rich and powerful city of Thebes sent just 400 men, a tiny fraction of their army. At this point in the campaign, Thebes did not want to break too openly with Athens and Sparta. Neither did the city want to anger Xerxes by fighting him. The city government perhaps thought it prudent to send a few soldiers to join the campaign and so try to keep both sides happy. Or it may be that the 400 men were volunteers who chose to march to war in defiance of their government's orders.

When he arrived at Thermopylae, probably around 5 or 6 August, Leonidas had with him some 7,000 men. It was not much of a force to face the vast hordes of Asia being led south through Thessaly by Xerxes. As we have seen, however, Leonidas did not intend to defeat the Persian army. All he needed to do was pin it down, then wait for hunger and disease to do their work.

Nor were Leonidas and his men alone. Waiting for him was an Athenian galley under the command of the experienced seaman Habronichus. He brought news that the Greek fleet was already at Artemisium. The task of Habronichus was to carry messages between Leonidas and Eurybiades and the fleet in his fast ship with its single bank of oars.

The Greeks were in position to face the enemy, but there was plenty of work to do.

Cavalrymen depicted on a frieze at the Parthenon. The tens of thousands of Persian cavalry played little part at Thermopylae because of the ground the Greeks had chosen.

CHAPTER 10

The Killing Ground

The Middle Gate seen from the east. The Phocian Wall was attached to the rock face on the left and ran across to the sea. The ancient coastline was located just to the right of this picture.

When he arrived at Thermopylae, King Leonidas of Sparta knew he had a tough job to do. He was, however, a grizzled veteran some 50 years of age with many campaigns behind him. We can be certain that he did not waste the time that he had before the Persians arrived. His task was to halt the army of the Great King, and the Pass at Thermopylae was his chosen instrument.

To understand what happened over the following days, knowledge of the ground over which the battle was to be fought was like is essential. The first thing to realise is that the Pass of Thermopylae is not really a pass at all. It is, or rather was, a narrow strip of land between the sea and the mountains of the sheer heights of Mount Kallidromos. At the time of the battle, the strip of level ground was very narrow indeed. Today silting of the shallow Malian Gulf means that more than a mile of marshes and salt flats now separate the mountain from the sea.

The pass itself is some 8km long. The eastern end of the pass is marked, then as now, by the village of Alpeni, though it is today generally referred to as Thermopylae. Located in the territory of Phocis, this village was fully behind the resistance to Persia, so Leonidas knew he could rely on the active co-operation of the villagers. Just west of Alpeni the road from Phocis to Thessaly entered the pass. The width of the flat ground here was very narrow indeed, barely four metres wide.

After 200 metres the pass widened dramatically to form a plain some 1 km long and 400 metres wide. It then narrowed again to about fifteen metres wide for a short distance. Beyond this the pass widened again to form a second, larger area of open ground. This was perhaps 2 km long and some 500 metres wide. The pass narrowed for a third time, again to about four metres wide for a short distance.

To the west of the pass, the direction from which the Persians would come, lay the plains of the Rivers Asopus and Spercheius. Between the two rivers stood the small town of Trachis, overlooking the flat ground from a bluff on the lower slopes of the towering Mount Oeta. The road from Lamia, down which the Persians would march, ran south along the coast to cross the Spercheius, run beneath the walls of Trachis, then turn east to cross the Asopus and enter the pass.

In drawing up his defensive plans, Leonidas therefore had a choice of good defensive positions where the pass narrowed. These were known as the East Gate, by Alpeni, the direction from which the Greeks were advancing, the West Gate, towards which the Persians were marching, where the pass opened out in front of Trachis, and the Middle Gate in the centre of the pass. Leonidas chose the Middle Gate and his reasons for doing so were clear.

At the narrower East Gate the slopes of Mount Kallidromos are steep, but not sheer. It would be possible for lightly armed infantry to get up on the slopes and work their way around the hoplites on the flat ground below. Much the same was true of the West Gate, which had the additional disadvantage of facing directly on to the open plain where Xerxes could marshal his troops.

The Middle Gate, by contrast, had sheer walls of inhospitable rock on its left side. Not even a mountain goat had much chance of scaling such rugged terrain, never mind a Persian soldier carrying his weapons. Added to the narrowness of the pass, this made the Middle Gate preferable.

Nor was that all. By putting his main defensive line at the Middle Gate, Leonidas would have plenty of warning of a Persian attack. It would be impossible for the Persians to camp on the open ground between the West Gate and Middle Gate as this would be to invite a night raid from the Greeks. Only the plain around Trachis was large enough, safe enough and provided with enough water for the Persian army.

Consequently, any force marching to attack the Middle Gate must first negotiate the West Gate, then advance for some 2km across open ground in full view of defenders at the Middle Gate. And at some point in the advance, the invaders would be forced to halt to reform their lines out of the column four men abreast necessary to pass through the West Gate. All this would take time and give Leonidas the opportunity to organise his defence. If he were to put a small scouting force in the West Gate, as he probably did, he would have had even more notice of any attack.

The Middle Gate had other advantages too. The smaller open plain behind it offered a convenient camping ground for the Greek army. It was all the more attractive as a spring fed water into a small stream on the lower slopes of Kallidromos on the plain's southern flank. Herodotus indicates that this is exactly where Leonidas put his men when he says that the Greek commander used the village of Alpeni "as a source of supplies". If the men had been billeted in the village, Herodotus would probably have said so. Since he did not, the only other place for the army to have camped was on the small eastern plain in the pass.

With his troops camped here, Leonidas could organise an efficient rota system of duties. A few men would be on duty at the Middle Gate, keeping an eye on the West Gate for signs of attack. In the camp, a force of men able to guard the Middle Gate would be armed and ready for action. When an attack developed, this force would be brought up to the Gate. A second squad would then be ordered to arm and prepare for battle while the rest of the army continued to rest or eat. When the first squad began to tire, it could be replaced with the second and sent back to camp to rest. A third squad would then be ordered to arm and prepare to advance.

With careful organisation and forethought, Leonidas could ensure that he always had an adequate force of fresh, armed men ready to go into action. With their main camp some 3km away, the Persians would not be in such a position.

There was another reason why Leonidas may have chosen to fight in the Middle Gate. On the western plain, between the West Gate and Middle Gate were a series of hot springs that gave the pass its name: "thermopy-lae" meaning "hot gates". These springs poured forth an endless stream of boiling hot water throughout the year and were famous in the area for their medicinal properties. The waters are not only hot, but rich in sulphur which gives them a distinctive and deeply unpleasant smell that sticks in the throat. Of particular interest to Leonidas would have been the fact that they were held to be sacred to Heracles, a small shrine to the demi-god standing beside the springs.

Heracles was born the son of Zeus, king of the gods, and Alcmene, a beautiful woman of Thebes. He is best known as being a demi-god of superhuman strength who undertook the famous Twelve Labours, or impossible tasks, to atone for a multiple murder he committed while in a fit of madness sent by the goddess Hera. But there was much more to Heracles than that. He was widely believed to be a link between men and gods. His help was invoked whenever men were suffering at the hands of the gods – be it disease, earthquake or violent storm. Given that the Persians were supported by Zeus, according to the Delphic Oracle, his son Heracles might be a useful demi-god for the Greeks to have on side in the coming battle.

Crucially, Leonidas was supposed to be a direct descendant of Heracles. According to legend Aristodemos, great grandson of Heracles, had founded the royal family of Sparta about 80 years after the Trojan War, the date of which was unclear. The Spartans themselves counted backwards using the number of years each king had reigned to date the founding of their kingdom in the year we would call 1102BC.

The author is convinced that Leonidas would have believed these leg-ends. He would have known with certainty that Heracles was his ancestor and that the demi-god who lived eternally among the Immortals had the power to intervene directly in the coming battle. One of the first acts of Leonidas upon arriving at Thermopylae would have been to go to the shrine of Heracles and pay his respects. He would have taken a goat to the shrine and, as the sun dipped below the western mountains, slit its throat so that the blood ran over the altar. The goat's head would then have been buried outside the door of the shrine and the carcass taken back to camp for a ritual meal.

Thus did the King of Sparta seek the aid of the gods for his army. The second and less metaphysical task undertaken by Leonidas was to launch an extensive raid into the land west of the pass. The raid was probably undertaken on the first night the troops were in the pass. They spread out across the plains of the Asopus and Spercheius, right up to the walls of Trachis. The granaries were emptied on to carts which, together with all livestock, were driven back to the Greek camp. This would keep the small army of Leonidas in food for some time and also make the supply problem of Xerxes that much more difficult.

Leonidas was not the first man to have noted the defensive possibilities of the Middle Gate at Thermopylae. Many years earlier the Phocians had been at war with the Thessalians and in fear of invasion. They too had decided to halt the invasion at the Middle Gate. Having rather more time to prepare than did Leonidas, they had built a strong defensive wall across the pass.

This Phocian Wall, as it is known, was to play a key part in the battle that followed. This makes it all the more odd that most historians give it barely a second look. They say it existed then pass on, but this approach is misleading. The Phocian Wall was at the centre of the fighting and its importance must be understood if the fighting is to make sense.

Herodotus does not say much about the Phocian Wall other than to state "The wall had been built a very long time ago and most of it had fallen into ruin through age. Now, however, it was decided to repair it and to use it to stop the Persians from getting through into Greece." Nothing now remains above ground of this wall and an archaeological excavation in 1939 revealed only the traces of fortification works of the later Hellenistic and Byzantine periods.

It is possible, however, to describe the height of the wall with some accuracy; and even its materials and construction. At one point Herodotus tells us that a Persian scout approaching on horseback was unable to see over the wall. Given that Persian horses of this date were fairly small, around 13 hands, this must mean that the wall was at least 2.5 metres tall. At another point, Herodotus mentions that Persian infantry, working together, were able to scramble over the wall. An officer in the Royal Marines who has studied the problem of battlefield tactics in arms and armour of various periods concluded:

"Crossing a six-foot (1.8-metre) wall is pretty easy for a relatively fit male on his own, unaided. The difficulty increases if carrying equipment, wearing armour (difficult – due to weight and inability to drag up wall), carrying weapons (very difficult – as have no free arms). Given the light equipment of the Persians, they could scale a six-foot wall on their own, unaided, without much difficulty.

"At the other extreme, I would expect a group to easily cross a 12-foot wall with equipment (that is with weapons slung from straps rather than carried in their hands). The way we would do this today is the first man puts his back to the wall and knees up number 2 who uses his shoulder and head as steps. Number 3 follows, with a pull up from number 2. Number 4 then repeats and can proceed straight over to the other side or allow number 2 or 3 to drop down and assume their place. If number 1 is to go over, 2 and 3 lie flat on the top of the wall and he jumps up and grabs a hand and is dragged up. This may sound a bit complicated but is actually quite easy for trained men. However – if there are defenders on top, I assume that this would all be very difficult."

The height of the wall was therefore most likely something under 12 feet, or 3.6 metres. Herodotus gives no indication of its design, other than the fact that there was a gateway without a gate. Fortunately, archaeological digs elsewhere have revealed a fairly typical design for a defensive wall in Greece at this date.

As discussed earlier, the Greeks preferred short, sharp wars that gave a decisive result. They preferred open battles to sieges and, as a consequence, had not much skill in siege warfare. The walls with which they surrounded their towns did not need to be able to withstand prolonged punishment from catapults nor to be so tall as to make siege towers impotent. They needed only to be able to withstand an attack by infantry with ladders. As a result they tended to be fairly rudimentary compared to defensive works in other areas and of different periods.

A typical wall would have been about two or three metres thick. The facing would have been of carefully cut masonry blocks about 30cm thick, but the interior was filled with rubble, gravel and sand. As the outer facing walls were built, the space between was filled in and pounded down with wooden piles so that the loose material was compacted solid. The wall was topped with a walkway of flagstones. The parapet was sometimes of stone, but might just as easily have been of mudbrick.

Wherever possible, these walls were built on top of cliffs or steep slopes, which was not an option at Thermopylae. Weak points were strengthened with towers which projected forward and stood some two metres taller than the wall itself. These allowed defenders to outflank attackers as they reached the wall. Such towers were, however, fairly new innovations in Greece, so it is unlikely that the ancient Phocian Wall had any towers along its length.

The picture of the Phocian Wall so far is clear; but there is a serious problem as to its actual site. On the southern end the wall would have been built flush to the almost sheer mountainside, but at the northern end the sea gave a much less secure flank. The coast here was one of sandy beaches, and it is impossible to build a stone wall on a sand beach without it collapsing in the first storm to hit. Any attackers would simply need to wade into the sea to their waists and walk around the right flank of any wall built at the Middle Gate.

Clearly the Persians did not succeed in doing this, so the Phocian Wall cannot have just stopped at the edge of the beach. The easiest solution would have been to bend the wall back as it approached the sea. This would have meant that any troops seeking to outflank the wall by walking in the waves would have exposed their vulnerable, shieldless right side to the defenders. The wall would need to have been built back along the shore for only about 50 metres or so to be effective.

Alternatively, the builders of the wall may have relied upon temporary defences to render the surf impassable to hostile infantry. It would have been relatively easy to make wooden fencing, bristling with thorns. Weighted down with stones, these would have remained in position in the sea for some weeks before being washed away and were easily replaced when they did. Such a barrier would not have been impassable to determined men, but it would have been a slow job to cut it down with axes. The defenders would, of course, have used this delay to inflict casualties on the men seeking to cut a way through the fencing.

As we have seen, Leonidas decided to repair this wall before the Persians arrived. With thousands of men to hand, labour was not going to be a problem. However, the presumed dearth of skilled stonemasons present is a limiting factor. It is likely that the defenders had time to remove misplaced stones from the face of the wall that would have given the attackers a leg up and to rebuild a parapet along the top of the wall. If the wall had tumbled down in any places there would no doubt have been an attempt to rebuild the damaged sections to the same height as the rest of the wall as it stood in 480BC.

The villagers of Alpeni would have been persuaded, one way or another, to lend their tools. A farming village always has more tools for woodworking that stone dressing, so it should be assumed that much of the repair work was done in timber. Perhaps the final shape of the Phocian Wall was of a reasonably solid wall with a sheer face in most places topped by a timber battlement. At places, however, there would have been more crudely constructed sections where the soldiers had hurriedly piled up the stones that lay to hand, buttressed with timber supports. As for the missing gate, this was presumably easily replaced with a timber construction that could be shoved into place when required. As we shall see, it was a key part of Leonidas's battle plan that the gate could be opened.

However solidly the defenders were able to repair this Phocian Wall, Leonidas had good reason to worry. Unlike the Greeks, the Persians were highly skilled at siege warfare. The cities of Mesopotamia had for more than two thousand years been protected by towering walls. The ability to break through such walls was an essential feature of warfare in the region. Xerxes would have known that he might need to batter some Greek cities into surrender during this campaign and would have brought along siege specialists.

Leonidas would have been only too well aware of the siege skills of the Persians. Prior to the battle at Marathon ten years earlier a Persian force had landed on the island of Naxos in the Cyclades. The walls around the city of Naxos were as good as any in Greece, and the inhabitants retreated to the city in the expectation that they could hold out until the enemy moved on. They were wrong. Within a matter of days the Persians had built siege engines such as the Greeks had never seen before. The walls of Naxos fell and the city was plundered. As professional soldiers, the Spartans made a habit of inspecting and learning about anything new in the art of warfare so it is more than likely that they closely questioned the survivors from Naxos about Persian siege warfare.

These unfortunates would have told of battering rams built from tree trunks and topped with iron sheathing. Covered with a roof to protect the men operating them from missiles thrown from above, these rams were able to batter a hole through a stone wall in a relatively short time. There were also machines able to throw heavy stones more than 200 metres. Operated by teams of men tugging on pivoted beams of wood, these were relatively inaccurate. But the damage inflicted by an impact was tremendous. The Persians could afford to miss most of the time so long as a few shots found their target.

Leonidas would have been under no illusions about the ability of the repaired Phocian Wall to withstand Persian siege engines. It would not have stood up for more than a day or two to a determined assault. However, Leonidas would also have known that the most effective siege machinery was large, heavy and cumbersome – and that it was moved by means of brute muscle power. The engines were mounted on solid wooden wheels and axles able to take their great weight and pushed into position by teams of soldiers.

Herodotus tells us what Leonidas did with this knowledge. He "diverted the water of the hot springs over the pass, to cut up the ground into gullies". Using shovels and picks, acquired presumably from Alpeni, Leonidas had his men dig a series of trenches and ditches across the open plain in front of the Phocian Wall. The hot spring water was then diverted so that it ran through and over these depressions. Given a few days the water would soak into the ground to create a muddy morass quite impassable to the heavy Persian siege engines.

Leonidas would have been well aware that this was no permanent solution. Teams of Persians could come forward under the protection of armed guards to tip load after load of gravel into the ditches or lay wooden planking over the mud. Sooner or later the obstacles would be overcome. But anything that caused a delay was to the advantage of the defenders. As we have seen, they did not need to halt the vast Persian host indefinitely. The pass needed to be held only long enough for Persian supplies to run low or for disease to break out. A week, or perhaps two, might be long enough.

Another defensive measure that Leonidas may have adopted was designed specifically to counter the Persian cavalry. We are told by Herodotus that the trick had been devised by the Phocians a few years earlier when fighting another of their wars against the Thessalians. On that occasion, the Phocians had moved north of Thermopylae and had been moving through open country, where the Thessalians should have been able to use their great superiority in cavalry to deadly effect.

Preparing for battle, the Phocians had decided in advance where to place their hoplite phalanx. They had then gone out the day before and dug a series of pits in front of the agreed position. Into each pit was put an upside down earthenware pot. The earth was then poured back around the sides of the pot and stamped down. Finally a thin covering of earth and grass was put on top. To a casual inspection it looked as if the ground was undisturbed.

In fact the ground concealed a deadly trap. The pots had been chosen so that they would support the weight of a man, but not that of a horse.

When the battle began it at first seemed that all was going well for the Thessalians. The Phocian hoplites advanced, but began to retreat when they caught sight of the massed Thessalian cavalry. They fell back to the prepared position and waited. Having marched back and forth over the ground, the infantry had demonstrated that the ground was relatively flat, level and – apparently – free of obstructions. But when the Thessalian cavalry charged they soon discovered the trap. As the horses reached the hidden pits, the pots gave way and the horses were brought down. Many horses had their legs broken and had to be destroyed. It was a terrible defeat.

If Leonidas had not heard of this ruse before arriving at Thermopylae we can be certain that the supportive Phocians would have told him about it at once. Given the fact that the Persian cavalry was famously effective, it would be surprising if Leonidas had not strewn the ground in front of his position with such traps.

However, Leonidas had no intention of simply standing on the defensive. While he intended to allow the Persians to waste their strength attacking the wall, he was equally determined to launch attacks of his own. Herodotus describes these as "Making sorties from behind the wall to the land in front".

Most probably, Leonidas was intent on using his men to pursue the Persians as they withdrew from an attack. Launching a determined and organised hoplite attack on a disorganised and retreating enemy could be devastating. To make such a counterattack effective, the hoplites would need to be operating on fairly flat, obstruction free ground. We can assume that the land between the Phocian Wall and the muddy morass of the hot springs was cleared of bushes or small trees and any large boulder rolled aside. This would be the killing ground.

Leonidas would also have wanted to clear the Persians out of the plain in front of his wall after each attack and drive the Persians back beyond the West Gate. It was essential to keep control of the land in front of the Middle Gate so that the Greeks continued to enjoy the advantage of getting good warning of any attack. It would also allow them to redig the ditches where the hot springs flowed. Moreover, with control of this area, Leonidas could repeat his sunset sacrifice on the altar of his divine ancestor. Such things were important.

It was a good position that Leonidas was improving with skill and determination. So it must have come as a shock to him when he was told by the Phocians that there was another pass from Trachis to Alpeni.

This second route through the block of Mount Kallidromos was little better than a goat track. It was quite incapable of coping with the vast army of Xerxes, still less with the carts and pack animals that came in its wake. But it was good enough for infantry to use. And if infantry could use it, they could get behind the Middle Gate and render all the defences of Leonidas useless.

The path ran up from the Asopus past a hillock and into the oak woods that at that time blanketed the upper slopes of the mountain. The path then plunged through the forests, over rocky slopes and through defiles to emerge into a hidden valley. The top of the Kallidromos massif was not a single sharp ridge, as it appeared from below, but two ridges close together with a narrow but relatively flat valley between them. At the eastern end of this valley the path dropped down through an even narrower and rougher track to emerge on the open hillside just above Alpeni.

The fact that there was a path over Kallidromos seems to have been fairly well known in the area. But its actual course and how to find it was known to only a few shepherds. Nobody else ever went up to the forested heights and travellers always went through the pass of Thermopylae.

The revelation of the existence of this path at once presented Leonidas with a problem. If Xerxes discovered the path, he could send a force over it to take the Greeks from the rear. All the careful preparations at Thermopylae would count for nothing. The path had to be guarded, and guarded well.

On the other hand, the way to find the path was known to only a few men. If Leonidas drew attention to the route this would only serve to alert Xerxes to the fact that it existed. He would then send his vast thousands up into the hills until one of them found something. Meanwhile, so long as Xerxes did not know about the track over the mountain, the full weight of the Persian attack would be thrown against Thermopylae. Leonidas would need as many men as possible there, not twiddling their thumbs up on Kallidromos.

Leonidas had another problem that few modern commanders have to face. He had no absolute right to give orders to most of his men. Leonidas was King of Sparta and the 300 men of his bodyguard were honour bound to follow his commands unto death, as were the few hundred non-Spartiate hoplites from Sparta. But the men of Corinth, Tegea, Thespiae and elsewhere served under their own commanders and were loyal to their own towns. It is true that the delegates of the League meeting at Corinth had agreed that military leadership in the field should belong to Sparta, but that counted for little in the lonely pass of Thermopylae, with the Persians approaching. Leonidas might be the senior commander, but his power was not absolute. He needed to be able to persuade the other contingents to follow his lead. It was time for a council of war.

To modern military men it is difficult to understand the function of one of these councils of war. So it must be remembered that the men of each state fought in their own units and under their own commanders. It was expected that those commanders would share with their men details of the situation in which they found themselves and the plans for the future. If the commanders were to be obeyed they needed the confidence of their men. The commanders would also have been given instructions by their governments before marching to war. None of the other commanders would have known what these were, so there was always room for suspicion and doubt.

At a council of war it was possible for the various commanders to put forward their views and opinions. They could state that certain plans were incompatible with the orders given by their governments. They could argue for what measures they thought were most likely to succeed and point out the flaws in the plans of others. The hope was that it would be possible to end by settling on a course of action that was understood and supported by everyone present.

This particular council of war called at Thermopolyae did not run smoothly. All the commanders present will have known that their task was to keep the Persian army out of Boeotia with its rich stores of food and other supplies. There was a large war fleet at Artemisium which would be fighting to keep the Persian supply fleet out of the Gulf of Pagasae. If the army did not halt the Persians, the fleet's actions would be in vain. But the news of the pass over the mountains changed things.

Some of the Peloponnesian commanders suggested abandoning the whole idea of holding the Persians at Thermopylae and Artemisium. They put forward the old idea of falling back to the Isthmus of Corinth and fighting there. No doubt the stale old arguments that had been gone over time and again were gone through again. And, as before, the same conclusions will have been reached. This time the Phocians, Locrians and Thespiaeans were on hand to make the point forcefully that if the pass were to be abandoned then their homes would be destroyed by the Persian hordes.

Habronichus of Athens, who commanded the ship with which Leonidas liaised with the fleet, would have put the Athenian viewpoint.

At some stage in the debate the Phocians offered to defend the mountain pass. It was, after all, only a goat track and they knew the hills better than anyone. It was a good offer, but not enough to satisfy everyone. Leonidas then put forward a second suggestion. He would send messengers to the various cities of the League asking for reinforcements. It seems to have always been the plan that the main Spartan army would march north once the Carneia Festival was over. The other Peloponnesian states would have sent their main forces north alongside those of Sparta. Athens, of course, had most of her available manpower aboard the fleet at Artemisium. Now Leonidas was asking the cities to send some more men immediately. It was a wise decision.

The meeting broke up with general agreement. The Phocians were to march into the mountains and guard the goat track over Kallidromos. The rest of the army was to stay in its camp on the eastern small plain of Thermopylae to await the Persian attack.

But when the Persians first appeared, they did not come by land. They came by sea.

The hot springs that gave Thermopylae its name. The flow of water, channelled, proved to be a feature of the battlefield.

CHAPTER 11

First Blood

*A Greek merchant ship from a contemporary vase. The lack of oars makes this vessel
dependent on the wind. The merchant ships in the Persian fleet would have been similar.*

When they heard that Xerxes and his vast army were over the northern mountains and advancing through Thessaly, the people of Delphi finally decided to approach the Delphic Oracle themselves. The reply they received was one of the shortest and clearest the oracle ever uttered. "Pray to the winds, for they are the friends of the Greeks."

As usual, the Delphic Oracle was passing on gossip from the gods as much as advice. In this case Apollo would have known what he was talking about. He had many centuries earlier taken as a mortal mistress a beautiful Athenian maid named Creusa. She had an equally beautiful sister, Oreithyia, who married the god Boreus, the north wind. Thus the north wind was related to the Athenians and might have been supposed to be well disposed toward them. The fact that he lived, so it was believed, in a cave in Thrace, so recently added by conquest to the Persian Empire, may have also prodded him into action. Whatever the reason for the Oracle's belief that the winds were friendly to the Greeks, it certainly turned out that way. But it did not, at first, seem so.

The League fleet was at Artemisium by about 3 August. This place took its name from a temple to the goddess Artemis, twin sister of Apollo, which lay on a hill beside the beach. This beach is probably the two-kilometre long stretch now known as Pefki. The fleet had only just arrived when a fresh squabble broke out over the command structure. The League had decided that the Spartan admiral Eurybiades would be in command, but now the contingents from the various states were assembled together, the sea captains decided that they did not care for this arrangement. There seems to have been some doubt over the ability of Eurybiades to handle a large fleet in battle. The Athenians, as before, demanded the right to command the fleet as their ships were by far the most numerous.

In the end it was Themistocles, the Athenian admiral and politician, who calmed tempers. He spoke to confirm that the League's decision had to stand, but reading between the lines of what Plutarch has to say about this episode, and what Herodotus says about later events, Eurybiades' authority had been undermined. He seems to have been persuaded that he had to hold conferences involving all the commanders of the different fleets before reaching a major decision. It was an unwieldy and complex arrangement, but it kept the fleet together and at Artemisium.

It was unfortunate that the first decision to be made turned out to be a mistake of a fairly basic kind – modern officer training warns against it right at the start of instruction. The Greeks assumed that the Persians would behave as they would do if in the same position. For some it was to be a fatal error.

Eurybiades (as commander he must take responsibility even if the decision was a consensual one among the naval council of war), assumed that the Persian ships would advance down the coast, round the rocky headland of Cape Sepias and up the Trikeri Straits to reach the Gulf of Pagasae. Such a route would take them between the mainland and the island of Skiathos. Working from this assumption, three Greek galleys were sent to Skiathos to watch the channel between that island and the mainland. When the Persians arrived, men stationed on top of Skiathos hill were to light a fire. The galleys were to make a count of the enemy fleet, then race back to Artemisium with the news.

What Eurybiades had forgotten, if he knew, was that the Phoenicians in the Persian fleet did not follow the Greek habit of hugging a coast. The Greeks preferred to land to eat their midday meal, to rest and to sleep. The Phoenicians were happy to remain at sea all day and even overnight if the need arose.

As we have seen, the senior Persian admiral and brother to Xerxes, Achaemenes, had sent a small force of ten fast Phoenician galleys ahead of the main fleet. Herodotus tells us that they did not hug the coast, stopping off for meals, but instead "set a course direct for Skiathos". This would have brought them down on the island from the open Aegean Sea to the north of the island, not from the mainland coast to the west, which is where the Greeks were looking for them. The Phoenicians ships seem to have got quite close to the island before they were spotted. When they were sighted the signal fire was lit and the three Greek ships – one each from Troezen, Athens and Aegina – put to sea.

Eurybiades would have seen the signal and would, no doubt, have given orders for his ships to prepare to put to sea as soon as the three scout galleys arrived. They never did. Apart from the smoke from the signal fire far to the northeast, there was only an ominous silence from Skiathos. Later that day a fast messenger galley was sent out towards Skiathos to find out what had happened. There was no sign of the three scout ships nor of the Persians, though the signal fire still burned. Probably rather circumspectly the ship put into Skiathos harbour to learn what had gone on. The news was as depressing as it could be.

The men of Skiathos had watched while the three Greek galleys put out from land and the ten fast Phoenician ships raced down from the open sea. The ship from Troezen was caught almost immediately and surrounded by several of the enemy. The Phoenicians swarmed aboard the Greek ship, cutting down the crew and taking the survivors prisoner. As the horrified onlookers from shore watched, the Phoenicians then singled out the tallest and best looking man on the Troezen ship and dragged him to the prow of the captured vessel. The Phoenicians pushed him forward so that he hung over the waves, then slit his throat. The blood gushed down to the sea, swiftly followed by the corpse.

The Greeks recognised the unfortunate man as Leon and thought that the Phoenicians had chosen him as a sacrifice for his impressive physique and handsome features. They may have been right. Baal Eshmun, the god of the sea worshipped at Sidon, demanded regular sacrifices of bulls, rams and other male animals. Each had to be perfect and unblemished by even the smallest physical mark. There can be little doubt that the Phoenicians did sacrifice the unfortunate Leon to their gods, human sacrifice being not uncommon in Phoenicia, to gain divine aid in the battles to come. One can easily guess that they had visited their home temple before setting out and pledged to sacrifice the finest of their first prisoners to the sea god on whom they would rely.

Meanwhile, the other two Greek ships were hurrying away southwest towards Artemisium. The ship from Aegina was overwhelmed next. Perhaps having seen the fate of Leon of Troezen made the Aeginaeans desperate. For whatever reason they fought hard and long before being overpowered. This time the Phoenicians behaved quite differently. Pytheas, a hoplite who was seen to fight most bravely even after he was the last Greek still putting up resistance, was treated well by the Phoenicians who were seen to dress his wounds and treat him most tenderly.

The fight put up by the ship of Aegina gave that from Athens time to get away. It was cut off from Artemisium by the enemy craft, so it turned north and raced away up the coast. The last the men on Skiathos saw of the Athenian ship, commanded by a man named Phormus, it was disappearing over the horizon pursued by three or four of the Phoenician vessels. The remaining Persian ships spent some time nosing around the waters off Skiathos. Three ran aground on a reef between Skiathos and the mainland, which they duly marked with a stone cairn. They then headed off north in the wake of their fellows who were pursuing the lone Athenian galley.

It was some weeks before the Greeks learned what had happened to Phormus and his Athenians. They had managed to keep ahead of the Phoenicians as they ran north along the coast, but by the afternoon it was clear they would not be able to pull clear of their dogged pursuers. Phormos therefore steered his vessel into the mouth of the River Peneus and ran it ashore in the gathering dusk. The men bolted up into the mountains to evade the Phoenicians. But the enemy did not chase them. The Phoenicians instead dragged the Greek ship back out to sea, manned it with a skeleton crew and took it off as a prize of war to show to their commander back at Therme.

Phormos and his men were now stranded many miles behind enemy lines. Remarkably they managed to walk back home, evading Persian patrols as they passed through occupied Thessaly. Perhaps they were helped by Thessalians who wanted to assist their fellow Greeks. Perhaps Phormos had a purse of money with which to buy such help. However they managed it, these Athenians undertook a remarkable journey against the odds. It is a shame we don't know more about how they got from the Tempe Pass back to Athens.

None of the ancient writers gives us a date for the naval skirmish off Skiathos, but it clearly fell between the date Xerxes left Therme with his army and when Achaemenes was due to leave with the fleet. It makes sense for Achaemenes to have intended to send his logistics team to Halus in time to get things organised and report back before the main fleet put to sea. This means that they would have been off Skiathos on or about 4 August.

What is beyond doubt is that the Greek prisoners would have been persuaded to reveal to their captors where the main Greek fleet was and how large it was. Before he was due to leave Therme, therefore, Achaemenes would have known that his route to Halos was blocked at Artemisium by a Greek war fleet some 300 strong. With some 600 first class warships under his command – the older vessels had been used to build the bridges over the Hellespont – Achaemenes cannot have been too worried about the possibility of defeat by the Greeks. But he did have a serious problem.

He needed to get his merchant ships, loaded with the food on which Xerxes was relying, into the Gulf of Pagasae. But he could not do this while the Greek fleet was intact and at Artemisium. And so long as the Greek ships were hauled up on the beach, Achaemenes could not engage and defeat them in a naval battle. Even if the Greeks did launch their ships to fight, the narrow channel of the Trikeri Straits would restrict his ability to overwhelm them with numbers.

Throughout the war, whenever the chroniclers tell us about Achaemenes he is taking or suggesting a sensible, even cautious, approach and warning Xerxes against rash options. He would, most likely, have opted for the cautious approach to the problem presented to him at this point. Herodotus was not much of a seaman himself. As a consequence his accounts of the naval side of the campaign are frustratingly short and vague. At this critical point he makes no mention at all of how the Persians reacted to events. We must reconstruct their action from what we know of Achaemenes' cautious nature and the few available facts.

It is reasonable to assume that Achaemenes left the vulnerable merchant fleet at Therme while he led the fighting ships to the Trikeri Straits to deal with the Greek fleet. There would be various option open to him. He might land soldiers on Euboea to attack the Greek ships by land, or he might try to lure the Greeks out to fight by pretending to make mistakes. Or, for all Achaemenes knew, the Greeks might be rash enough to attack him in the open sea and lay themselves open to crushing defeat. All would become clear once Achaemenes got his fleet to the scene of action.

It does seem, however, that Achaemenes chose to hedge his bets. He took with him at least some of the merchant ships. This would make sense. The men on the warships needed supplies, and he could have brought down the coast those ships carrying the supplies that would be needed most urgently by the army. Then, if the Greeks were defeated or simply fled, these ships could be pushed quickly into Halus while messages were sent back to the main fleet at Therme. If, on the other, hand the Trikeri Straits could not be forced, only these few merchant ships would be left bobbing about on the open sea at the mercy of the elements.

Probably on 12 August, Achaemenes was at the Trikeri Straits with the vast majority of his 600 war galleys – no doubt some had been left at Therme to guard against a Greek naval raid. The first thing he would have realised was that old Artabanes had known what he was talking about when he warned Xerxes months earlier that there were no ports large enough for the fleet.

The best available was at Aphetae, now Platania. There are two beaches here, the larger one to the west, where up to a hundred galleys could have been hauled ashore and the small bay offers sheltered anchorages for as many more. To the east the sheltered sandy beach at Kastri offers another safe haven for almost a hundred galleys. Beyond that the refuges become more exposed. The beach at Katiyiorgis is tiny, but the bay is sheltered and has a firm bottom to hold anchors.

On the exposed east coast north of Cape Sepias are the twin beaches of Pralia which are sandy and shelving, but offer no secure anchorage off shore. North again, Paltsi would have been less suitable as it has a ridge of jagged rocks cutting it in two and running out to sea to lurk treacherously just beneath the waves. Melani and Potistika are safer to approach but neither is very large.

Between them, these various beaches and anchorages could probably have accommodated most, if not all, of the ships Achaemenes had with him. They are, however, strung out across more than 30km of coast and the mountainous hinterland ensures that none is within sight of any of the others. If Achaemenes had scattered his fleet into a series of smaller forces he would have risked laying them open to being destroyed piecemeal by the League ships. Instead he opted for the cautious alternative and chose to keep the fleet together, apparently at the northern beaches on the first night, while he assessed the situation for himself and decided what action to take next day. Only some of the ships could be accommodated on the beaches, the rest were anchored off shore.

It was at this point that a messenger from Delphi arrived at the League fleet with the message from the Oracle to pray to the winds. The Athenians would have known that Boreas, the north wind, was related to them by marriage. Indeed, some of the Athenians remembered an old utterance of the Oracle from some years earlier that had never made much sense before. This had told the Athenians to "seek the assistance of their son-in-law" if in danger. Now, the two messages seemed to refer to each other and to make sense. The Athenians set up a temporary altar and offered sacrifices to Boreas.

For some reason, Eurybiades had pulled his main force back from Artemisium to Chalcis in the sheltered channel between Euboea and the mainland. Herodotus says it was because he had been frightened by the crushing defeat suffered by the three Greek ships off Skiathos and by reports of the vast size of the Persian fleet. This was a potentially disastrous move as it left Leonidas and his army exposed at Thermopylae. Perhaps it was that, with their local knowledge, the League captains had some idea of what was about to happen. In any case, Eurybiades clearly had no intention of abandoning his position at Artemisium. He left lookouts and signal stations at Artemisium and along the Euboean coast.

August is a notoriously difficult time in the Aegean for the weather. Over the previous weeks of predictably unbroken blazing sunshine the land and sea has been heating up. Hot air sits like a blanket over the Greek peninsula and nearby islands. So long as the air remains stable, all is well. But if a slight change takes place in the upper atmosphere, the hot air will rise suddenly and dramatically. This movement sucks in vast quantities of air from the cooler areas to the north. This produces a howling northeasterly gale that tears across the Aegean with terrifying speed under a still cloudless sky. The Greeks called it a Hellesponter as it seemed to come from that direction.

Herodotus, as usual, does not seem to understand the naval events he now describes. Any local seamen would have understood what was happening, but in his writing Herodotus seems amazed that such a fierce gale could strike apparently without warning although the weather was calm and sunny. Nor is his account of the effect the gale had on the Persian fleet much better. He tells us some of the places where wreckage was washed ashore – probably because he was told by the local population – and it is an interesting spread. He mentions the village of Casthanea, which lay near the mouth of the Peneus to the north, and Cape Sepias, which are some 120km apart. Otherwise he simply states "It was a storm of the greatest violence and there was no chance of riding it out".

The storm struck early on the morning of 13 August. As dawn broke on 14 August the lookouts that Eurybiades had left on the hills of northeastern Euboia began to sight storm-battered Persian ships being driven south before the winds. Wreckage and broken timbers came ashore on the beaches, together with bodies and bedraggled survivors. The lookouts sent messengers racing down to the League fleet at Chalcis with the news. The Greeks hurried to offer prayers and libations to Poseidon, god of the sea, in thanks for his work. Then they climbed into their ships and rowed back up the Euripus, the strip of water between Euboea and the mainland. They swept past Leonidas and his men as they laboured on rebuilding the wall and digging ditches. The oars glinted in the bright August sunlight as the fleet powered on into the choppy waters of the Trikeri Straits to take up its position once again at Artemisium.

The amount of damage suffered by the Persian fleet has long been a contentious issue. For the League it was the first sign that any of the gods might favour their cause. It made useful propaganda to boost the morale in those states already committed to fighting Persia and would have been a useful debating point when approaching those which were still wavering. Herodotus makes much of the storm, but this might be because he faced an inconsistency in his own account. He needed to explain the small size of the Persian fleet which was to fight here at Artemisium, when he had originally said it numbered 1,207. Could he say all the missing ships had been destroyed by the storm? It seemed a lot. Actually he had not deducted the ships used to build the bridges at the Hellespont, which was why his numbers did not seem reasonable.

It is true that wreckage and bodies were washed up on beaches over a wide area. It is also undeniable that in the following days Achaemenes did not behave like a man who had just seen a huge proportion of his fleet smashed to pieces. He behaved like an admiral who had a battered, damaged but largely intact fleet. In any case, he had a job to do. As soon as the storm had blown itself out, on 14 August, he set about doing it.

Achaemenes began by moving the bulk of his warfleet around Cape Sepias to Aphetae. As already noted the beaches and anchorage here could not accommodate the entire war fleet. From what follows it seems that Achaemenes left a large number of his ships on the northern beaches, though no doubt they were pulled up on to the sand to be out of harm's way. None of the accounts of the days that followed make any mention of the supply ships. Presumably those that had survived the storm were sent back to Therme to await developments.

The move to Aphetae was accompanied by a setback for the Persians. A squadron of fifteen ships from Cyme in Aeolis, a state on the western coast of Asia Minor, were the last of the Persian allies to put into the Trikeri Straits. Seeing the Greek fleet at Artemisium, their commander, a man named Sandoces, mistook them for the Persian fleet. It was a relatively easy mistake for a man who had just weathered a storm to make. Many Greek-looking ships from the Greek cities under Persian control were in the Persian fleet, and Sandoces may have been brigaded with these. In any case, he led his squadron straight towards Artemisium and was swiftly captured along with all his ships. It would be fascinating to know, still better to see, the exact moment – the precise distance from the enemy fleet – when he realised his mistake

By later afternoon on 14 August the bulk of the Persian fleet was safely ensconced at Aphetae, Kastri and Katiyiorgis in the Straits, with smaller squadrons at Pralia, Paltsi, Melani and Potistika outside the straits. No doubt Achaemenes sent off messengers to make contact with his imperial brother and report the situation. Meanwhile, he waited and eyed up the Greek fleet opposite his position.

Xerxes was, by this time, marching from Lamia to Trachis. He was fully aware that his path was blocked by Leonidas at Thermopylae, but may not have realised the situation of the fleet until the messengers sent by Achaemenes caught up with him that night or the following morning. The King of Kings seems to have been in the vanguard of his army, keen to see the situation for himself. As soon as he arrived on the banks of the River Asopus, Xerxes sent a scout forward to probe into the narrow pass.

The horseman got through the West Gate without any trouble and trotted over the plain where the hot springs and shrine to Heracles were located. He seems to have got past the broken ground where the hot water was gathering in pits and ditches, but then came to a halt. His was the first glimpse by any of the Persian forces of the preparations made by the hostile Greeks that they had come to fight.

From his position, the Persian could see the repaired Phocian Wall, but he could not see beyond it. He was therefore unable to see the Greek camp nor to count the size of the army gathered there. If he was an experienced scout, and we must presume he was, he may have been able to make an accurate guess as to the size of the enemy army from the number of columns of smoke rising into the sky from the cooking fires, but it would have been only a guess.

However, the scout did see a group of men in front of the Phocian Wall and they astonished him. For one thing the Greeks made no attempt to catch him or even drive him away. These men were the 300 Spartiates. They were stripped for exercise, spending their time running, leaping and stretching. Others were sitting on the ground combing each other's hair to ensure it was in immaculate condition. No wonder the Persian was startled. Having seen all he could, the scout rode back over the small plain to pass through the West Gate and report to Xerxes. The Great King was as amazed as the scout. He promptly sent for Demaratus, the exiled King of Sparta, to ask his opinion. As ever, Demaratus began with a straightforward view of the situation.

"These men," he said, "have come to fight us for possession of the pass, and for that struggle they are preparing. It is the custom of the Spartans to pay careful attention to their hair when they are about to risk their lives." Perhaps seeing from the expression on Xerxes' face that this had not gone down well, Demaratus added "But I assure you that if you can defeat these men and the rest of the Spartans who are still at home, there is no other people in the world who will dare to stand firm or lift a hand against you."

Xerxes was unconvinced and bewildered. He told Demaratus bluntly that he did not believe that such a small handful of men would dare fight against the vast Persian army. Demaratus merely shrugged "My lord," he replied. "Treat me as a liar if what I have told does not take place." Xerxes waved him away.

There was a second visitor to the Greek position who arrived after dark, probably on this first night. His name has not been recorded, but he was a native of Trachis favourably disposed to the League. He had watched the Persian army arriving all day and had questioned the officers as to how many more men were to come. He was alarmed and made his way to the Phocian Wall. He was stopped by the lookouts and brought to King Leonidas.

In front of the king, the man poured out his story of the sheer size of the Persian army. Clearly the Spartan king and his officers appeared unmoved, for in an effort to get his point across the Trachian then declared. "There are so many Persians coming against you that when they shoot, their arrows they will hide the sun." Dieneces, a Spartiate standing beside Leonidas, grinned. "This is pleasant news," he said smiling. "If the Persians hide the sun, we shall have our battle in the shade." It is no wonder that the Spartiates, those ancient inhabitants of Laconia, have given modern English the word "laconic".

With both armies at Thermopylae and both fleets in the Trikeri Straits, the scene was set for battle. But not yet.

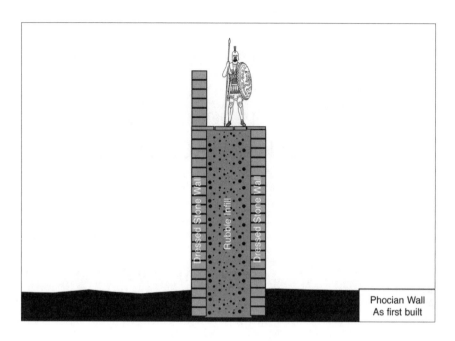

Phocian Wall
As first built

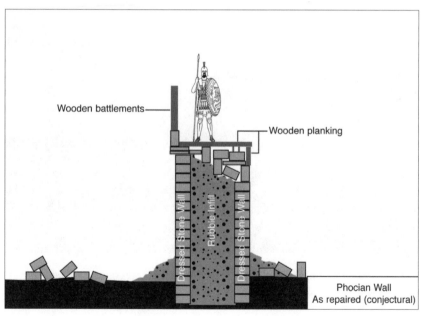

Wooden battlements

Wooden planking

Phocian Wall
As repaired (conjectural)

CHAPTER 12

The Waiting Game

The Greek camp ground at Thermopylae seen from the hillock beside the Middle Gate. The ancient coastline ran approximately along the route of the road.

Before the fighting began at Thermopylae, there was a curious lull. Neither the Greek fleet nor the army was in any hurry to start proceedings. Their task, after all, was simply to keep the Persians pinned down. If the Great King decided not to attack, so much the better. But why was Xerxes hesitating? The answer is that he was not. It was that his activities could not be seen by the Greeks.

Xerxes was an experienced commander and he had taken the trouble to surround himself with capable men with local knowledge. He was not one to make rash mistakes. At dawn on 15 August, the morning after he arrived at Trachis, the situation facing Xerxes was not particularly alarming, though it was undoubtedly frustrating to have his path blocked by the impudent Spartans and their allies. He will have realised that to fight his way through the Pass of Thermopylae would be a costly battle, but Xerxes will also have been aware that he had alternatives. This was the time to investigate them, for it would take several days for the entire Persian army to arrive at Trachis.

No matter how effectively defended a pass might be, there is always a way around it. Xerxes had sent his spies throughout Greece long before setting out on his invasion, and he now had the supportive advice of the Thessalians. He will already have known about, and discounted, the long routes around the western end of the Parnassos Mountains. If Xerxes did not already know of the footpath to Delphi, he would no doubt have learned about it from the Thessalians. This route could carry infantry over the mountain and put them in a position to attack Leonidas from the rear; but there were difficulties.

Once on the far side of the mountains, the force would be bereft of cavalry support or of supplies. Persian armies were accustomed to marching with plenty of both and would have been reluctant to abandon such safeguards in hostile and unknown territory. The route would also have involved a march of approaching 200km to get back to Thermopylae. This would take many days even in friendly territory, but with the risk of ambush at every turn it would take much longer. Xerxes wanted to be through the pass quicker than that, so this idea must have been discounted.

Xerxes needed a route around Thermopylae that was much closer to hand. It is possible that he had picked up rumours of such a path as he advanced, but he clearly had no idea where the path was, even if he knew it existed. He will have sent men up the valleys of the Spercheius and Asopus with instructions to scout the ground thoroughly. It was a sensible precaution to make sure that no hostile force lurked in the upper valleys and if something as useful as a path was found, so much the better.

While his men combed the hills, Xerxes decided to try the second standard gambit to get through a defended pass without fighting: bribery. Xerxes will have known that he faced a motley collection of troops from various allied states. He would also have known that many of these states had old quarrels with each other. Although these had been put on one side to face the greater threat of the Persians, there would have been underlying suspicions and feuds. Xerxes decided to exploit them.

Writing some 450 years later, but apparently drawing on contemporary records now lost, Diodorus of Sicily gives the most detailed account of what followed. As the morning sun climbed into the sky, probably on 15 August, a Persian herald rode through the West Gate and approached the Phocian Wall. He called out that he wanted to talk to the commanders of the Greek armies. He was not to be fobbed off with meeting only Leonidas, but wanted his words heard by all the commanders.

When the Greek leaders had gathered, the Persian herald announced "Xerxes, King of Kings, orders all to give up their arms, to depart unharmed to their native lands and to be allies of the Persians. To all Greeks who do this, he will give more and better lands than they now possess."

It was a tempting and clever offer. The Greeks in the pass will by then have been aware of the great size of the Persian army. All the previous day they will have watched the endless column of men and horses marching down the road from Lamia to Trachis, and now for a second day the stream of armed humanity was passing without pause. To be offered the chance to retreat alive and unharmed must have been attractive. And if that were not enough, the Great King was offering to enrich the home state of any contingent that pulled back. Territory would be taken from other Greek states, presumably from implacable Athens and Sparta, and handed over to the co-operative cities.

Diodorus tells us that Leonidas replied "If we should be allies of the Great King, we should be more useful to him if we kept our arms. And if we should have to wage war against him, we should fight the better for our freedom if we kept them. As for the lands which he promises to give, the Greeks have learned from their fathers to gain lands, not by cowardice, but by valour."

It was a good reply, but not so laconic as the words later to be inscribed on the statue of Leonidas at Sparta. According to this version of events, Leonidas replied to the request to hand over his weapons with the words "Come and get them." Whatever his precise words, Leonidas made his intentions very clear. He would fight.

Xerxes now turned to his third option to avoid a battle in the pass: his fleet. Communications between Xerxes and his brother Achaemenes would have been of prime importance when co-ordinating action. But Xerxes could not simply pick up a phone to talk this brother, and links between the two could not be quick. Sending a top secret message by galley along the disputed Trikeri Straits would be fast, but risky. A roving Greek warship might intercept it and learn all the innermost secrets of the Persian high command.

More secure would be to send a messenger on horse to Halus, by boat across the Gulf of Pagasae and then on horseback again over the hills to Aphetae. The journey was over 140km, which even with changes of horse must have taken a day each way. Thus it would have been 48 hours before either Xerxes or Achaemenes received a reply to a message they sent to the other. The army and navy would be making decisions and acting with at best only a hazy idea of what the other was doing. Without transcripts of the messages the brothers exchanged it is impossible to be certain, but it seems to have been at least 16 August before the two had made contact and exchanged views and ideas. Given the slow communications between the two, it is likely to have been Achaemenes acting on his own initiative rather than obeying orders from Xerxes that began the next phase of the campaign.

As the later afternoon sun began to dip down over the mountains of Greece, a force of 200 warships detached itself from the main Persian fleet. The ships rounded Cape Sepias and headed north between Skiathos and the mainland. Where such a powerful force was heading must have been a mystery to Eurybiades and Themistocles watching from the beach at Artemisium. This was, after all, about a third of the Persian fleet apparently heading back towards Therme. Perhaps there was trouble at home that demanded a strong force of warships.

In fact the ships were heading north only as a feint. As soon as they were out of sight of Artemisium they turned around to run south on the seaward side of Skopelos. The ships were then to head south to round the bottom end of Euboea to enter the Euripus Channel from the south.

The Persian captains would have known what they were about. In 490BC, the Persians had landed on southern Euboea on their way to meet defeat at Marathon and had captured the city of Carystus. No doubt Achaemenes will have selected for this voyage captains who had served in the earlier campaign so that they would know the waters.

Once into the Euripus, the 200 ships were to sweep north. Men were to be landed on Euboea to climb to a hilltop and light a signal fire. When he saw this signal, Achaemenes was to put to sea and head to Artemisium. He hoped to lure the Greeks out to sea, then hit them from behind with the force coming up from the south. It was a plan that relied on good timing to work properly, but was not beyond the abilities of either the ships or the captains of the Persian fleet. Given the distance to be covered, Achaemenes will have expected to see the signal fire on 19 August. Meanwhile, he would wait.

Over the straits at Artemisium all was not going well for the League. Now that the true size of the enemy fleet could be guessed at, some of the Greeks present were deeply unhappy. They had clearly hoped that Boreas, the god of the north wind, had done their work for them. Now they could see that the storm had only damaged the enemy fleet, not destroyed it. Eurybiades called a council of war to discuss the situation with the commanders of the various fleets from different states.

According to Herodotus, who is here drawing on his Athenian sources, it was the Athenians who wanted to stay and fight while the Spartans and Corinthians wanted to flee. He then recounts a long and involved story about what happened behind the scenes. As ever with Herodotus when he is writing about what is supposed to have taken place in secret, his account must be treated with caution. There is no independent confirmation of this story – Plutarch for instance merely repeats the story adding the words "according to Herodotus". It has, however, become well known so it is worth repeating.

The council of war, says Herodotus, decided to abandon the position at Artemisium before the Persian fleet destroyed them all. The Greek fleet was to put to sea that night and row away as quietly as possible in the hope that the Persians would not realise they were gone until dawn, by which time pursuit would be impossible.

The Euboeans who were bringing supplies down to the League fleet heard what was afoot. Realising that this would leave them at the mercy of the Persians, they hurriedly found Eurybiades and begged him to stay at least long enough for the Euboeans to get their women, children and livestock to safety. Eurybiades refused, insisting the fleet would leave that night.

The Euboeans then went to Themistocles who, as leader of by far the largest part of the allied fleet could be relied upon to have some influence. Moreover, he was known to be in favour of staying at Artemisium. The Euboeans handed over 30 talents of silver to Themistocles on the understanding that he would keep the fleet where it was.

Themistocles then went to see Eurybiades and slipped him five talents. This, Herodotus says, was enough for the Spartan admiral to announce a change of heart. The other commanders were surprised, none more so than Ocytus, commander of the Corinthian ships. Themistocles then confronted Ocytus openly in front of the other commanders and shouted "Never shall you betray us by leaving. I will give you more for staying with us than the Great King of Persia would pay you to desert us." Themistocles then privately handed over three talents of silver to the abashed Corinthian. The wily Athenian then pocketed the rest of the 30 talents for himself.

The story may be suspect as it deals with events supposed to have happened in private and portrays the Corinthians and Spartans in a poor light. By the time Herodotus was collecting information, the Athenians would have wanted to hog all the glory for themselves and had fallen out badly with both Corinth and Sparta. It is suspicious that the only states named as wanting to flee were the two which Athens would have wanted to denounce by the time Herodotus was writing.

It is clear, however, that all was not well. Another writer, Phanias of Lesbos, recorded a dispute between Themistocles and another Athenian named Architeles. According to Phanias, Architeles was commander of the sacred state galley. He was, therefore, a man of much influence and probably a priest of some kind, though this is not entirely clear. He may have been one of those who believed that the Delphic Oracle's "wooden walls" referred to the Acropolis, not the fleet. Architeles may, therefore, have been at Artemisium under protest. In any case, he now announced that he had to sail back to Athens as he did not have enough money to pay his crew to stay at Artemisium any longer.

Themistocles managed to stir up trouble among the crew of the sacred galley to such a pitch that the men snatched dinner out of the hands of Architeles. Architeles denounced his crew and went into a sulk. Themistocles then sent a messenger to the aggrieved commander carrying a box of bread and meat, hidden at the bottom of which was a talent of silver. Themistocles told him to pay his crew and stop causing trouble, or that he would be denounced for having taken a bribe from the Persians.

Again it is impossible to judge the truth of this. The key events are supposed to have taken place in secret and we have only one source for the story. Clearly, however, there was trouble of some sort among the commanders of the fleet once they realised the vast size of the armada which was come against them.

At this point a professional diver named Scyllias from Scione in Thrace arrived at Artemisium. Scione was a Greek city that had formerly been an ally of Athens and had become home to many men from Athens looking for a better life elsewhere. It had, however, fallen under Persian control along with the rest of Thrace, which is presumably how Scyllias found himself at Aphetae diving on Persian ships wrecked in the recent storm to retrieve pay chests and other valuables.

Given his home city, Scyllias may well have had Athenian parents. In any case he was on the side of the League and on the morning of 17 August he arrived at Artemisium. The man claimed to have swum all the way from Aphetae underwater, a distance of about 16km. Herodotus says he does not believe a word of it and says that Scyllias must have travelled by boat, though that does not explain how he would have got past the Persian patrol boats. Given that Scyllias was acknowledged to be the finest diver of his generation, and that skilled craftsmen tend to keep trade secrets to themselves, it is not impossible that Scyllias had used a snorkel or some similar device.

However he did it, Scyllias did arrive at Artemisium. He began by telling his eager listeners the precise state of the enemy fleet and the damage it had suffered in the storm. He then revealed the destination of the 200 ships seen heading north past Skiathos.

The Greek commanders again held a council of war, but this time there was no talk of retreat and little in the way of argument. Eurybiades sent scouts to keep an eye open for the Persian squadron coming up the Euripus. When it was learned that this fleet was approaching, the Greeks planned to put to sea and head south to defeat it. This was sound military sense. The Greek fleet outnumbered the 200 ships coming from the south and so could hope to win a victory.

Like Achaemenes and the Persians, Eurybiades and the Greeks settled down to wait. Some distance away, Leonidas and his men were also waiting – though we can assume that they were making good use of their time by preparing the ground in front of them. And Xerxes was also waiting.

The sun came up, the sun went down. Time passed. Men fingered their weapons. Birds flew through the skies. Time passed. The hours dragged by while everyone knew that fighting and bloodshed on a vast scale was close. Death hung over everyone's head. It must have frayed the nerves badly on all sides.

But as the hours passed and men waited, the inexorable forces of which Artabanes had long since warned Xerxes came grindingly into play. By 18 August, as so often in warfare, it was the logistical situation that prompted action.

By that time the enormous Persian army had been arriving at Trachis for over three days. Whatever the precise numbers of the main army by this point, there have been tens of thousands of men camped along the shores of the Malian Gulf and along the rivers Spercheius and Asopus. The army had passed through Thessaly, eating up the fruits of the land as they marched. Xerxes had counted on having access to the vast stocks of food from his supply fleet by this date, but as yet there was no sign of either fleet or supplies.

Xerxes would by then have learned that his brother in command of the fleet had embarked on a plan that would not yield any results until 19 August at the earliest, perhaps later. Whatever food the army had brought with it must have been running low by this point. The area around Trachis had been stripped by Leonidas, and the stores of food in the city itself would have been stretched to supply its own citizens until the harvest was in – or until the war rolled on and supplies could be bought in from elsewhere.

It might be thought that Xerxes could have ordered his supply fleet to unload at Therme and send the food overland. Or perhaps supplies could be gathered across Thessaly and transported to Trachis. But the land transportation systems of the time made either approach unrealistic. Military supplies are heavy and bulky, needing stout carts to carry them. An average four-wheeled farm cart of the period could carry about 400kg of cargo and required a crew of two men and eight oxen to keep it moving. A distance of some 18km covered in a day was considered pretty good going on flat ground. In hilly regions, and Greece is nothing if not hilly, a mere 8km might be considered a daily average. The men and oxen, of course, needed food and water to keep them going. In normal times this could be found along the roadside, but if large numbers of carts were trundling along a single road the wayside grass would soon be consumed. A road-based supply system meant that not only the army had to be supplied, but also the supply train.

We can assume that the Persians of 480BC would have eaten a similar amount of food to soldiers in the 18th or 19th centuries, from which precise records survive. Unlike those later armies, however, the Persians did not have the padded horsecollar that enabled draught horses to pull heavy wagons – that was not to be invented for centuries. So each 10,000 men in the Persian army would have needed 50 contemporary ox cart loads of food every day. Even if the carts were densely packed nose to tail, this caravan would occupy over a kilometre of road. Given that the likely size of the Persian army as it arrived in front of Thermopylae was around 200,000 men this means that a 20km procession of carts would need to arrive every day to keep it supplied with food.

The organisational and logistical demands of receiving, unloading and turning round so many carts in a day would have been phenomenal. Then the carts would have needed to be sent back where they had come from. If the place where food was being loaded on to the carts for transportation was more than a day's march away a duplicate convoy of ox carts would be needed so that they could be on the move while the first was returning to base for reloading.

Then there was the problem of feeding the oxen. Within a day any available roadside fodder would have been stripped clean. Other carts would be needed to carry fodder for the oxen pulling the supply carts – and these too would have been pulled by oxen which needed feeding. Each cart was able to carry enough fodder to keep a team of oxen going for just three days. Our 50 carts carrying food for 10,000 men would need another 17 carts just to feed the oxen, and those 17 would need another five to keep them going, which in turn would need two more. Multiplied up by the numbers needed to keep the entire Persian army in food, this shows that it was a total nonsense to try to feed the army by road. In any case, there were not that many carts in all Greece, never mind in Thessaly.

Xerxes had provided carts to march alongside the army, but these were not intended for long distance transport. Instead they were expected to carry out short term duties only. Within the Persian Empire they would have carried supplies from one pre-prepared supply dump to the next. In Greece, where there were no such prearranged food supplies, the carts would have been intended to carry food from a port where the fleet had put in to the army camped a short distance away. In hostile territory they could have carried supplies looted from the local populace.

Some idea of how bad road transport was in the ancient world can be gathered from events in the Roman province of Coele, now northern Syria, in AD362. A drought struck the area and famine resulted. The drought had not affected the entire region and large stocks of food were available in granaries at Tyre some 70km away. But the drought that had caused the famine had also dried off all fodder crops, effectively halting the ox carts. Unable to transport food to the people, the government ordered the people to walk to the food. Thousands died along the road, but there was nothing that could be done to help them.

This then was the problem facing Xerxes. His food was running out and he had no way of getting any more except to batter his way through the Pass of Thermopylae to the rich, fertile plains of Boeotia beyond.

The time of waiting was over. The time of killing was about to begin.

Ploughing on the great, fertile plain of Thessaly. No matter how rich, the plain could not feed an army the size of the Persian invaders for long. The supplies with the merchant fleet would soon be required if Thermopylae was not taken.

CHAPTER 13

The First Day of Battle

*Darius I of Persia enthroned. Herodotus tells us
that his son and successor, Xerxes I, to whom
he had left the task of taking revenge against
Athens for their interference in the Ionian revolt,
watched the battle from his throne.*

It can be a frustrating business reading ancient accounts of battles. There is plenty of detail and description in the writings, but it is so often of apparently irrelevant matter or unimportant incidents, while so much of the real action is skated over with barely a mention. Only rarely are events explained, still less do the reasons why commanders do certain things get given much space.

The cause is that the people for whom Herodotus, Plutarch and the rest were writing did not need the details that we need today. They knew all about the weapons and tactics of their times. They did not need to be told why a commander behaved in a certain way in a particular situation because they understood perfectly well already.

Imagine that a modern writer were producing an account of a skirmish in Iraq in 2006. He would not need to explain what a grenade was, nor what it did and still less what soldiers would do if one were to be thrown at them. Nor would he need to explain that American soldiers in the skirmish would be wearing helmets, nor that they carried rifles, nor who Osama bin Laden might be. So it was with the ancient writers. They could assume that the people for whom they wrote knew and understood a great deal of information that we in the 21st century do not.

However, with a knowledge of weapons and fighting tactics of the time, and having studied the ground at first hand, it is possible to put together a, hopefully, fairly accurate and detailed account of the battle at Thermopylae. What is needed is to take the bare bones of the account given in Herodotus, cross-reference to other accounts and read this in conjunction with knowledge of how battles were fought at the time gleaned from other sources. To take as an example the first movements of the Persians after dawn on that fateful 18 August. None of our sources say what happened. So what can we surmise?

Herodotus mentions later that Xerxes sat watching the battle all day long from his throne. It is obvious that Xerxes would not want to risk his own life, so he would not arrange to be too close to the deadly spears of the Greeks. Comfort and convenience might have tempted Xerxes to watch the battle from close to his own tent. However, Xerxes could not have had a view of events from the Persian camp. Not only was the distance of six

144

kilometres a long shot before the days of telescopes, but the shoulder of Mount Kallidromos would have been in the way.

It is possible that Xerxes may have positioned himself near the mouth of the Asopus River. From there he would have had an uninterrupted view across the Malian Gulf (now silted to form salt marsh) to the Middle Gate where the fighting would take place. However, he would be looking across water into the rising sun of a bright August day. The glare of the Mediterranean sun would have bounced and sparkled off the rippling waters in dazzling fashion until well past mid-morning. And he would still have been some 5km from the action. All he could have seen – if the sun let him see anything much at all – would have been the backs of his own soldiers.

A much better view could have been obtained from the lower slopes of Mount Kallidromos just to the east of the West Gate. From this position, Xerxes would have been about two kilometres from the Middle Gate and Phocian Wall. A man with average eyesight would have had no difficulty following the course of a battle at this distance. At a suitable height, the Great King could have seen over the heads of his men to the wall itself and the actions of the Greeks in the immediate vicinity.

Plutarch, when writing about the Battle of Salamis fought a month or so later, tells us that Xerxes had had his throne brought all the way from Persia so that he could sit on it when conducting official business. The Great King sat on this throne to watch Salamis, so it is reasonable to assume he sat on it at Thermopylae also. It was a magnificent creation in gilded timber that must have been both heavy and bulky. And it would have needed a fairly flat piece of land on which to stand. There would also have to be space around the throne for Xerxes' generals and advisors to stand, plus the cupbearers and food servers that would have been considered essential by the King of Kings arrayed in his full splendour.

Xerxes' decision to sit on this throne was not mere ostentation. He came from a society in which the ruler was a being of great majesty and splendour, akin to a god in the eyes of many of his subjects. If Xerxes were to appear in front of his army, he had to dress for the occasion and that involved display on a grand scale. It was probably likely that the sight of the King of Kings watching enthroned thus would encourage the men to fight better. We know it was the habit of Persian monarchs to get their secretaries to write down the names of anyone who fought particularly well. Xerxes would have had his secretaries to hand to make such notes.

Of course, nobody in the Persian army would want their king to see them acting with anything except the most daring bravery and absolute loyalty. When leaving Sardis at the start of the campaign they had marched between the severed halves of the hapless son of Pythius, who had failed to show the required degree of loyalty. Fear was always a motivator used by the Persians.

But getting a heavy wooden throne part way up the steep slopes of Mount Kallidromos, levelling a parcel of land for it to stand on and getting supplies of food and water into position was going to take some time. It would be unthinkable to allow the sacred throne of the Great King to fall into enemy hands, so the workmen would need to be protected from a sudden Greek raid.

As the sun set on 17 August all was apparently quiet at Thermopylae, though Xerxes must have already decided to attack the following day. No doubt some preparations were going ahead in the Persian camp. As yet, however, no Persian soldiers had entered the pass except for the envoys rebuffed so laconically by Leonidas. It could have been that Leonidas had fleet-footed scouts posted in the West Gate to keep an eye on things.

The first signs of action would have been a force of Persian troops marching out of camp towards the West Gate. These men would undoubtedly have been royal guards from the unit known as Immortals. On campaign most Persians wore the more convenient dress of the Medes, but these men would have been drawn from the crack 1,000 Royal Guards and they were there to make a show. It is likely, therefore, that they marched into action arrayed in the finery of the Persian nobility.

These robes swept down to the ankle and wrists with great billowing folds of brightly coloured cloth. Each man had his own pattern of embroidery and patchwork so that the mass must have shimmered like a rainbow on the march in the early morning sun. Each man carried a brightly decorated quiver over his left shoulder which contained his bow as well as his arrows. The two-metre spear was tipped with an iron head, burnished to a silvery sparkle, while the butt end was a gilded silver pomegranate as large as a man's fist. The men habitually carried the spear point downward so that the gilding of the butt would catch the sunlight as they marched. Behind this imposing display of armed might would have come a small army of workmen. No doubt these men were drawn from the ranks of the more primitive nations marching with Xerxes, such as the Mysians or Milyae. These men were poorly armed and may have been brought along to undertake exactly this sort of ground levelling manual labour.

The Greek scouts in the West Gate will have fallen back before the Persians. One would have been sent scampering back to the Phocian Wall to alert Leonidas, while the others kept a wary distance from the advancing Persians.

But the glittering ranks advanced only a short distance on to the plain from the West Gate. There they formed a defensive line and came to a halt. Behind them the workmen swarmed up the hillside to begin their work. Attacking the ground with shovels, pickaxes and spades they would have cleared and levelled an area of ground on which the throne could sit. Then the throne would have been manhandled up the slope and put into place. Tents, banners and sunshades would have followed until the small platform of level ground resembled nothing so much as a gorgeous and brightly coloured pavilion.

Finally, Xerxes himself would have appeared. Accompanied by his officers and advisers, plus a host of servants, the Great King would have walked through the West Gate, turned to his right and mounted the hill to take his place on his throne. Secretaries sat at his feet ready to write down whatever was Xerxes' will. Messengers hung around nearby to take his orders to the army. Commanders waited patiently for the king's pleasure. All was at last ready.

All this can be reconstructed from the single sentence in Herodotus that "Xerxes watched the battle from his seat," from studying the topography of the battlefield and an understanding of how the Persian army operated. In a similar way, it is possible to construct a plausible account of much of the course of the fighting.

Behind the Phocian Wall, Leonidas was likewise getting ready for the battle. He brought a young female goat to the wall, watched by the commanders of the other troops. The flautists who played the marching songs of the Spartans began to play sacred hymns. Leonidas called out to the skies, invoking the aid of Artemis Agrotera, the Roman goddess Diana, the goddess of hunters and the forest. (She was also the goddess most associated with revenge.) Then he killed the goat with a single stroke of his sword. The religious preliminaries over, he set to work ordering his forces to meet the attack that was obviously coming.

Xerxes had already decided on the plan of attack and must have discussed it at some length with his senior officers. Foremost among these were Mardonius and Hydarnes. Mardonius had commanded the army that had put down the revolt of the Ionian Greeks and had long been a supporter of war with Athens and Sparta. He was the son of Gobryas, one of the six Persian noblemen who had organised the coup that put Darius on the throne. This made Mardonius a member of one of the richest and most noble families in Persia, so it is no surprise that he was married to the daughter of Xerxes. He was now in overall command of the infantry.

Hydarnes was in command of the Immortals, the elite unit of the entire army and had responsibility for the 1,000 Royal Guards, although these men were under the direct control of Xerxes and stayed with him at all times. Like Mardonius, Hydarnes was a highly placed Persian nobleman. His father, also named Hydarnes, had joined Gobryas in the coup that put Xerxes' father on the throne. He was never far from the Great King and there are clues that he was more of a professional soldier than some others on the expedition.

The other two men who formed the high command with Xerxes were the brothers Harmamithras and Tithaeus. These noblemen commanded the cavalry, so their men were not to be heavily involved at Thermopylae. No doubt the cavalry were busy elsewhere, perhaps patrolling the surrounding areas, keeping an eye on the Thessalians to the rear or scouting the roads to the west. The brothers were sons of Datis, the commander of the Persian army at Marathon who had been killed by a Spartan executioner after the battle. They would have taken a very keen and personal interest in the Spartan hoplites now facing the Persians at Thermopylae.

Of rather more immediate importance was one of the second rank commanders: Tigranes. This man was a member of the royal family, but seems to have come from a fairly junior branch as nobody bothers to record the names of his parents. Perhaps he was illegitimate. In 490BC, Tigranes was in command of the Median infantry. The Medes were tough mountain men who were counted almost as Persians within the empire, enjoying many of the honours and privileges of the ruling nation. It was Tigranes that Xerxes now ordered to advance with his Medes to attack the Phocian Wall. The Medes had been chosen by Xerxes and his commanders as they believed these men had the best chance of success.

Attacking a defended fortification is a tricky and dangerous business in any period of history. Facing up to elite troops such as the Spartans who have had several days to prepare the ground was a tough mission. Casualties were going to be high, but then Xerxes had plenty of men to lose.

Xerxes would have known it would be useless to give the task to second rate men such as the Bactrians or Caspians. Trained and experienced men were needed, but Xerxes would not have wanted to risk his best men – the Immortals – in the first encounter. The enemy might have prepared traps and tricks that would not be revealed until the fighting began. And so the reliable, but not indispensable Medes were chosen.

It would have been mid-morning by the time the Medes marched through the West Gate. They could have come four abreast for there was not room for a wider column. Moving out in front of the Royal Guards, the Medes would have formed up for the advance. No doubt small bodies of men would have been sent ahead of the main body to drive back the Greek scouts and search around in the undergrowth for any unpleasant surprises. They would probably have pushed forward only as far as the boggy, cut up ground of the hot springs. Beyond that stretched the firm, cleared killing ground on which no ambushes could be laid.

Behind these skirmishers would have come the main body. The wall to be assaulted was some 15 metres wide. This would have allowed a frontage for no more than 20 men. It would be reasonable to assume that an attack column might be 20 men wide and perhaps up to 15 men deep. But the Medes did not intend simply to surge forward against the wall. That would have been suicidal and the Persian army was both professional and experienced. The assault would have been carefully planned.

As already noted, the men brought by Xerxes to Greece were chosen for their missile weapons more than anything else. The Medes carried small bows made of a composite construction mixing a wooden core with horn on the back and sinew on the face. This complex design greatly increased the force that the bow delivered to the arrow. Sinew will snap back to position when stretched, as it was on the front of the bow, while horn reacts in the same way when put under tension such as it experienced on the rear of the bow. These bows may have had a range of about 100 metres or perhaps a little less.

Given that siege machinery could not be brought forward over the morass of the hot springs, the Medes needed to find another way of capturing the Phocian Wall. As seasoned professionals, we can assume that Tigranes and his officers would have adopted the standard routine of the day.

The first move was to deluge the enemy on the wall with missiles. Unable to get their siege machines within range, the Medes would have used their arrows. The arrows were not intended only to inflict casualties on the defending Greeks, but also to act as what is known as 'suppressing fire'. This means that the arrows would have made it difficult for the Greeks to launch their own missile weaponry at the Medes. Suppressing fire works only if the sheer volume of missiles outweighs that of the defenders. At Thermopylae this was not a problem for the Medes. Every man in the Mede forces had a bow and arrow, while missile weapons were a rarity among the Greeks.

In fact, Leonidas will have been in something of a quandary in deciding how to man the Phocian Wall to meet this attack. He had with him several hundred Helots and other poorer Greeks who would have had missile weaponry of various kinds.

A Greek slinger could use his leather weapon to hurl a lead shot weighing about 30 grams. Slingers could achieve some accuracy over a distance of about 100 metres, less than that of the range of the enemy's arrows. The lead shot could break an arm or inflict a nasty flesh wound if it struck an unarmoured man. Even if it hit armour, it could cause painful bruising and could concuss a man if it hit him on the helmet. However, the limited range was a handicap compared to that of Persian arrows.

Javelin throwers were also present in the League army at Thermopylae, though again we do not have accurate numbers. Perhaps there were 500 or so. Javelin throwing was an Olympic sport, so the skill was obviously of recognised importance. The distance over which the weapon was useful was less than that of the sling at about 40 metres or so. The weapon did, however, have the advantage of being easy to make from materials that lay readily to hand. Greek archers would have been more useful to Leonidas, but archery was a rare skill among the Greeks outside Crete and there is no evidence that Leonidas had any men armed with bows with him.

Even if he had been well supplied with archers, Leonidas may have hesitated to line the wall with them. A barrage of arrows directed at an advancing enemy would be useful for inflicting casualties, but lightly armed men such as archers or slingers would not be able to hold the wall. Hoplites would be needed for that task. Given the ruined state of the wall, the parapet walk is unlikely to have been either spacious or even. Exchanging one group of men for another would not be easy under enemy attack.

It is likely that Leonidas would have put on the wall enough hoplites to ensure one man per metre of wall to form a secure defence against direct assault. Events were to prove that these hoplites were almost immune to the Medes' missiles. The arrows were short and light, with broad arrowheads. These were designed for use against enemies equipped in similar fashion to themselves. The arrowheads were able to pierce light armour and plunge into the living flesh below, where the broad flanges made them difficult to extract. Against the thick armour of the hoplites, however, the arrows were useless. The light weight meant they had little momentum and what force there was was dissipated across the full width of the arrow head. Narrow, pointed arrowheads are needed to be effective against heavy armour. These the Medes and Persians did not have for the simple reason that they had never before needed them.

Leonidas would have added as many slingers as there was space for. It is also possible that a small number of slingers may have been stationed in front of the gateway. From there they could shoot at an advancing enemy, then slip back through the gateway in time for waiting comrades to push the wooden barrier into place. Timing was critical, but the manoeuvre would not be too difficult.

But under the strain of Mede suppressing fire there would be little the Greek slingers could realistically achieve. They would swiftly have been reduced to huddling behind the wooden parapet, peering through to keep an eye on what was going on. They had to sit there and take it.

What would be happening in front of the wall would not come as much of a surprise to the Greeks, but the timing of it could not be second-guessed. While one force of Medes continued to pour arrows at the parapet, another would make ready to assault the wall. Assuming the wall was between 1.8 and 3.6 metres tall, it would not be realistic to expect infantry to get up it in the face of opposition unaided. They needed, quite literally, a leg up.

The most obvious aid the Medes would have used were ladders. These were easy to make and light enough to carry over the hot spring morass and up to the Phocian Wall without difficulty. Men on a ladder to assault a wall are able to use their arms to wield their weapons, though their footing is of course insecure. They would be at a clear disadvantage to the Greeks on the wall walk, but not ridiculously so. Fortresses have been carried by escalade throughout human history, though the attackers needed to be lucky to achieve success.

As the assault force got ready to attack, the archers pouring in the suppressing barrage would have continued their work right up until the last moment. Archery was always an inexact art. With changeable breezes and arrows that varied in flight from one minute to the next, it would have been impossible for the Medes to have shot with great accuracy. They would probably have ceased loosing off their shafts when their attacking force got to within three or four metres of the foot of the wall.

Peeping through chinks in the timber battlements, the Greeks would have seen the attack coming. As soon as the arrows stopped falling, javelin throwers and slingers would have sprung up to shoot at close range into the advancing mass of Medes. At a distance of only two or three metres it would have been difficult for the Greeks to miss, but these throwers were present in small numbers – perhaps no more than ten on the wall. And the Medes did not have far to run before they were in action. So time for throwing was limited.

Once at the foot of the wall, the Medes would have pushed their ladders up against it. Even at its highest likely height of 3.6 metres, the Phocian Wall would have been within easy ladder reach. While two men stood at the foot of the ladder to hold it steady, a third would have scrambled up. Gripping his lightweight wicker shield in his left hand and his two-metre spear in the other, the man would have headed for the top.

There he would be met by the defending hoplites. It is likely that ladders could have been erected at a density of only one per two metres of wall because of the need for men to stand at the bottom and hold them steady. This means that each man on a ladder was facing two or three on the wall. These were heavy odds against the Medes, but other things made them far worse.

Medes wore little in the way of body armour. The most that seems to have been usual was lightweight scale armour. This consisted of large numbers of small flat pieces of metal, perhaps five centimetres by two, sewn on to a leather or cloth jerkin so that they overlapped. This armour was flexible and comfortable to wear, but was only reasonably effective at blocking weapons. As with the broad arrowheads, the Medes had found this type of armour effective to that date because of the enemies they had faced.

At Thermopylae, the Medes were up against the Greek dory, or heavy thrusting spear. This weapon could punch through the Median armour with ease. Nor was the standard Mede shield much use. The wicker work was proof against the light weaponry of Asia, but simply fell to pieces when struck a determined blow by a dory. Worst of all for the Medes was the awful realisation that the Greek dory was about 20cm longer than the Mede spear. The Greeks on the wall could deal death and injury while the Medes could not get a blow in at all.

Even if a Mede did manage to get near the top of a ladder and land a strike on a Greek hoplite with his spear, matters did not improve much for him. Unlike the Mede wicker shield the Greek *aspis*, or large circular shield, was made of jointed sections of wood glued together and held under stress by the outer bronze covering. It could turn aside or simply stop a thrust from a Mede spear.

Taking into account the quality of the weaponry and numbers of men that could be brought into action at the wall top it is hardly surprising that the conflict on the ladders went the way of the Greeks. After some minutes of savage struggle, the attack force of Medes must have been disordered and would have taken heavy casualties. No body of men can be expected to continue to attack in such circumstances, so the Medes would have pulled back either to reform their ranks or to be replaced by another squad.

It is likely that this would have been calculated in advance by Xerxes and his commanders, though not necessarily told to the men sent forward to do the actual fighting and dying. The Great King cannot have expected to win the wall in the first rush. Instead the plan would have been to launch repeated waves of assaults up the ladders, with archers deluging the parapet with arrows between each attack. This would keep up a constant pressure on the defending Greeks. If they were not being picked off by a hail of arrows, they were engaged in the exhausting business of fighting from the parapet.

Presumably the Persians were hoping this perpetual attack would make it difficult, if not impossible for the Greeks to withdraw one force of defenders and replace it with another. The best they might manage would have been to push up fresh defenders to replace those killed or wounded in the fighting. And even the toughest and most resilient men would eventually tire. As the men grew tired they would be more prone to make mistakes.

It must have been on this that Xerxes pinned his hopes. By keeping up a constant assault of arrow barrages and ladder assaults, the Medes would exhaust the Greeks on the wall. Then one Greek might make an error and one Mede would get on the wall itself. Once one attacker is on a defended wall, it is much easier for a second to get up beside him, easier still for a third to get in position. Unless the defenders can launch a swift and effective counter attack the wall will be captured.

Xerxes must have hoped the battle would be over in a couple of hours. He had reckoned without the iron discipline of the Spartans and the effective use to which their King Leonidas put them. As Herodotus tells us, the Spartans spent the day "making sorties from behind the wall". These sorties were an essential part of Leonidas's battle plan. Xerxes had fondly imagined that the Greeks would stay behind their wall, perhaps overawed by the vast size of the Persian army. Leonidas had seen the danger in that plan and avoided it.

Every time a battered force of Medes pulled back from the fatal ladders, they would have fallen back over the flat, cleared ground to get beyond range of the javelins and sling shots that they could expect the Greeks to send after them. This meant pulling back some 100 metres or so. In the circumstances, it is likely that the Medes would have made off as fast as they could. Given the need to carry their wounded and carry their ladders, their formation would have been completely disordered and most would have had their backs to the Phocian Wall.

That was when Leonidas would have struck. The timber barrier blocking the gateway would have been torn down and the Spartans would have surged through. Expertly trained men such as the Spartans would have had no difficulty keeping tight formation at a jog, nor in deploying out from column into line with great speed. Taking up formation in a small phalanx, the Spartans would have charged.

The massive impact of a solid wall of heavily armoured hoplites advancing at the run would have shattered the already disorganised Medes. Once the Medes were scattered, killing them in large numbers was easy work to the battle-hardened Spartans. Casualties would have been huge and, as Herodotus says, "The Spartans had their losses too, but not many." This was slaughter indeed.

But there was danger for the Greeks as well. If the pursuit of the fleeing Medes was carried any distance, the Spartans would have got too far from the Phocian Wall. They would have been vulnerable to being outflanked or even surrounded by a well organised Mede counterattack. Even the retreat back to the wall would be dangerous under the hail of arrows the Medes could loose on them. Armoured though they were, the Spartans were not encased in armour. Some arrows would find a mark in exposed sections of arm or leg.

It was at this point that the iron discipline of the Spartiates really showed itself to advantage. Men with their blood up and chasing a broken enemy are notoriously difficult to halt and get back into formation. Not so the Spartiates. Leonidas needed only command his men and they obeyed. Long before they got into trouble, the Spartans would halt their charge and return to the cover of the Phocian Wall.

Herodotus records that "in the course of the attacks three times, in terror for his army, Xerxes leapt to his feet". Presumably this must mean that the Medes were three times driven back by a Spartan counterattack. Not only did these sallies by the Spartans inflict heavy casualties on the Medes, they also broke up the formations of the enemy and would have badly affected morale among those waiting to take their turn in the attack. The effect must have been to delay the next wave of the ladder assault for some time.

This in turn had two great advantages for the defending Greeks. The increased time granted to them between each assault by the Medes meant that there was plenty of time to change the guard on the wall. Herodotus tells us quite explicitly that "Each contingent took its turn." In this way, Leonidas ensured that none of his men were pushed to the brink of exhaustion, so the breakthrough hoped for by Xerxes never happened.

The second advantage was that the Medes needed to spend rather more time shooting arrows at the wall than they had expected. Each Mede quiver could carry about 30 or 40 arrows. This would supply enough ammunition for about 10 minutes or so of shooting. The static nature of this battle meant that, unlike in more fluid encounters, the Medes could not pick up their arrows to shoot again. And since the Greeks had no archers, there were no Greek arrows to shoot back. It would not be long before a quiver of arrows would be used up.

The Medes had been on the road for months, carrying their weapons all the way from Sardis. Inevitably accidents will have happened and arrows become broken. Even if each man had set off with two quivers of arrows – which was certainly standard practice in later years – he would soon have exhausted this immediate supply at Thermopylae.

It is difficult to be certain, but there are thought to have been about 10,000 or 12,000 Medes at Thermopylae. As each archer ran out of arrows, a new man could be pushed forward to take his place. Given the topography of the land in front of the Phocian Wall on which the Medes were deployed, it is likely that around 250 or 300 could bring their arrows to bear on the wall at any given moment. Using the above calculations for the rate of shooting and number of arrows that each man could be expected to have, the Medes would have run out of ammunition after about 5 hours of fighting.

Where, the Medes may have wondered, were all the spare arrows that their officers had assured them were going to be available for use once the fighting began? They were on the transport ships that could not get past the Greek fleet at Artemisium. It was not just hunger that the Greek ships were inflicting on the Persian army.

It would now have been about mid-afternoon on that hot August day. Sitting up on his throne near the West Gate, Xerxes was losing patience. He must have expected to have taken the wall within a couple of hours of the attack starting. Even if there had been additional defences behind the Middle Gate, Xerxes must have been confident that he would have overcome all resistance by this time. He had even given his men orders to bring him some live Greeks for interrogation before supper.

Yet here he was no further forward. The cautious and sensible move would have been to withdraw the Medes and send in the Hyrkanians or Kashshites. These men, like the Medes, were as well armoured as men in the Persian army were likely to be. They came from wealthy lands that could afford rudimentary training for their young men and were experienced, reliable troops.

But Xerxes seems to have lost his temper – or at least his patience. He called for Hydarnes and sent in the Immortals.

These 10,000 men were the elite of the entire Persian army. They were professional, full time soldiers who underwent detailed training and remorseless drilling. If anyone could brush aside these impudent Greeks, Xerxes must have thought, it was the Immortals. But although superbly trained veterans, the Immortals carried only the same weaponry as the Medes. Like them they suffered from having short spears and broad-bladed arrows that made little impact on the Greek armour and from having wicker shields and light armour that collapsed under the heavy Greek spears.

Brave and determined, the Immortals pushed forward to the attack. They shot their arrows and assaulted the wall, but to no effect. Their discipline made them less vulnerable to Spartan sallies than had been the Medes so they lost fewer men, but they could not take the wall. After some furious fighting these men too were withdrawn.

With the sun setting behind Trachis and the long shadows of the mountains spreading over the pass it was time to pause, but not for long. Leonidas soon had his men at work. The wounded had their injuries bandaged up and were carried back to camp. The dead were dragged out of the way and prepared for cremation on heroic pyres. Weapons were cleaned and cared for. Squads of men were sent forward from the Phocian Wall to drag aside the enemy dead. The killing ground between the wall and the hot springs had to be kept clear for Spartan hoplites to manoeuvre on.

Whether or not the League troops would have pushed beyond the hot springs and shrine to Heracles is uncertain. No doubt Leonidas had intended that they should do so, but Xerxes now had his throne set up on Mount Kallidromos. It would have been an unacceptable sign of defeat to have had the throne manhandled back to camp and even worse to allow it to be seized by the Greeks. Most likely it was left in position together with a powerful force to guard it. The scrub-covered plain between the hot springs and the West Gate must have become a form of no man's land.

Leonidas must have been pleased. His plan had worked to perfection. Perhaps he made his way forward to the shrine of Heracles to offer thanks to his semi-divine ancestor. Certainly he would have talked events over with the commanders of the men from other states and prepared for the fighting that would surely come next day.

The Persian army was also busy. They had few wounded to treat. The Spartans had seen to that by killing them off during their sallies, but there were some. There were also weapons to repair and clean, meals to be eaten and comrades to be mourned. Xerxes must have been both angry and disappointed. His finest men had been beaten back in humiliating defeat. He will have met with his commanders Mardonius, Hydarnes, Harmamithras and Tithaeus to discuss what to do next. No doubt Tigranes was there to explain what had gone wrong for the Medes and offer his opinion on what could be done next. Demaratus, exiled King of Sparta, seems to have kept out of the way. Perhaps he judged that Xerxes would not make a Spartan welcome after the events of that bloody day.

But one thing that both Leonidas and Xerxes would have done was to cast an anxious eye across the darkening waters of the Malian Gulf to the north. What, they wondered, were the rival fleets doing in the disputed Trikeri Straits?

These Greek hoplites hold their spears overhead. This vase painting dates to 50 years before Thermopylae. Note the flautist playing suitably martial music.

CHAPTER 14
In the Trikeri Straits

Dawn at Artemisium. A Victorian view of the Greek fleet as it prepares for battle against the Persians. In reality the masts were left ashore so that the ships were as light as possible to ensure the oarsmen could achieve maximum speed in combat.

While men were killing and dying at Thermopylae, time passed peacefully in the Trikeri Straits. As the sun climbed up over the eastern hills anxious eyes on both sides of the water scanned the hills to the south. There was no sign of any signal fire sending its column of smoke up into the cloudless August sky. The Persian fleet sent to sail around Euboea was not yet advancing up the Euripus.

On the northern shore of the Trikeri Straits, carpenters and shipwrights were busy on the Persian ships repairing damage caused by the storm that had raged just a few days earlier. On the Greek side, there was less to do. The ships were in perfect condition, the men ready to fight. It was just a matter of waiting.

All the ancient accounts of what was to follow make a point of mentioning the temple of Artemis that gave its name to this beach. No doubt some of the Greeks made their way there to offer their respects to this vengeful, virgin goddess. The temple stood in the wooded hills just behind the beach. A particularly dense patch of woodland surrounded the clearing where the temple stood. Inside the clearing was arranged a circle of upright marble slabs. It is made clear that these were not columns, but standing stones and that they were very ancient indeed. Plutarch records that "if you rub this stone with your hand it gives off the colour and odour of saffron" – saffron being a plant sacred to this goddess. Perhaps there was a type of lichen growing on the stones in the shaded, damp forest clearing.

The temple was obviously quite unlike anything else in contemporary Greece. It may have dated back to the Mycenaean period of prehistory about 1400BC. Certainly Artemis was one of the oldest deities worshipped by the Greeks, and also one of the most quirky. She is goddess of the moon, hunting and wild places. Most of the legends about Artemis revolve around hunting and her murderous rage if a mortal beheld her naked. Her powers and interests went much further than this, however, for she looked after women in childbirth, caused plagues in sheep and loved music and dance. She was notoriously fussy about the way in which ceremonies were carried out, sending revenge on any who made a mistake and death to any who forgot to pay her suitable homage.

Her complex character was made brutally clear at Limnaion, near Sparta. At some date before written history the people of Limnaion found a statue of the goddess standing upright in a thicket. They took the statue to the city square, but were at once struck down by madness. An old holy man advised the citizens to tie a youth to the statue and flog him. This was done and the madness passed. At the time of Thermopylae, the battered old wooden statue still stood in Limnaion and each year a youth was flogged in front of the goddess.

It was to this bloodthirsty goddess that the Greeks would have paid homage on that hot August day. To confuse matters, Artemis had a major temple in the Persian Empire, at the Greek city of Ephesus. This city had sent ships to join the fleet now facing the League fleet across the Trikeri Straits. The men must have wondered which side the violent goddess would favour.

Meanwhile, the Greek commanders were deep in discussion at a council of war called by Eurybiades. The diver Scyllias had brought them news about the Persian ships still at Aphetae, as well as those which had sailed away. He had said that most of the remaining ships had been damaged to a lesser or greater degree in the storm. And the Greeks could see with their own eyes that the enemy fleet was scattered among several beaches and anchorages.

Themistocles was keen to strike a blow against the Persians and believed that a favourable opportunity had come. Some of the others seem to have been more reluctant to face an enemy fleet larger than their own on the advice of a renegade diver. In the end a compromise was reached. The League fleet would put to sea in the later afternoon and head towards Aphetae. At this date naval commanders never fought at night, and travelled in darkness only when they absolutely had to do so. By delaying an attack until late in the day, the Greeks hoped to make the fight a short one. The Persian ships beached further away would not have time to intervene, so with luck numbers would be about equal on both sides. And even if things went badly, darkness would bring an end to the battle and allow the Greeks to escape.

Herodotus tells us that the sally was planned "with the intention of testing Persian seamanship and tactics". The campaign of 490BC that ended at Marathon saw no naval actions of any size between the Greeks and Persians. It is unlikely that any of the captains or commanders in the Greek fleet had seen Phoenician or Egyptian ships in action, never mind had an opportunity to learn much about them.

The League captains were probably buoyed up by the fact that they had at their disposal a new tactic which they were confident would come as a surprise to the enemy. This was the kyklos, a defensive formation that put the ships in a huge circle with prows facing outward. This in itself meant that the Persians would be unable to use their superior numbers, assuming enough ships got into action before nightfall, to carry out a periplus manoeuvre. The weather must have been calm and the sea flat, for the planned kyklos was vulnerable to bad weather.

The Greeks usually put a number of ships with more skilled and experienced crews on station within the kyklos. These ships were then a constant threat to any Persian vessels which attempted to dart between the Greek ships and carry out a diekplus attack. A defensive formation such as the kyklos was no way to go about winning a battle, but it did offer the Greeks the opportunity to test their enemy without any undue risks to themselves. It was a good plan, but nobody knew if it would work in practice.

Some time after the main heat of the day had passed, perhaps at 5pm, the Greeks manhandled their ships into the sea. On the far side of the Trikeri Straits, the Persian lookouts would have spotted the move. Achaemenes must have been puzzled. There was no signal from the hilltops to tell him that his flanking fleet was on its way, and in any case he did not really expect it until the following morning. It was just possible, he might have thought, that the Greeks had got wind of his plan and were preparing to flee while they could still get away.

Whatever the Greeks were up to, Achaemenes would have known his best move was to get his ships out to sea as well. Fast galleys would have been dispatched to Kastri, Katiyiorgis and the bays and beaches to order all ships fit to fight to put to sea and gather off Aphetae. If the Greeks were fleeing, the Persian fleet would have to move fast if they were to give chase. It was while Achaemenes was getting his ships from Aphetae into formation that he saw with utter amazement that the enemy fleet was forming up to attack.

The straits here are a little over 10km wide. Each ship in the League fleet was about 16 metres wide, from oar tip to oar tip. It was usual for ships in line abreast to keep about 50 metres or so from their neighbours to allow room for manouevre. This means that the 291 ships of the Greek fleet would have filled the Trikeri Straits from side to side in one complete line, with a second line almost complete behind it. In the event, it seems likely that the Greeks formed up in two lines of equal length. This left gaps between the end ships of each line and the shore.

We don't know exactly how many Persian ships got to sea in time to form up on the flagship of Achaemenes, but Herodotus and Plutarch both tell us that the League was outnumbered. The Greeks had got to sea first, so they were probably better formed than the Persians. Perhaps we should picture around 350 or so ships under Achaemenes. Most would have been formed up in a line abreast, but others were bunched together untidily and others were coming up in column to join the battle after it began.

Herodotus tells us that as the fleets approached each other the Persians "developed a move to surround the enemy". This sounds like a standard periplus. The ships on the flanks would be moving forward faster than those in the centre to get around the flanks of the Greek fleet. They were, no doubt, pushing fast into the gaps between the Greek lines and the shores of the straits. They would have hoped to get into this gap, then turn inward to ram the outermost ships of the Greek lines. The Greek formation could then have been expected to crumble from the edges into the centre. The Phoenician galleys would have the opportunity to move in to ram and sink as opportunity arose. The Egyptian ships, meanwhile, would trap and board the enemy to capture their ships intact.

But the Greeks had left the gaps deliberately and now put their plan into operation. While the ships in the centre of the lines continued to move slowly forward, those on the flanks rowed backward. As the flank ships moved back, they steered in towards the centre of the formation and away from the coasts. The Persians pushed forward thinking that the enemy ships were fleeing. In fact the Greeks were pulling their flanks back to form the kyklos. As the circle closed, the ships of the Persian fleet were left floating haplessly and in a rather disorganised state around the League fleet. It was soon obvious that the kyklos had come as a complete surprise to the Persians. Neither Achaemenes nor any of his commanders had any idea how to counter the Greek tactic.

Once this was clear, the Greeks were confident enough to begin the battle proper. Whenever an enemy ship got too close, a Greek ship would dart out to make a ramming attempt. If other Persians came up to support their comrade, the Greek ship would simply back water to return to the protective embrace of the kyklos. The first such attack to be successful was that carried out by the ship commanded by Lycomedes of Athens. He managed to cripple and capture an enemy ship, and was decorated for valour after the battle.

It is clear that some captains in the Persian fleet made attempts to break the deadlock. They may have sought to dart in between the outer Greek ships, perhaps hoping to smash oars and drive a ship off its station. The Egyptians in their heavy ships may have tried ramming a Greek ship head on, hoping the impact of ram on ram might damage the lighter enemy.

One man who we know tried to break the Greek formation, though we don't know how, was Philaon, who commanded 150 Cypriot ships in the Persian fleet. Philaon was the brother of King Gorgos of Cyprus. Ironically, Philaon was descended from Teucer, a citizen of Salamis near Athens. The Cypriot royal family were proud of this connection to the extent of naming their chief city Salamis Altera – meaning "the Other Salamis". Perhaps the Persian aristocrats who ran the empire doubted the loyalty of men such of Philaon, which may have prompted his rash action.

Whatever his motives, Philaon failed to break the Greek kyklos. His ship was disabled and he was captured. He was not alone. In all 30 ships were captured by the League fleet before night closed in and brought an end to the fighting. In the gathering darkness one of the ships from the Greek island of Lemnos, which was serving in the Persian fleet, slipped away from its comrades and made for Artemisium where the crew defected to the League. The captain, Antidorus, was later given an estate by the grateful Athenians. This defection is rather surprising given that Lemnos had an old and violent feud with Athens. According to legend, the trouble had begun some 400 years earlier when the crew of a Lemnian ship visiting Athens kidnapped some local women. Back at Lemnos, the crewmen married the women but later killed them and all their children. The enmity between the two states would last for some generations after 480BC. Perhaps Antidorus had his own private reasons to desert Xerxes.

When they returned to the beach at Artemisium after dark, the Greeks must have been jubilant. They had succeeded in their raid, captured 30 enemy ships and escaped without serious casualties. No doubt the temple of Artemis was visited again to give thanks. But Themistocles, Eurybiades and the Greek commanders had more to think about. They had been studying the enemy ships for their abilities, skills and tactics. It must have been apparent to them that the Phoenician vessels in particular were faster and more manoeuvrable than their own ships. They will also have noted the large numbers of armed men on the Egyptian ships. The kyklos had proved to be an effective defensive measure, but it could not be relied upon forever. Sooner or later the Persians would develop a successful counter-tactic, or a Greek mistake might lead to disaster.

The Greek commanders seem to have drawn a grim lesson. In open water their ships would be outmanoeuvred by the Phoenicians. In confined waters they would be trapped and boarded by the Egyptians. What was needed was a stretch of water where there was room for the Greek ships to move, but not enough space for the Phoenicians to race about. The sea area off Artemisium was too spacious for the Greeks to fight an aggressive battle there with any hopes of success. But Artemisium was where they were and where they had to fight.

Even as the council of war was continuing, dark clouds were seen banking up over Euboea to the south. Lightning crackled across the skies and thunder rumbled over the hills. Soon heavy raindrops began to fall and a gusty southerly wind got up. By the early hours of the morning a violent thunderstorm was lashing the whole area. The heavy rain falling on the hills, rushed down the steep valleys causing flash floods. At Aphetae a small stream runs down a wooded valley to enter the sea across the beach. The flash flood that tore down here damaged several of the ships hauled up on the shore.

Some 120km to the south, things were much worse for the invaders. The 200 ships sent by Achaemenes to round Euboea and race up the Euripus were just off the southern tip of the island when the storm struck. The blow was short but exceptionally violent and was driving the ships straight to the sections of the Euboean coast known as The Hollows. There were two ports here, at Karystos and Marmari, which could offer shelter.

No doubt some of the Persian ships managed to get safely to harbour and others may have been able to ride out the bad weather. Others, however, were driven ashore and wrecked.

As with the earlier storm, it may be that the Greek writers exaggerated the damage done to the Persian fleet. Herodotus claims that every single ship rounding Euboea was destroyed, which seems unlikely and is probably another attempt by him to explain the reduction in the size of the Persian fleet between the start of the campaign and the battle at Salamis.

However many ships were wrecked and whatever the damage to the survivors, it is clear that the unnamed commander of the expedition called off any attempt to steer up the Euripus to attack Artemisium from the rear.

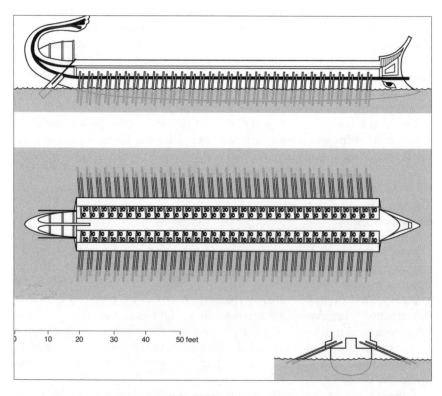

Three views of a Greek bireme warship of about 490BC. These craft were nimble and fast in combat and could be dragged up on to any convenient beach. By the time of the Thermopylae campaign the bireme was being superseded by the trireme, which had three banks of oarsmen and was quicker in action.

The periplus was one of the first naval tactics to be developed in the ancient Mediterranean. It was designed to aid a larger fleet to overwhelm a smaller one.

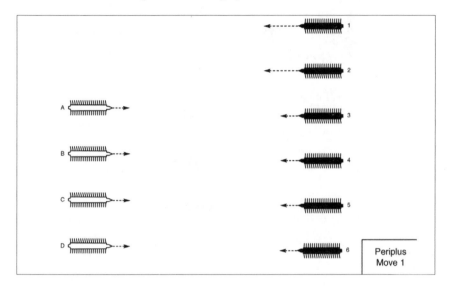

1) Fleet A - D and Fleet 1 - 6 have both adopted the usual line abreast formation. Fleet 1 - 6 has more ships and is about to perform the periplus. As it moves forward, ships 1 and 2 increase speed to pull ahead of the main line.

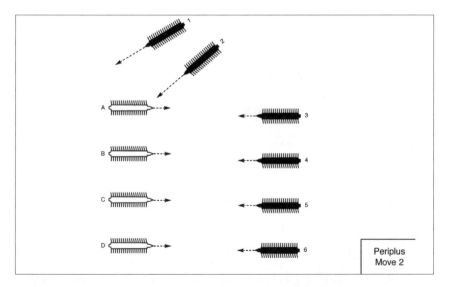

2) As the fleets approach each other, Ship 2 turns inward to take up a position from which it can ram Ship A. Ship 1 moves to row around the rear of Ship A

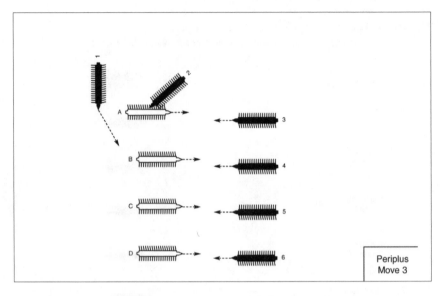

3) *The fleets meet. Ship 2 rams Ship A, which is holed and loses way. Ship 1 continues around the rear of Ship A to take up a position to ram Ship B.*

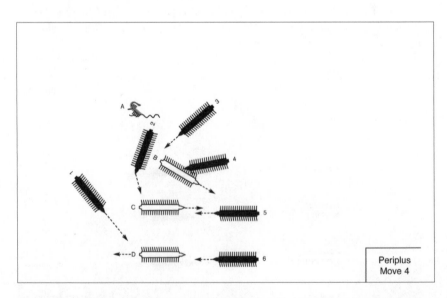

4) *Ship B turns to starboard to present its less vulnerable stern to the fast-approaching Ship 1, but in doing so exposes its flank to Ship 4, which increases to ramming speed and attacks. Ship 1 then turns to starboard to similarly threaten Ship D. Having sunk Ship A, Ship 2 is now getting up speed to attack Ship C. Ship 3 follows Ship 2. The left wing of Fleet A - D has been destroyed at no cost to Fleet 1 - 6.*

The Diekplus was devised to give a smaller fleet the advantage over a larger one. It called for a high degree of co-operation between the ships and for great skill in manoeuvrability, especially in the lead ships.

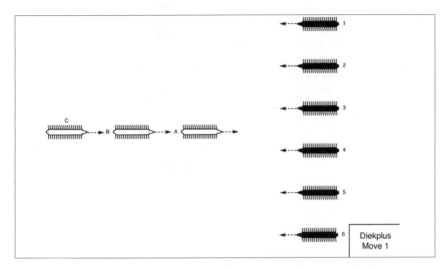

1) *Fleet 1 - 6 has adopted the usual line abreast formation. Fleet A - D is in line ahead, with Ship D out of sight behind Ship C. The admiral of the smaller fleet, in Ship A alters direction frequently as he approaches the enemy so that it is unclear precisely where he will strike the enemy line.*

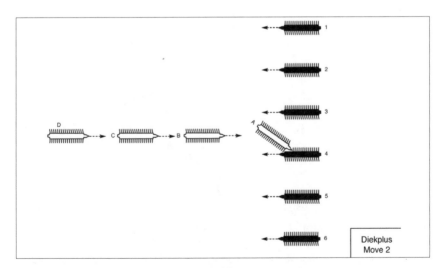

2) *As the fleets meet, Ship A turns aside at the last moment. The turn is not sharp enough nor performed at a high enough speed for ramming. Instead the intention is to slice off the oars of Ship 4.*

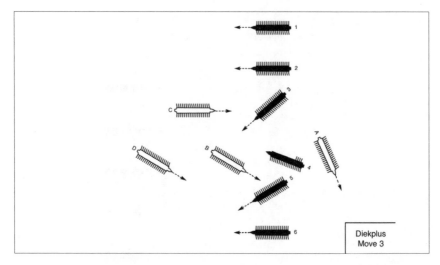

Diekplus
Move 3

3) *Having crippled Ship 4, Ship A continues through the enemy line, increasing speed as it turns to starboard. Ship 5 turns to port to avoid collision with Ship 4, but in doing so exposes its flank to Ship B, which increases to ramming speed. Ship 3 seeks to ram Ship B, but exposes its flank in turn to Ship C, which now rapidly increases speed to get into position. Ship D, seeing Ship A turn to starboard follows suit.*

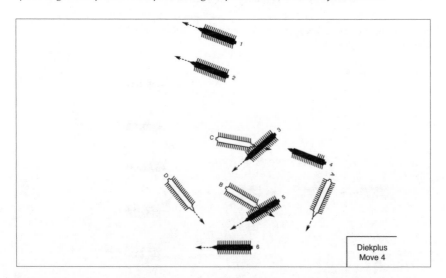

Diekplus
Move 4

4) *Ship 4 continues to drift while its crew desperately try to move oars from the port to the starboard side so that it can get underway. Ship C rams Ship 3. Ship B rams Ship 5. Ship A and Ship D converge on Ship 6 from different directions so that one of them will approach from the side and ram successfully. Ship 4 will be finished off later. Ships 1 and 2 flee. Two-thirds of the larger fleet has been destroyed without loss, but only because the smaller fleet was able to move more swiftly and turn more quickly than their opponents.*

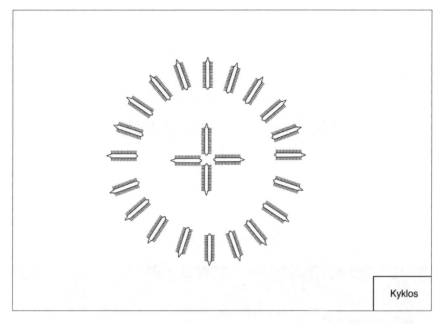

Kyklos

The Kyklos was designed as a defensive posture to be adopted by a numerically smaller fleet against a larger. By forming in a ring with their prows pointing outward the ships each protected the vulnerable flank of their neighbours. If the enemy made a mistake, a ship could dart forward to ram before rowing backwards to reassume position. A smaller number of ships formed inside the circle, again facing outward to be in a position to fill gaps or deal with any enemy that did break through.

CHAPTER 15

The Second Day of Battle

One of the relief panels on the modern monument at Thermopylae showing the Spartans in battle. The older, unarmed man is the seer Megistias.

By dawn on 17 August, if not earlier, King Leonidas had with him at Thermopylae one of the most famous men in Greece: Megistias of the family Melampus. Megistias is not very well known today, certainly not so celebrated as scientist Archimedes, the philosopher Plato or the playwright Aeschylus. This is because the skills at which Megistias excelled are not highly valued in the 21st century. But in his day, Megistias was counted one of the greatest men of Greece. He was a seer.

Unlike the Oracle at Delphi, or that at Didyma, seers did not claim to be able to pass on messages from the gods. Instead they predicted the future, using a variety of techniques and devices to do so. Some watched the flight of the birds to predict weather, others watched the stars; Megistias inspected the remnants of sacrifices after the sacred rites were completed.

This great seer derived his powers from his ancestor Melampus, who lived about 900BC. Melampus had rescued a nest of baby snakes after their parents had been killed by his servants. He fed them milk and, in return, the snakes licked his ears while he slept. This gave Melampus the gift of understanding the language of the birds. Later devotion to Apollo gave Melampus the ability to predict the future, which he passed on to his descendants.

Megistias was at Thermopylae not out of any burning desire to serve Greece, but because his son was there serving in the ranks of the hoplites from Pylos, a small state in the Peloponnese. As a religious man, King Leonidas of Sparta was not one to ignore any advantage the presence of the seer may offer, so he asked Megistias to inspect the remains of the dawn sacrifice of a goat to the goddess Artemis. The great seer did so and told Leonidas that the signs were favourable. This was a good day to fight. This was just as well, for it was not long before Xerxes was seen to take his place on his gilded throne on the slopes of Mount Kallidromos.

Then a cry went up from the Greek camp. Advancing steadily up the Euripus Channel was a sizeable fleet of warships. The oars dipped and splashed, causing the early morning sun to glitter off the water. At first nobody was certain what ships these were. Leonidas must have dreaded that they were the squadron sent by Achaemenes to round Euboea.

Xerxes too will have seen the ships from his vantage point. This was about the time that the Persian ships were expected to arrive. He must have been deeply relieved. With the League fleet crushed at Artemisium the Persian supply ships could at last get into the Gulf of Pagasae to solve the army's problems.

It would not have taken more than 30 minutes for the ships to get close enough for them to be recognised. They were Athenian warships, 53 in number. As they swept up the Channel towards Artemisium, one of them peeled off to carry a message to Leonidas. The ships had been detached from that portion of the Athenian fleet guarding the approaches to Athens itself. Their initial mission was to act as a forward defence force, but having learned of the destruction of the Persian ships off southern Euboea, their commander decided that they were no longer needed where they were and would be more use at Artemisium.

The news must have been a boost to the morale of the Greeks at Thermopylae. Perhaps they cheered and broke into song. For Xerxes, however, there was no way of knowing what this new arrival meant. He saw the fleet of Greek ships heading north when he had been looking for a force of his own. Xerxes could not know what had happened but he must have guessed it was bad news of some kind.

It is unfortunate that neither Herodotus nor Plutarch give much detail about the fighting on the second day of the battle. The account written by Ephorus in about 350BC was much more detailed, but no copy of it survives. However, many later writers referred to the great History of Ephorus, which chronicled the wars between Greeks and barbarians from 1100 to 350BC. It is possible to piece together something of the events of that day.

After the Greek ships had swept past Thermopylae, Xerxes gave the order to attack. This time he did not risk his best troops, but sent forward second rank units. These were not the tribal levies that seem to have been used for manual labour on the campaign; they would have been mere cannon fodder to be killed without inflicting much damage.

The Kashites fought at Thermopylae, so too did the Hyrkanians, Indians and Bactrians. Of these the Indians and Bactrians were only lightly armed and would have been little use when assaulting a wall. But they may have been useful nonetheless. The Kashites and Hyrkanians were not dissimilar in equipment and training from the Medes who had launched the assault on the Phocian Wall. They carried two-metre long spears with wicker shields for close fighting and bows and arrows for missile combat. However, they are thought to have been less armoured, perhaps they were unable to afford coats of scale armour to wear beneath their tunics.

It must be assumed that these men went forward with much the same tactical plan as did the Medes and Immortals on the previous day. Xerxes had no choice other than to try to grind down the resistance of the Greeks by inflicting casualties and causing exhaustion to set in. He must have known that the Greeks were taking far fewer casualties than his own army, but the Persian host outnumbered the Greeks by about 28 to 1. Xerxes could afford to lose men at a high rate.

The hapless men who were expected to be lost would not have faced the prospect quite so calmly as did their monarch. Autocratic monarch he may have been, but Xerxes would have been aware of the realities of the situation. He needed to persuade the men allotted the task of assaulting the wall to do so with the utmost vigour. Otherwise they might make a half-hearted try then retreat before the vicious spears of the Spartans as they surged out of the gate to massacre them.

This could have been where the lightly armed Indians and Bactrians came in. Neither had shields nor armour, but both had bows and arrows. It is possible that they were sent forward to accompany the ladder assault forces to provide additional archery cover. If so, they would have found the land close to the wall rather cramped. This may not have mattered too much if their primary purpose was to improve morale among the unfortunate Kashites and Hyrkanians.

Before sending his men forward, Xerxes had a proclamation read to them. This reminded his men that the Great King was watching them personally and that he had sitting at his feet his secretaries. Those men who fought bravely, the proclamation declared, would be given rich rewards. Those who did not would be executed.

As an added precaution to ensure his men fought with the required enthusiasm, Xerxes backed up the attacking forces with a solid line of reliable men. These may have been the Medes who had fought the previous day. Whoever they were, they completely blocked the path of retreat with sharp spears and grim determination. They must have had orders to kill any of the Great King's soldiers who dared to flee from the battle.

Thus encouraged, the Kashites and Hyrkanians advanced to the attack. Predictably they did even less well against the armoured hoplites manning the Phocian Wall than did their comrades the previous day.

It was probably against these less experienced and less well trained troops that Leonidas felt able to use the battlefield ruse of the Spartans: the feigned retreat. This is a difficult manoeuvre to manage successfully, but with his highly trained professionals facing relatively inexperienced conscripts, it could be used with little risk.

Given that the Spartans were launching sallies from the broken gate against bodies of enemy troops as they withdrew, the opportunities for a feigned retreat seem limited. Certainly there was little point in springing the trap on men already defeated. It is far more likely that the ploy was used in slightly different circumstances.

If the Spartan hoplites had driven off an attack with the usual slaughter and bloodshed, they might then have formed up in a phalanx some distance in front of the wall. There they would have waited to receive the next attack of Kashites or Hyrkanians. As soon as the battle was joined we should imagine the rear-most Spartans slipping away, perhaps back to the foot of the Phocian Wall.

On a prearranged signal, the remaining Spartiates would have turned and run, apparently fleeing before the soldiers of the Great King. Inexperienced men can rarely resist the sight of an enemy in flight, so the Persians would have surged forward. As they did so they would have lost formation and cohesion. By the time they realised that they had been tricked it would be too late. At the foot of the Phocian Wall they would be met by the levelled spears of the Spartan hoplites, while being deluged with javelins and sling shot from above. The carnage would have been awful.

Herodotus tells us that the Spartans used this ploy and implies it was done on the first day of the battle. However, it seems unlikely that the Immortals would have fallen for such a trick. The Kashites and Hyrkanians seem far more likely victims.

As on the previous day, Leonidas used the intervals in the assault on the wall to change the guard. He removed the men of one state and replaced them with those of another to ensure that the defenders were always fresh and fit for duty. But on this second day, things did not go quite as smoothly as on the first. The task of killing the enemy was so much easier that several hoplites refused to give way to their relief until forced to do so. Ephorus puts this down to love of country, but it may just as easily have been the heat of battle and the scent of easy victory that caused this action.

It is clear that Xerxes was becoming desperate. Towards the end of the day he would have received a messenger from Aphetae telling him about the naval action of the previous day. He knew that more time must pass before his supply ships could come in. Meanwhile, the hoplites in the pass of Thermopylae were holding out just as resolutely as before. His only option was to continue to batter at the Phocian Wall with his men and hope that, sooner or later, the Greeks would take so many casualties that they would give way.

Morale among the Persian troops was, however, at rock bottom. They were running low on food, on arrows and other military equipment. A fleet of Greek warships had rowed by with impunity when they had been expecting the invincible armada of the King of Kings to come to their aid. They were stuck on a sun-baked plain in front of a miserable little town with nothing to do except get killed for the glory of their monarch.

Xerxes was not much better. Herodotus tells us: "How to deal with the situation, Xerxes had no idea". Ephorus states that the Great King "was in a state of dismay". He had to go on, for the only alternative was to accept defeat and retreat. Yet he could see nothing in front of him except bloody defeat.

Meanwhile, at Aphetae, the survivors of the force sent to round Euboea were arriving in their battered ships. Now Achaemenes knew that his plan had failed and he would be forced to bludgeon his way through the Trikeri Straits. He would be aware by now that the land forces of the Great King had failed dismally to get through Thermopylae on the previous day. How the fighting at the pass was going this day, Achaemenes had no way of knowing. But he did know that his sovereign lord and brother was an angry man.

Achaemenes knew the army needed the supplies loaded on the merchant ships that waited at Therme for the order to sail. He knew that the entire invasion could falter if the Greeks were not defeated at either Thermopylae or in the Trikeri Straits. And he knew that the wrath of Xerxes could be frightful. The Great King was not going to shoulder the blame for failure at Thermopylae when he could blame his brother for failure at sea. Achaemenes will have summoned his commanders and begun to plan a way to defeat the Greeks.

First, however, there was to be a fresh blow to Persian prestige. For some reason, that is not recorded, some of the 100 Cilician warships put out into the straits. The Cilicians of southern Anatolia were reckoned good war sailors, but not the best. A group of fast Greek warships that had been kept ready for instant action were sent out in pursuit. The conflict seems to have been short and sharp. The Cilicians were overwhelmed and several ships captured. The Greeks got back to base without loss. The whole event had been played out in sight of both fleets. The engagement must have cheered the Greeks every bit as much as it depressed the Persians. And so twilight closed in on the Trikeri Straits. Not much had changed since the previous day, though the Greeks were now stronger and the Persians weaker. And Achaemenes was preparing his orders for a major attack to take place the next day.

Twilight also closed in on Thermopylae. But here everything had changed. The battle for the pass was taking a dramatic new turn.

During the later afternoon, apparently after the Great King had ordered his troops back over the muddy hot springs and into camp, a local man came to the Persian camp. This, in itself, was not unusual. Over the previous days many men had come to the Persians for all sorts of reasons. Some came to sell food, others to complain food had been stolen. Any army in foreign territory gives rise to all sorts of disputes and problems. This man, however, was different. His name was Ephialtes, son of Eurydemus, from the city of Malis close to Trachis. Although we do not know his profession it is clear that he was intimately familiar with the hills around Trachis. Perhaps he was a shepherd or a woodcutter.

In any case, arrive he did and the news he brought ensured that he was quickly ushered into the presence of Xerxes himself. Ephialtes told Xerxes that there was a footpath over Mount Kallidromos that led to the rear of the pass at Thermopylae. More importantly, he knew the route and was prepared to show the soldiers of the Great King the way. Herodotus tells us with some understatement that "Xerxes found Ephialtes's offer most satisfactory." The Greek had come in hopes of a rich reward and it must be assumed that Xerxes was only too happy to pay any price for this piece of information.

However, there were problems with the offer of Ephialtes to guide Persian troops over a secret path to the rear of Thermopylae. It could, Xerxes must have thought, have been a clever trap. Ephialtes himself confirmed that the path was no better than a goat track in places. And narrow mountain gorges are ideal locations in which to spring an ambush on an unsuspecting enemy.

Even if Ephialtes was as honest as he appeared and entirely trustworthy, a peasant such as he could have no idea about military campaigning. What to him was a useful path around Thermopylae might turn out to a long and arduous journey for men carrying heavy weapons, or it might come down from the mountain a day or more march from the rear of the pass. Finally, the Greek army in Thermopylae was unlikely to have left the path unguarded. Xerxes would have known that the Phocians in whose land the mountain lay were enthusiastic supporters of the League. They would surely have told Leonidas about the path.

Nevertheless, the offer was too good to turn down. It would have been no good sending anything but the best on this mission over a secret path. If there were an ambush or a defending force, it would take courage and skill to get through. The units which had fought in the pass that day had needed both threats and promises to make them fight. They could not be trusted with a dangerous and important mission.

Xerxes sent for Hydarnes, commander of the elite Immortals unit. The two men discussed the plan – probably with input from Ephialtes when required. It was decided to delay the departure of the Immortals until dusk – "about the time when the lamps are lit" in the evocative phrase of Herodotus. This timing had two advantages. First, any Greek scouts were less likely to see the men go. Second, if Ephialtes could be trusted, the Immortals would be arriving at the East Gate of Thermopylae sometime around noon. This would give Xerxes plenty of time to arrange something to keep the attention of the Greeks firmly fixed on the land to the front of the Phocian Wall, not to the rear.

So as the sun sank below the mountains of Greece and the gloom of dusk drew in, several thousand men got to their feet and set off up the valley of the Asopus River.

Herodotus, "the Father of History", has also been called by some historians and philosophers "the Father of Lies." Modern archaeological and ethnographic investigations have, however, tended to support his accounts of expansion of the Persian Empire.

CHAPTER 16

The Third Day of Battle – Morning

*Themistocles, of whom Plutarch would observe some
440 years after his death "... it is evident that his
mind was early imbued with the keenest interest in
public affairs and the most passionate ambition for
distinction".*

175

At dawn on 20 August 480BC, in Sparta and cities all across the Peloponnese, the Carneia Festival was coming to an end. Men were gathering in town squares and village streets by the thousand. Each man came with weapons of war: the Spartans with their famous red cloaks. Young men were waved off to war by weeping wives and mothers, or by grim old fathers telling them sternly "come back with your shield or on it". Dust rose into the cold grey air as thousands of feet pounded the roads. Columns of men snaked away over the hills leaving behind cities empty of young men. All were heading north toward battle.

At Aphetae on the northern shores of the Trikeri Straits thousands of men sprang into action as the sun rose out of the dead calm sea to the east. Their admiral, Achaemenes brother to Xerxes, had decreed that this would be the day on which his mighty armada would put to sea in force to smash the League fleet to pieces. Achaemenes had announced that he had a plan to ensure victory. The Trikeri Straits would be won for Persia and supply ships would at long last be able to sail into the Gulf of Pagasae.

Across the waters at Artemisium, on the south side of the Trikeri Straits, the activity at Aphetae will have been noticed by the Spartan admiral Eurybiades and the Athenian commander Themistocles. They too will have ordered their men to prepare for battle. Meals were eaten and ships inspected. Oars were got ready and equipment carefully checked. The League commanders had their own plan. They had learned from the previous fighting and were determined to block the progress of the enemy fleet.

At Thermopylae, King Leonidas of Sparta once again performed his dawn rituals. He took one of the goats that he had brought along for this purpose and prepared to sacrifice it to the goddess Artemis. As usual the commanders of the allied contingents were invited to attend and, as on the previous day, Megistias the seer was asked to inspect the sacrificial victim for signs of the future.

In the chill dawn air, with the sun still hidden behind the hills of Euboea, Leonidas drew his knife and called out to the goddess. Then he dispatched the goat and handed its carcass over to Megistias. The great seer must have blanched at what he saw. He could foresee only death. Death for Leonidas. Death for all the Spartans. And it was a death that was going to be not long delayed.

Leonidas must have been alarmed, but also puzzled. As a religious king of a religious people, he would have believed what Megistias told him. As a professional soldier he must have known that death was a constant risk, but as he looked at the intact Phocian Wall, the confident League army and the piles of Persian dead he must have wondered how death could come to him as quickly as the seer foretold. And then his eyes may have strayed up to the heights of Mount Kallidromos where the 1,000 Phocian hoplites were guarding the secret path over the mountain.

Up on Mount Kallidromos it had been a quiet night for the Phocians, as had all the others since they had climbed up from Alpeni over a week earlier. They had spent tedious days on the forested heights of Kallidromos. Messengers would have passed back and forth. Men would have carried supplies up from Alpeni, then returned again. The men would have been bored, listless and relaxed.

Certainly the Phocians were not professionals, like the Spartans. These were farmers, potters and merchants who had put aside the tools of their trade to don the arms and armour of war. They were probably only too happy to leave the fighting in the pass to the scarlet-cloaked hard men from the south. Up here all was quiet. On the night of 19-20 August they slept soundly and set no lookouts to keep an eye on the path as it wound up through the dense forests of oaks that blanketed the upper heights of Kallidromos in those days.

As dawn broke, the Phocians began to wake. Some stirred cooking fires into life, others may have left camp to look for firewood or to fill their flasks with water. And then they heard something quite remarkable. Although it was a still dawn, with not a breath of breeze drifting over Kallidromos, the leaves of the oak forests began to rustle as if a wind were blowing through them.

Slowly the truth dawned on the horrified Phocians. It was not the wind stirring the branches that made this noise. It was the tramp of thousands of feet through the leaf litter on the forest floor. The Persians were coming. A messenger, perhaps more, was hurriedly sent off to run down the track to pass the information on to Leonidas while the Phocians raced to grab their weapons.

At this moment the head of the Persian column emerged from the forest. Looking across the mountain meadow in front of him, Hydarnes, commander of the elite Immortal unit, was shocked to see a force of hoplites preparing to meet him. He turned in anger on Ephialtes. Perhaps it had been a trap after all. His men had already fought the Spartans once before in a narrow pass, and they would have had no wish to do so again. He demanded that the man from Malis who was guiding them should tell him if these were Spartans.

Ephialtes will have known that the Spartans marched to war in scarlet cloaks and tunics. One glance at the motley collection of colours in front of him will have told him that these were not Spartans. He may even have recognised them as Phocians. Reassured, Hydarnes ordered his men forward to an immediate attack.

There has been endless speculation as to where, precisely, on the track over the mountain this confrontation took place. In fact there are three or four places which fit the sketchy descriptions and clues that have survived, but the layout of the battlefield and progress of the fighting are clear enough.

Leonidas had posted 1,000 hoplites accustomed to fighting in standard phalanx formation to guard the pass. Citizen armies, such as that of Phocians, tended to form up in a deeper phalanx than did the better trained armies. Assuming the Phocians formed up twelve men deep, the phalanx would have covered a frontage of 75 metres or so. It must be assumed, therefore, that the flat or slightly sloping ground here was about that width. It may well have been narrower.

Leonidas probably neither expected nor ordered the Phocians to halt a Persian attack permanently. He would have wanted them to hold the mountain track only long enough for a messenger to get down to Thermopylae and for a reinforcement force to get back up the hill. It would be reasonable, therefore, to put the Phocians near the eastern end of the mountain track. Such a site can be found near the modern hamlet of Palaiodrakospilia, but the place will probably never be located with certainty.

For the first time in the war the two styles of fighting would be tested in open combat without a defensive wall to cloud the issue. Professionals that they were, the Immortals were ready first. They marched forward across the grassland in their open, loose formation while the Greeks hurried to form up in a dense phalanx. At a distance of perhaps 100 metres from the Phocians, the Immortals came to a halt. They laid their wicker shields and short spears on the ground, then pulled out their bows and arrows.

When the Immortals let loose, Herodotus records, "the arrows flew thick and fast". This was not something the Phocians would have ever encountered before. To make matters worse for the defenders, it seems that many of them had not yet had the chance to don their armour. The broad arrow heads that had proved to be so useless against the Phocian Wall and heavy shields of the men who defended it, were horribly effective plunging into the exposed flesh of the Phocians. Nasty, jagged wounds were inflicted, many of them fatal.

Something close to panic seems to have gripped the Phocians. Huddling together for protection, they edged back up the mountainside. Perhaps they were seeking tree cover that would protect them from the plunging arrows. Whatever the reason, they abandoned the path they were supposed to be guarding. One man at least knew his duty. He took off as fast as his legs would carry him to warn Leonidas of what was happening.

Hydarnes probably posted a squad of archers and another of spearmen to face up to the Phocians while his main column marched past. Then the flank guard will have edged away to form a rearguard and follow their comrades down the hill. It seemed that Xerxes had been right to put his trust in men armed with missile weapons. Greek hoplites – heavily armed, close combat troops that they were – must have seemed outclassed.

Soon after Megistias delivered his doom-laden prediction, a man named Tyrrhastiadas from the city of Cyme came trotting up to the Phocian Wall from the direction of the Persian army. The city of Cyme lay in Asia Minor, near the modern city of Izmir. It was a Greek city and was generally reckoned to be one of the most beautiful in the world with its fine temples and monuments. This Tyrrhastiadas brought news that Hydarnes had set off the evening before from the Persian camp, apparently to follow a traitor who was leading them over the mountain.

Leonidas must have hoped that the Phocians would hold the mountain track as ordered, and would have begun marshalling a force to go up the track to reinforce them. It was not long before he was put right in his thinking. The messenger who had fled as the Phocians pulled back arrived to give the bad news.

Leonidas now had no choice but to call a council of war. The situation had changed drastically and he had to consult the commanders of the other contingents about what to do next.

In assessing what did happen next at Thermopylae, it is important once again to remember the geography. The Greek camp was on a small plain between the Middle and East Gates of the pass. There were a couple of springs that fed a tiny stream. The Middle Gate was defended by the Phocian Wall and had shown itself to be virtually impregnable to assault. The East Gate was very narrow, but had no wall and was flanked by a slope along which lightly armed men could walk without too much difficulty.

It is also important to realise that the sacrifice to Artemis that had so alarmed the seer Megistias was made by the King of Sparta for the sake of his own men only. Whatever message the sacrifice revealed referred to the Spartans, not to their allies. Leonidas and his men were marked for death, but not the others.

With this information the commanders of the League forces gathered to discuss their options. Leonidas spoke out for staying where they were. We do not know exactly what he intended to do, but it is not difficult to put together a likely scenario. Leonidas knew that the Middle Gate could be held. The problem was the East Gate. He must have known that it would be more vulnerable to attack, but probably hoped to be able to defend it reasonably well. He had a few hours in hand before the Persians arrived. There will have been carts to hand and limitless amounts of scrub to cut down and push together into a rough stockade.

Even allowing for casualties and the Phocian detachment, Leonidas must have had 5,000 men with him in the pass. A force of 1,000 could be put to man the wall at the Middle Pass, which would allow for changes of guard, though they would not be as frequent as before. That would leave 4,000 men to guard the East Gate. Leonidas must have reasoned that this was good enough.

There was a good water source in the camp and it is reasonable to assume that there were stocks of food as well. Leonidas would have known that his men did not need to hold out forever. This day, 20 August, was the end of the Carneian Festival. The main army of the League would be leaving their homes and marching north to join him and his men at Thermopylae. Sparta was more than a week's march away, but Corinth was closer and so were other, smaller cities.

In any case, Leonidas had sent out messages some days earlier telling the League cities that he needed reinforcements. Even now these men might be marching towards Thermopylae. Who knew when they might arrive? Leonidas clearly thought that there was a chance of holding the pass for several days, even if the Persians did send an infantry force over the mountain path. And a few days might be enough.

Others did not see it that way. By barricading the East Gate they would be accepting that they were surrounded by an infinitely larger army. There would be nowhere to retreat to and no escape if things went wrong. Understandably, it was an unappealing prospect – especially for those who had always wanted to defend the Isthmus of Corinth further south. And if the Spartans were all to die, many would have concluded that those who stayed with them would share that fate.

The debate was heated and prolonged and could reach no general agreement. In the end the army broke up, with each contingent doing what they thought was best. Apart from the Spartans, all those from the Peloponnese marched off, passing through the East Gate and heading along the coast towards Boeotia. The Locrians also went, presumably to get their families and goods into the mountains to be safe from the vengeance of the Persians that would soon be sweeping over their land.

Those who went always maintained that they had been ordered to leave by Leonidas to save their lives and allow them to fight another day. This might be true, but it seems unlikely. It was always the case that, in the last resort, the armed forces of a state obeyed their own officers and followed the instructions of their own government. Leonidas had been ordered to hold Thermopylae for as long as possible, the others may have received more circumspect orders.

We shall never know the truth, but one fact indicates what may have happened. When the allies were gathering their equipment and preparing to leave, Leonidas ordered Megistias to leave, perhaps thinking that the seer would be more use to the League alive and giving predictions than lying dead at Thermopylae. Megistias refused to leave but asked that his son should go instead. This might indicate that he sought Leonidas' permission for the young man to go with honour, implying the rest left without the permission of the commander.

Only the 700 Thespians and 400 Thebans stayed with Leonidas. This was a brave act indeed. With the others gone there was much less chance of holding the East Gate. For the first time the task of holding Thermopylae could be seen as a suicide mission. And yet these men stayed voluntarily.

Perhaps they hoped reinforcements would turn up. Perhaps they thought the fleet would take them off. Or perhaps they accepted that death was their lot. We have no way of knowing.

With his 300 Spartiates, the other hoplites from Sparta and the Helot skirmishers, Leonidas probably had approaching 2,000 men left with him. There was no sign of movement from the Persian camp, so Leonidas may have guessed that the attack from that direction would be timed to coincide with that of the force coming over the mountain. He set his men to prepare the ground as best they could with their reduced numbers, then told them to eat a meal. The Spartiates may have chosen to comb their hair for the coming fray. "Eat a good breakfast," Leonidas called to his Spartiates. "Tonight we dine in Hades." No doubt he was recalling the message from the Delphic Oracle that either Sparta must burn or a Spartan king must die. Now he knew which it would be.

As the column of League hoplites trailed away along the coast they marched through the village of Alpeni. In the village were two Spartiates, Eurytus and Aristodemus. Both men were suffering from acute inflammation of the eyes and had been sent back to the village by Leonidas to recover. Hearing the unmistakable sound of marching soldiers, the men called their Helot servants and asked what was going on. When they learned that there were no Spartans among the retreating mass, they at once guessed what was afoot.

Eurytus ordered his Helot to fetch his armour, while Aristodemus instead told his servant to gather up their belongings and follow the retreating army. There was a short argument between the two, but neither would change his mind. The Helot of Eurytus later told of how he led the Spartiate warrior to the East Gate just as the Persian Immortals were coming into sight down the mountain path. He saw his master take his place in the line of battle, then fled.

When Aristodemus got back to Sparta, he was in disgrace. Almost blind he may have been, but the honour code of the Spartiates was unforgiving. It had been his duty to support his king in battle and he had failed. None of his fellow citizens spoke to him and he was openly called a "Trembler", a euphemism for coward. Aristodemus seems to have been genuinely surprised by his reception. At any rate, he begged permission to march with the army next time it went to war to redeem his honour.

A third Spartiate, Pantites, had left Thermopylae even before the Persians arrived to carry a message to some Thessalians who were loyal to the League. On his return he found the entire Persian army blocking his path back to Thermopylae so he took one of the remote footpaths over the Parnassos Mountains. Completely unaware of what had happened, he returned to Sparta. When he realised that he had missed a great battle, Pantites hanged himself for shame.

By the time Eurytus came blind into the ranks, King Leonidas had finished composing his final message to the government of Sparta. He turned to a fellow Spartiate and asked him to carry the message, "I came with you to fight, not to carry messages" was the reply. Leonidas asked a second hoplite only to be told, "I shall do my duty better if I stay here, and the news will be better if I stay here". Leonidas finally turned to a Helot, who was probably only too grateful of the chance to escape the closing trap.

Meanwhile, in the Straits of Trikeri, the rival fleets were preparing for battle. It is difficult to be accurate on the strengths of the fleets at this moment. The original Persian fleet had been hit by two storms and had lost ships to the Greeks in the earlier fighting. Perhaps Achaemenes had close on 500 warships under his command. The Greeks had been reinforced the previous day, but some of their craft must have been damaged by battle or storm and been unfit for combat. Eurybiades may have had some 300 ships to put to sea.

Herodotus alone among ancient authors gives any detail on the naval fighting on this day, but he is rather vague and his account lacks detail. Herodotus begins by saying that the Greek fleet "was fighting for the Euripus", meaning the channel between Euboea and the mainland and goes on, "The Greek cry was to stop the enemy from getting through, while the Persians aimed at destroying the defending forces in order to clear the passage." This does not sound very much like the naval fighting of two days earlier. On that occasion the Greeks had launched a raid, then pulled back to form a defensive kyklos formation. However strong a kyklos might be, it most certainly does not "stop the enemy from getting through" nor would an enemy need to "destroy the defending forces in order the clear the passage". Faced by a kyklos, an enemy commander could simply send his ships around the sides.

Although Herodotus does not say as much, it rather reads as if the Greeks were here adopting a very different plan. Faced by a massively overwhelming number of enemy ships, the Greeks will have sought constricted waters where the enemy could neither outflank their fleet nor use the faster Phoenician ships to outmanoeuvre them.

There was just such a stretch of water close to Artemisium, the entrance to the Euripus a few kilometres to the west. The channel here was much narrower than were the Trikeri Straits. We have already seen that the Greek fleet could not block the Trikeri Straits with two complete lines of ships spaced at the usual intervals. But they could block the entrance to the Euripus. Indeed, they could manage not two, but three complete lines of warships.

It could be argued that by abandoning the Trikeri Straits and so the entrance to the Gulf of Pagasae, the Greeks were not fulfilling the entire purpose that they were there. This is not the case. The prime objective of the Greek fleet was to stop the Persian merchant ships from bringing supplies to the army of Xerxes. So long as the Greek fleet was intact and in the vicinity of the mouth of the Gulf of Pagasae, the merchant ships could not get through. Any attempt to do so by Achaemenes, even with heavy warship escort, would have ended with substantial losses to the merchant fleet – and it would not have been at all certain that any would have got through at all.

Assuming that the Greeks did fall back to the narrower waters of the Euripus to meet the attack of the repaired and complete Persian fleet, the course of the action is a little easier to understand from the confused comments made by Herodotus. "Then the Persians adopted a crescent formation and came on" he tells us, "with the intention of surrounding the enemy." This probably means that Achaemenes was pushing forward his flanks along the coasts in an attempt to perform a periplus on the smaller Greek fleet.

A similar attempt two days earlier had failed when the Greeks adopted their kyklos. It may be argued that this shows a remarkable lack of imagination or flexibility on the part of the Persian admiral. In truth, however, there was not much else he could do. Just as the Greek's main object was to keep their fleet intact, Achaemenes' main object was to destroy it. He may have felt that only the coming of night had robbed him of victory two days earlier.

Furthermore, on that previous occasion, the Persian fleet came into action piecemeal and in smaller numbers. It is probable that Achaemenes blamed his lack of success on the fact that the Greeks had had the time and space to adopt their novel kyklos formation. He may have planned to deny them both by pushing powerful forces forward on the flanks at the very start of the action. If these flank forces were able to carry out a diekplus on the opposing Greek ships, they would be able to break through and turn inward before the Greek flanks could drop back and adopt the kyklos. In these circumstances Achaemenes could hope to get the League forces disorganised and surrounded in the first half hour or so of battle. Then it would just be a matter of using overwhelming numbers to destroy the enemy that had escaped him so far.

This did not happen. The Persian flanks failed to break through and the battle degenerated into a slogging match between the rival fleets. Speed and manoeuvrability counted for less than strength and brute force. Ramming was an effective weapon only on rare occasions when the opportunity presented itself. More useful was boarding and bloodshed.

In such a combat the advantages each side had over the other tended to cancel out. Much skill was called for in positioning the ships and manoeuvring them for action. The objective was to board a ship that the attacking crew would be able to overwhelm, perhaps in co-operation with another ship. Equally, captains sought to avoid being boarded by superior numbers. At slow speed and in a confined space filled with other ships, neither was an easy task to achieve.

Once boarding had taken place, fighting was largely down to the marines, though the officers and sailors would be expected to take part as well. Rowers were mostly armed with only a knife and would have been ineffective in combat. Greek marines were equipped as were their land hoplites – so they had heavy armour, long spears and large shields. This made them just as effective at boarding combat as on land.

When a Greek ship boarded a Cilician, the advantage lay clearly with the Greeks. The Cilician marines had light rawhide shields, two throwing javelins and a short sword. They would be no match for the Greek hoplites. The Lycians would have been similarly outclassed in a boarding action, being armed with bows and daggers and having only a goatskin jerkin for protection. The Phoenicians would have fared rather better. Their marines had metal helmets and armour of bonded, layered linen However, their shields were lightweight and their javelins made for throwing rather than thrusting. As their ships were fast and nimble, the Phoenicians were armed for pursuit and chase rather than close combat.

The Greek states within the Persian Empire, of course, supplied ships that were built and crewed in the Greek fashion. This would have put them on a level footing with the League ships and marines in this sort of fighting. But the best on either side were the Egyptian ships. The Egyptian marines wore helmets that Herodotus describes as being made up of several pieces. This may mean that they were of the conical shape preferred by some Asian peoples in which segments of metal were rivetted or forged together at the seams. Their shields, said by Herodotus to be "concave and broad-rimmed" seem to have been very similar to the Greek apis. As offensive weapons the marines carried highly effective thrusting spears and heavy axes. Even the rowers had bonded linen corselets and long knives with which to attack the enemy.

Quite how many ships of which nation Achaemenes had left in his fleet by this time, we have no way of knowing. He was, however, sufficiently confident to push in to the attack without delay. Or, as Herodotus has it, he may have been so concerned about the reaction of Xerxes to failure that he may have been more frightened of not attacking than he was of combat itself. Whatever the case, the Persian fleet moved forward to attack, while the Greeks patiently awaited them. At the last minute the Greeks got underway to give themselves momentum for the clash. With a grinding thump of timber on timber, the combat began. It was about mid-morning.

Back at Thermopylae, the fighting began at about the same time, described by Herodotus as "the time when the market place is filled". On a hot day in August, this would be after farmers had had time to get their goods on to carts and into town, but before the noon sun drove people to seek rest in the shade: Perhaps 10.30 or 11am.

Xerxes had already carried out his religious duties to his god and, we must presume, had taken his seat on his throne to watch what he hoped would be the end of the matter. Herodotus does not name the troops sent forward this morning, but makes it clear that they were understandably reluctant to attack. "The junior officers used their whips wildly, pushing the men forward."

Herodotus is, perhaps, being a little unfair on the soldiers of the Great King at this point. We know of two senior commanders who lost their lives in the fighting on the morning of 20 August, and they were among the most important in the Persian Empire. They were clearly leading from the front and died bravely serving their king.

These two men were the brothers Habrocomes and Hyperanthes, both of them half-brothers to Xerxes. Unlike Achaemenes and other half-brothers of the Great King who were commanding troops, these men were also cousins of Xerxes. Darius had married his own niece, Phratagune, to inherit the wealth of his brother Artanes and the boys were the children of this union. Such incestuous marriages were not usual among the Persians, but neither were they entirely unknown. These two men were, therefore, closely related to the Great King twice over.

Although they would have been considerably younger than Xerxes, himself about 40 at this time, and probably inexperienced in war, they would not have been in command of troops that did not fit their royal status. They may have been put over troops of a reasonably effective type and went to their deaths in a youthful attempt to impress their older and more experienced half-brother and cousin. The Thracians were at Thermopylae, but these men would have been known to Herodotus and so he is unlikely to have dismissed them merely as "barbarians". The Mysians and Ethiopians, in contrast, were probably too primitive and backward to be worthy of officers of such exalted rank.

More likely candidates are the Phrygians. Living in what is now central Turkey, the Phrygians would have been close enough to Sardis for it to have been practicable for them to send the entire available fighting force to join the invasion. Their equipment was typically a pair of light throwing javelins, together with a short thrusting spear for close combat and a dagger for use in desperate circumstances. For protection each had a helmet of tough, boiled leather and a small round shield of solid wood.

In the Persian army at this date, men such as the Phrygians were of the middle rank. Effective enough in combat, they were not elite troops to be reserved to missions requiring discipline and great skill. Phrygia had been under Persian rule for some 30 years, so putting them in the care of a close relative of the Great King may have been a wise move. Xerxes would have known their commanders were absolutely loyal to him and the Phrygians may have been flattered to be so closely linked to the King of Kings.

If it were the Phrygians who were sent to the attack across the hot springs and toward the Middle Gate at mid-morning on 20 August, it would make sound military sense. Xerxes hoped that the Immortals marching over the mountain path would take the enemy facing him entirely by surprise. Trapped in a narrow pass with no way of escape, disordered and surprised, the Greeks would be massacred.

This plan would work only if the Immortals got over the mountain without being seen and if the Greeks at Thermopylae had their attention firmly fixed on the land in front of them. Xerxes had no control over whether or not Leonidas knew of the secret path, nor of whether or not any stray Greeks might be up that way scouting or trying to catch a goat for supper. Like any sensible military commander he concentrated on what he could influence. By making a determined and serious attack on the Middle Gate, Xerxes hoped to fix all eyes among the League Greeks to the west. They would not see the Immortals until those professional troops were in the East Gate and had the Greeks firmly trapped.

Of course, Leonidas was aware of the path over Mount Kallidromos and had got men stationed there. He was, therefore, aware that the Immortals were coming – with the results we have already seen. Xerxes was not to know this and made his decisions accordingly. His attack needed to appear to Leonidas to be just as serious and determined as on the previous day. It had to look as if Xerxes was continuing with his policy of grinding down the Greeks through casualties and tiredness until they gave way.

As a consequence, Xerxes would not have wanted to push forward third rate troops who would have been easily driven off by the Greeks. He had to continue using second rate troops that were good enough to inflict casualties and yet not so important their their loss would damage the effectiveness of the army as a whole. This would explain the presence of royal princes such as Habrocomes and Hyperanthes.

On the League side, we have even less idea of what dispositions were made by Leonidas. We know for certain the position only of the elite Spartiates, led by King Leonidas in person. These men, the vast majority of whom seem to have still been able to take their place in action, were given the most important and hazardous duty available. Leonidas led them forward from the Phocian Wall and out on to the cleared killing ground. There they took up position in the traditional Spartiate phalanx. Herodotus tells us that Leonidas took this decision "knowing that they were going to their deaths". It seems that he reasoned that since Megistias had forecast their deaths, the Spartiates may as well take as many of the enemy as possible with them. And a great deal more killing could be done in the open, fighting in phalanx then standing on top of a wall waiting for reluctant enemy troops to climb up ladders. Leonidas was planning a brutal, heroic and bloody end for himself and his immediate command.

Herodotus tells us nothing about the positioning of the other troops, nor does any other ancient writer. The military history written by Ephorus, which alone may have included this detail, has been lost. However, it is possible to make an attempt to reconstruct the dispositions of the League Greeks, given what happened during the day's fighting.

Assuming Leonidas believed that he and his men would be killed that day, he would have needed to put a force on the Phocian Wall. These men would have had the task of defending the Middle Gate once the Spartiates had been killed on the open ground in front of the wall. It would make sense for the Lacedaemonians to be stationed here. These were the hoplites from Sparta who were not of the elite Spartiates but who were well-drilled as soldiers from birth to death. As such, these men were better trained than the hoplites from Thespia or Thebes and would have been known to and trusted by Leonidas.

Perhaps just as important, whichever of these men might survive would return to Sparta with a first hand account of the coming heroic death of Leonidas and his men. This would have been important to Leonidas, Dieneces, Eurytus and the rest. They wanted their friends and relatives to know that they died with honour and courage.

Meanwhile, the East Gate had to be guarded against the approaching Persian force that had marched over Mount Kallidromos. Leonidas may not have known that these were the Immortals, but he will have guessed that Xerxes would have sent good troops. The East Gate of the Pass of Thermopylae consisted of a very narrow stretch of flat land, no more than about four or five metres, between the sea and the slopes of Kallidromos. The slopes rise quite steeply but are not, at least lower down, impassable. Hoplites could keep their footing, but keeping formation in a tight phalanx would be difficult. As the hill rises, the slope becomes steeper. This land is better suited to lightly armed troops wearing less cumbersome armour and fighting in more open formation. Eventually the slope becomes sheer and impossible for humans to cross.

This would be the place to position the Thespians. Forming a tight phalanx, they could cover a frontage of about 75 metres. This would enable them to cover the flat ground and the sloping terrain where it was reasonable for hoplites to fight and still to have about half their men drawn up as a reserve. The higher, steeper slopes would be best left to those Helots from Sparta who had come as slingers and javelin-throwers rather than as servants.

The Thebans pose special problems. Herodotus tells us that Leonidas kept them at Thermopylae as hostages against the good behaviour of Thebes. On the face of it, this may make sense. The Theban government was known to be less than enthusiastic about the League and its war with Persia, and we now know with hindsight – as did Herodotus – that Thebes had actually promised to surrender to Xerxes. With a Persian force of some kind over the mountain path, Thebes may have been tempted to join the Persians openly and attack Thermopylae from the east. Leonidas would, surely, have wanted to guard against this.

On closer inspection, holding the Thebans as hostages does not make much military sense. Once the other League troops had marched away, Leonidas was going to need every man he had to fight the Persians. Detailing off several dozen valuable men to guard the 400 Thebans would have weakened his situation. Nor would it have been sensible to have such a large body of hostile men within the League camp. In any case, the Thebans had come voluntarily to Thermopylae. This may have been because they were those that favoured the League over Persia and had flouted their government's policy to do so.

In general it makes more sense that the Thebans, like the Thespians, remained at Thermopylae voluntarily. On the other hand, as the battle unwound, the Thebans did end up separated from the Thespians and Spartans during the day's fighting. There was something ambiguous about the Theban contribution that day. Herodotus may not have been entirely right, but he certainly picked up on some undercurrent.

Whatever the precise dispositions made by King Leonidas for the third day of fighting in the Pass of Thermopylae, we know that the battle began in the west where the Spartiates stood in armed phalanx awaiting the Persian onslaught.

When the attack came, it was in vast numbers. It was now about noon.

The West Gate seen from the Persian camp ground. The shallow angle of the lower slope of Mount Kallidromos at this point is clear.

CHAPTER 17

The Third Day of Battle – Afternoon

The small hill behind the Middle Gate to which the Spartans retreated to make their last stand. The hill is about 10 metres high.

By noon the fleets had been fighting in the entrance to the Euripus, if that is where the combat took place, for almost an hour. We know almost nothing about the progress of this naval battle, but by comparison with better documented combats in similar circumstances we can make some informed assumptions.

The combat would have begun, and for some time remained, confined to the ships in the front rank of each fleet. The Greeks clearly managed to block the attempt by the Persian wings to break through and get behind the League fleet. The ships would have edged warily around each other, making sudden darts forward to strike if the opportunity arose, or backward to avoid a blow from the enemy.

Those ships which had archers or javelin throwers would attempt to get close enough to an enemy vessel to shower the decks with missile weapons. The rowers had no protection and were densely packed. Wounds inflicted on them would reduce the ability of the enemy ship to manoeuvre or move at speed. With luck the ship's commander or another officer might be killed or injured.

When a ship was attempting to board an enemy, the marines would gather in the bows where a section of decking formed a platform. Although full ramming speed was rarely possible, there would still be a substantial impact as the ship ran on the enemy. The marines usually crouched down to avoid being thrown from their feet by the impact. Once the two ships were locked together, the marines would swarm to board the enemy. Their first targets would be the enemy marines, officers and sailors who would be on the decks with weapons in their hands. Sometimes the ships would drift or be pushed apart, forcing the invading marines to flee back to their own ship or be killed. At other times the ships would remain together and the fight would become one for possession of both ships. It was usual for the rowers to become the prisoners, along with their ship, if the marines and other fighting men were all killed. Naked and unarmed there was little they could do against a dozen or more fully armed men.

In a close combat of this kind it was inevitable that oars got smashed as ships ground against each other, or passed by close enough to brush oars. This was a dangerous time for oarsmen. An oar being snapped back by impact with a passing enemy ship would deliver a terrible blow to any oarsman who did not get out of the way in time. Broken bones were frequent injuries among oarsmen. And because the ships were built to withstand the blow of a successful ram, all the strength in the vessel lay lengthwise. Blows from the sides or quarters would cause timbers to buckle and seams to burst open. Under the pressure of the bumping and crunching that went on, some ships began to take on water.

Although a battle such as that being fought in the entrance to the Euripus Channel on 20 August 480BC produced few ramming attacks that would sink a ship, there was a great deal of wreckage about. Broken oars and dead bodies would be floating in the waters, while many ships would be limping along with only some of their oars in action, or with smashed timbers and wallowing deeply in the waters.

The most badly damaged ships would edge away from the fighting, their places being taken by ships pushing forward from the second rank. The damaged vessels would be steered toward the nearest available beach where they could be run aground. Wounded men would be hurriedly put ashore while the able crewmen went to work on the ship. Broken oars would be replaced by those spares kept stored along the keel and sprung seams hurriedly recaulked with bags of fibres kept on board for the purpose. A decision then had to be made whether to return to the fray or to flee to safer waters. If the ship was in reasonably serviceable order without any serious leaks and a crew only slightly below numbers, the captain might decide to return to battle. More badly damaged ships might be judged lucky to get home and would make haste to get away as quickly as they could. It was not unknown for two ships which had taken heavy casualties, but which were not badly damaged physically to combine crews to produce one fully manned ship that would go back to battle. The wounded and surplus crew would stay on the beach with the other ship to await events. This beaching and repairing of damaged warships was such an accepted feature of naval warfare, that enemies sometimes put men ashore at suitable beaches to ensure that they could be used only by their own ships.

Battles fought in this grinding manner usually came down to a test of numbers and morale rather than skill or tactics. In violent, bloody combat men are often willing to fight only so long as they believe they have a good chance of winning. If they see their own ranks thinning while those of the enemy remain full, the fighting men may conclude that they are not going to win. Morale falters and it becomes natural for men to attack with less gusto and to retreat more readily.

In the circumstances of the naval battle in the Euripus, the advantage should have been with the Persians. They had more ranks to draw upon, so when their damaged ships pulled back, there were plenty of replacements to come forward. Over the course of some hours' combat, this should have ensured that the Persian fleet kept its fighting front at full strength, while that of the Greeks suffered and fell below strength. At some point Greek morale would collapse and their fleet collapse into flight.

This is not what happened. Over the preceding two days there had been two naval actions fought out in the Trikeri Straits. Both combats had led to Greek success, albeit on a modest scale. Nevertheless this must have had a crucial impact on morale. The Greek League went into battle knowing that they had won the two previous encounters with the Persian fleet and confident that they could do so a third time. It was going to take a lot of evidence to shatter this confidence. Conversely the Persians had lost two actions. Their disappointment would have been all the greater because they must have expected their advantage of numbers to have given them victory. Their morale would have been shaken even before the battle began. They would have seen every reversal as an indication that third successive defeat was about to occur, so it would not have taken much to convince the Persian crews that their cause was doomed.

As Herodotus makes clear, there was another reason – though as usual in naval matters he is not very clear about what he means. He writes "The Persian fleet, by its mere size, proved to be its own greatest enemy as constant confusion was caused by the ships fouling one another". It may be that with some five or more ranks of warships lined up behind each other, the ships ran afoul of each other. The damaged ships seeking to get out of the fighting would have had to limp through these lines of ships with few working oarsmen and often with broken steering oars. The possibilities for collision and confusion were great.

However, the captains of the ships in the Persian fleet were experienced, professional naval men. They would have been used to the problems thrown up by combat. The commanders of the fully crewed ships to the rear will have known it was down to them to get out of the way of the retreating vessels. Most would have been more than able to do so. It is unlikely that simple numbers caused them to get in each other's way to such an extent that the fleet's fighting ability was seriously compromised.

It is more likely that the confusion in the Persian ranks which the Greeks saw and which Herodotus reports was caused by the command structure of the Persian fleet. Each contingent in the fleet of the Great King was commanded by its own admiral. Herodotus tells us that, "Every nation had as many commanders as it had towns," and gives the names of some of the more prominent. The ships of Sidon were commanded by Teramnestus, those of Tyre by Matten son of Siromus, those of Cilicia by Syennesis and the Carian ships by Damasithymus, son of Candaules. Each contingent was of a different size, so officers equal in rank might be in charge of drastically different numbers of ships. To make matters worse, there were a dozen different languages being spoken by the officers of the fleet. No doubt these sailors had picked up a few words of foreign languages in various ports, but it is unlikely that more than a handful were fluent in a tongue other than their own.

There would also have been problems which would be familiar to commanders of allied forces through history. The Phoenicians preferred fast-moving combat with missile weapons playing a role before ramming settled the issue. The Egyptians preferred slower fights ending in boarding attacks. Other nations no doubt preferred their own style of combat. It would not matter how much the captains were told they had to conform to an agreed plan and style. Once battle begins and imminent death threatens, men tend to revert to what they know and trust.

To impose some sort of order on this confusing picture, Xerxes had imposed a strict hierarchy of command with his brother Achaemenes at the top. Every ship had a Persian officer on board at all times. It must be assumed that this man could at least have made himself understood in the native language of the ship's crew even if he were not fluent. His duties would have been to act as a sort of liaison officer, trying to ensure the captain knew what was expected of him – and no doubt reporting back any signs of disaffection or unrest. Each commander likewise had a Persian officer at his side, again to serve as liaison and perhaps to be an interpreter as well.

Achaemenes himself was also formally the commander of the powerful Egyptian squadron, but it is not entirely clear how real was his power over his fellow Persian admirals. Whenever the fleet acts as a unit it is Achaemenes who seems to be taking the lead. His status as a full brother of Xerxes would have given him a moral authority, if nothing else, over the others. Megabazus and Prexaspes were non-royal nobles while Ariabignes was only a half-brother to Xerxes. But nepotistic authority may not count for much in the heat of combat. Any one of the other Persian admirals might have wished to drive forward to win honour, or to hold back for fear of losing his ships in a plan he considered rash.

In the circumstances it is not surprising that the Egyptian squadron did best in the fighting that day. They captured five Greek ships for no loss of their own. With heavy armour and effective weapons the Egyptians would have done well; and under the personal command of Achaemenes they would have followed the battle plan directly and on time.

It is most likely in the babel of languages spoken in the Persian fleet and the divided command that we are to find the cause of the confusion that soon became evident.

The Greeks were likewise divided into a number of independent squadrons over which the commander in chief, the Spartan Eurybiades, had a less than certain authority. They were, however, united by language and by style of fighting. There were no major differences in equipment or preferred tactics among the Greek contingents, nor was there going to be much confusion as to the meaning of orders as they did not need to be translated from one language to another. All this seems to have had a real impact on the battle fought in the mouth of the Euripus.

As the sun passed its height and the heat of the day reached its greatest, the naval battle raged on unabated. Ships were pummelled and men smashed as the desperate struggle for control of the sea route reached its bloody climax.

At Thermopylae, the noon sun also saw events reaching their culmination. Hydarnes and his Immortals were making their way down the last stretches of the mountain path towards Alpeni. The Thespians were manning the East Gate and fingering their weapons. The Phocian Wall at the Middle Gate was manned. King Leonidas and his Spartiates were drawn up in phalanx in front of the wall watching the masses of the Persian army forming up in front of them.

Dressed in their scarlet tunics and cloaks, the Spartans would have made a brave and stirring sight. Their bronze faced shields were painted with a variety of warlike devices such as scorpions, snakes, lions, gorgons, clubs or any of the mythical monsters with which Greek legends abound. Their helmets were topped by brightly coloured crests of horsehair that nodded and waved in the gentle breeze that came in off the Malian Gulf.

As they waited the Spartans will have sung the ancient songs of Tyrtaios. The men had known these songs since childhood, singing them in unison as an essential part of the bonding process that made them Spartan hoplites. Now the lyrics recalling heroic deeds and urging the singers to greater efforts drifted across the sun-baked plain towards the advancing Persian host. Given the bloodshed of the previous days and the piles of dead Persians that littered the ground, it must have been a chilling sound.

Whoever the advancing Persian troops were, they will have been equipped with both spears and shields for close combat and with bows or javelins for longer range fighting. As they came on across the muddy pools of the hot springs, these men must have wondered why the scarlet-clad Greeks were this time awaiting them in front of the wall, rather than behind it. They would soon find out.

As the Persians advanced, the Spartan singing will have reached a crescendo, then abruptly stopped. The Persians will have halted perhaps 100 metres or so from the Spartans if they had bows, or closer if they had javelins. The resulting cloud of arrows or spears would not have been dense enough to block out the sun, as the Spartans had been warned before the battle began, but it would have been heavier than anything the Spartans had before encountered. No doubt the Spartans crouched down behind their large shields to weather the storm. The light, broad-headed Asian arrows could not penetrate shield, helmet or greaves. Only a few lucky shots would have found unprotected flesh.

Then the Persians would have picked up their heavy thrusting spears and their shields to advance to close quarters. At this Leonidas and his men stood up once again. Their shields were brought forward to form a solid wall of bronze with the greaves and helmets. The spears of the first few ranks were hoisted up to the overarm position to bristle forward of the shields.

Then the Spartans began to advance. In silence at first they walked forwards, then began to trot. The formation of the phalanx would have been as solid and unbroken as only a Spartan phalanx could be. The advancing Persian formation would have been looser and less regular by comparison.

With a shattering roar the war cry of the Spartans will have torn the air as the Spartans gave full vent to their terrifying scream of battle. Then the phalanx would have surged forward at the run. The impact of the solid body of hoplites crashing into the Persian forces would have been immense. The first ranks of lightly armed Asians would have collapsed as the heavy spears punched through the light shields to kill the man behind. Those behind will have been bowled over by the momentum of the heavily armoured men coming on at the run. With the front ranks gone, the rear ranks would find themselves suddenly prey to the stabbing spear points of the Spartan hoplites pushing forward as their momentum carried them on into the Persian ranks.

It is unlikely that any of the Asians subjected to the full onslaught of the Spartan phalanx charging at full tilt would ever have seen or experienced anything like it before. And for many it was the last thing that they ever would see. The casualties would have been high and the bloodshed horrific. This was what Leonidas wanted for his men: the chance to deal out death in the manner for which they had trained all their lives.

As the momentum of the charge petered out on the fallen bodies of the soldiers of the Great King, Leonidas will have called a halt. Keeping tight formation was paramount to the success of the Spartan phalanx. With untold thousands of men waiting to advance against him, Leonidas will have wanted to keep his men in phalanx even if that meant allowing some of the enemy to escape when they could have been killed.

The attack will have been an object lesson to Xerxes and his advisers in how the Greeks, and the Spartans in particular, waged war. Xerxes must have recalled the conversation he had had with Demaratus, the exiled king of Sparta weeks before at Doriscus. Xerxes had asked if the Greeks, being few in number, would dare to stand against his vast army. Demaratus had replied, "Suppose a thousand of them take the field, then that thousand will fight you. So will any number be it more or less than that . . . Fighting together they are the best soldiers in the world." Xerxes had laughed at Demaratus then, but now he must have acknowledged to himself that the exiled king knew his own people.

Xerxes could not afford now to pull back and halt his attack. He knew now that he had Leonidas, commander of the Greek forces in Thermopylae, facing him in front of the Phocian Wall. While events beyond the wall were hidden, Xerxes will have wanted to keep Leonidas where he was. The only certain way to do that was to keep up the pace of the assault. Xerxes had no way of knowing that Leonidas had no intention of moving and that the continual advance of fresh Persians for his men to kill was exactly what he wanted.

Another Persian attack went in, then another. In one such assault the two Persian princes were killed. The Persians certainly did not lack courage in these encounters, but they were outclassed in terms of equipment, training and discipline. The heavy Greek hoplites were superior to the lighter Persian soldiers with their missile weaponry.

Each time the fighting ceased the Spartan phalanx would have been smaller than the time before. Superb soldiers they may have been, but the Spartans were not invulnerable. Nor was King Leonidas. At some point he was killed, his body falling to the ground in the front rank where he had been fighting. The Persians were encouraged when Leonidas fell and surged forward in an attempt to grab hold of his body. The Spartans pushed back and a terrific, if short-lived struggle raged for the body of the dead king.

Four times the Persians laid hands on the corpse of Leonidas, and four times the Spartans snatched it back. Eventually the Asian force was driven off, allowing the Spartan phalanx to reform itself once again, though smaller than ever. The body of Leonidas was carried away, through the Phocian Wall. It was probably laid out on the small hillock that stands behind the wall.

Then the fighting began again. Xerxes, scenting victory, sent a fresh wave of attackers surging up towards the Middle Gate, only for them to be driven back again in a welter of bloodshed.

Timings are impossible to establish clearly for events in the Pass of Thermopylae on this third day of the battle, but it seems to have been mid-afternoon when the Immortals got through the East Gate. Once this happened, the Greeks must have known that swift defeat was inevitable. The Spartans pulled back through the Phocian Wall for the last time and headed for the small hillock. Perhaps this was where the wounded were being cared for by the Helots. There the Spartans were joined by the Thespians, or such of them as still lived.

On this small hillock the League Greeks prepared to make their final stand. Forming a solid wall of hoplites, they faced outward against the gathering forces of Xerxes. The Persians pushing from the west scrambled over the Phocian Wall, while the Immortals marched up from the east. Still the fighting went on. By this time many of the hoplites had only broken spears, so they turned to their swords as tools with which to kill the enemy. A few lost even this last weapon and resorted to hands and teeth in the grim struggle that raged on.

When only a few Greeks remained on their feet and fighting, Xerxes called off his men. He ordered them to stand back and use their missile weapons to finish the job. And so the last few Spartans and Thespians died under a hail of arrows and javelins.

The Thebans, meanwhile, had become separated from the main body of their allies. They now threw down their weapons and walked forwards with empty hands held palms facing the front to show they were unarmed. It was the traditional Greek signal of surrender, but the Persians were now in no mood for pleasantries. They fell on the Thebans, killing several before the Persian officers got their men under control and called a halt to the slaughter.

As soon as he knew it was safe to do so, Xerxes hurried forward with his bodyguard and entourage. They crossed the muddy streams of the hot springs of Thermopylae into the cleared killing ground where so many of the Persians had died. They came through the broken gates of the Phocian Wall and arrived beside the hillock where the Spartans and Thespians had made their last stand.

Xerxes demanded that the body of King Leonidas be brought before him. When the battered corpse was located and dragged forward, Xerxes felt a fierce flush of anger. He ordered that the head be hacked off and put on an upright spike. This was set beside the road beside the hillock. He wanted his army as it marched through to pass under the grisly trophy so that they could all see what happened to men who dared defy the monarch of the Persian Empire, even if they were kings.

It was by this time late afternoon, perhaps about 5 pm or so. The fate of the Thebans was, at first, in doubt. Some Persians wanted them killed as an example to the rest of Greece, but Xerxes refused. He knew that Thebes had already promised to surrender promptly and had no wish to turn that powerful city into an enemy. Nevertheless, he could not allow the open hostility shown to him by these particular Thebans to go unpunished. He compromised by sparing their lives, but branding them as imperial slaves and sending them back to Persia to labour for the benefit of the King of Kings.

As the last Greeks died on the little hillock, the swift Athenian galley commanded by Habronichus waited off shore. Once he had witnessed the final scene, Habronichus ordered his men to bend to their oars and headed off towards Artemisium with the grim news from Thermopylae.

Making a maximum effort because of the urgency of their news, the galley could have reached Artemisium within six hours. Habronichus arrived after sunset to find a battered and badly damaged fleet pulled up on the beach. Several large funeral pyres were blazing with flames tens of metres high as wreckage from broken ships was used to carry away the souls of the dead heroes who had fought so hard that day at the entrance to the Euripus.

The battle had ended shortly before sunset in stalemate. Both fleets had been badly damaged in the fighting, but neither had given way. Of the Athenian ships, over half were so badly damaged as to be unfit for action. Herodotus tells us that Eurybiades and Themistocles were glad when gathering night put an end to the fighting, and reached the beach at Artemisium with much relief. As well they might. They had done well to hold their own in a straight fight against a fleet at least 60% bigger than their own.

The Greek admirals must have been discussing what to do the next day when Habronichus arrived. The news was terrible. The line had broken. The Great King was free to move his army on into fertile Boeotia where there would be plenty of food to be had. The trap that had been laid so carefully at Thermopylae-Artemisium was now broken. The vast Persian army would not starve at Trachis, nor turn back into Thessaly. The invasion would continue.

The news did, at least, solve the problem of what the navy should do. There was no point staying on at Artemisium. If the League fleet was to get away, they had to move fast while they had the cover of night and before the messengers of Xerxes could complete their journey overland to give the Persian fleet at Aphetae the glad news of Thermopylae.

Themistocles put heart into the tired, exhausted men by telling them that he had a plan that would reduce the size of the enemy fleet. Then orders were given that all crews should light their cooking fires as usual. All the sheep and goats in the area were promptly slaughtered and roasted, as much to keep them out of the hands of the Persians as to feed the crews.

As soon as everything was ready, the League squadrons put to sea. The crews rowed away to the west, turning south along the Euripus to put as much distance between themselves and the Persians as possible before daybreak. Night travel at sea was most unusual at this date, but this was an emergency.

As the Greeks fled to safety, Themistocles put his plan into operation. At every port or cove where the pursuing ships of Xerxes might put in for food or water, he landed and scrawled a message on the nearest convenient wall or rockface. "Men of Ionia," the message read in Greek, "it is wrong that you should make war upon your fathers and help to bring the Greeks into subjection. The best thing you can do is to join our side; if this is impossible, you might at least remain neutral, and ask the Carians to do the same. If you are unable to do either, but are held by a compulsion so strong that it puts desertion out of the question, there is still another course open to you: in the next battle, remember that you and we are of the same blood, that our quarrel with Persia arose originally on your account – and fight badly."

As psychological warfare goes, it was not particularly subtle. Nor was it very effective. After the Greeks fled Artemisium there are no signs that any of the Great King's Greek subjects abandoned his cause.

With both the army and the navy of the League hurrying south with the forces of Xerxes hard on their heels, the war must have appeared lost. But the Thermopylae campaign was not yet over. For the League, worse – and better – was still to come.

The Persian attack on the sacred Greek sanctuary of Delphi ends in disaster as the god Apollo hurls down rocks to destroy the barbarian raiding force. This is a Victorian view of the famous legend.

CHAPTER 18

The Fall of Athens

The Athens Acropolis photographed from the south in the 19th century, when the prospect of storming the high city was even more clearly daunting that it is today.

When the sun rose on 21 August 480BC, the battle of Thermopylae was over but the campaign still had some way to run. Xerxes, King of Kings, was determined to exact revenge on those who had stood against him and to continue with the original object of the invasion: the destruction of Athens and Sparta and the reduction of the rest of Greece to the status of a province of the Persian Empire. First, however, there was some tidying up to do; and manipulation of the news release, both for its effect on the rest of the campaign and for posterity.

Exactly how many of the Great King's soldiers had been killed it is impossible to say. Herodotus puts the total at 20,000, but this is probably just a guess. What is beyond question is that the casualties suffered by the Persian army were many, far more than those lost by the League army that had fought under King Leonidas of Sparta. But Xerxes wanted to present this battle as a great victory. He kept the bulk of his army and navy away from the battlefield while gangs of workmen dug large pits and hurriedly heaved the majority of the Persian bodies out of sight. Only then was the rest of the vast army allowed to march through the Pass of Thermopylae. They will have seen the spiked head of Leonidas beside the roadside, the bodies of his men and the far fewer visible bodies of the dead Persians. Relays of boats brought over men from the fleet to see the battlefield. Xerxes wanted the battlefield presented as a stunning Persian triumph in which the impudent Greeks had been crushed by the overwhelming might of the Persian host. The battlefield certainly looked that way, but far too many people knew the truth.

As Xerxes led his army in triumph through the pass and into Phocis, he was a busy monarch. Much had to be done and there was little time in which to do it. Getting past Thermopylae had taken up a valuable week of the campaigning season. Of prime importance was the need to make an example of Phocis. This was the first state reached by Xerxes which had not surrendered as soon as the Persian army appeared. Other Greek states needed to learn what it meant to defy the King of Kings. Powerful detachments of cavalry were sent out to race across the land to deal out the Great King's vengeance in brutal and ruthless fashion.

It was probably because they had known what to expect that the Phocians had got clear of Thermopylae as soon as they could after their bruising encounter with the Immortals. They had families to save, valuables to hide and work to do. If the Persians were determined, they could find anything given time. The Phocians must have hoped that the Persians would move on to Athens without stopping to search too carefully. For some the most obvious place of relative safety were the heights of the Mount Parnassos massif. Others chose to flee to Locris, which had opted to surrender to Xerxes, and hope that friends or relatives would keep them safe. With only hours to play with, the Phocians will have buried money, plate and grain. Some transportable valuables were loaded on to pack animals and driven along with the herds of livestock by the men, women and children all desperate to get away before the Persians arrived.

Even as the frantic Phocians were packing up to flee, they received a message from their old enemies the Thessalians. "Men of Phocis," began the message, "Now at last you must admit your error and own that you are not our equals. In the past, while it suited us to be one with the Greeks, we were always considered more important than you: and now our influence with the Persians is so great that a word from us would get you turned out of your country – and sold as slaves. Even so, we are willing to let bygones be bygones even though we have you completely in our power. Simply pay us 50 talents, and we undertake to divert the danger that is approaching you." To their credit, the leaders of Phocis found the time to put together a fittingly heroic response. They told the Thessalians that the Phocians could have joined the Persians just as easily as had the Thessalians had they chosen to do so, but that they preferred not to be traitors.

Not everyone made their escape in time. Herodotus tells us that several groups of refugees were caught as they fled to the mountains. The men were killed out of hand, the women raped first. The city of Neon went up in flames, as did Drymus, Charadra, Erochus, Trites, Pedies and Hyampolis. At Abae not only was the city torched, but so was the famous temple of Apollo, having been first stripped of its treasures. The thoroughness of the Persian havoc wrought on Phocis was, in large part, thanks to the Thessalians. Stung by the Phocian reply to their request for a cash bribe, the Thessalians had sent scouts to lead the Persian raiding parties.

In the far southwest of Phocis lay one very special place: Delphi. As the townsfolk hurried to pack their goods and flee over the Gulf of Corinth to the Peloponnese, their leaders went to consult the Delphic Oracle in the Sacred Precinct. Speaking through the Oracle, the great god Apollo advised them to look after themselves and not to bother about the temple and its treasures because "Apollo can look after his own". The great god had conspicuously failed to do so at Abae, but this may not have been known to the human inhabitants of Delphi at the time. The people of Delphi fled while the oracle priestess and her 60 attendants at the Sacred Precinct awaited their fate.

Quite what happened next has long been a matter of dispute. As Herodotus tells the story: "Just as the Persians came to the shrine of

Athene Pronaea [which stood within sight of, but downhill from the Sacred Precinct], thunderbolts fell on them from the sky and two pinnacles of rock, torn from Mount Parnassos, came crashing down on them, killing a large number. At the same time a terrible war shout came from the Temple [of Apollo]. All this caused a panic among the Persian troops, who fled. I have learned that some who escaped said that they saw two huge hoplites, taller than any mortal man, chasing them away . . . According to the Delphians these were Phylacus and Autonous, two ancestral local heroes."

Is there any truth hidden in all this? Of course, there may have been an earthquake that brought boulders down from the mountain into the path of the Persians, and the panic Herodotus mentions may have caused the Persians to imagine the rest; but this stretches credulity. Or it may have been a carefully contrived ruse by the priests of Apollo. Perhaps there were delicately poised pinnacles of rock that could be toppled by the judicious use of crowbars and muscle power. And some sort of megaphone system to boom a voice out of the temple would not have been beyond the skills of the Greeks.

Or it might all have been a story put about by the servants of Apollo to explain why the Sacred Precinct was not destroyed by the Persians that would boost the holy reputation of the place. Xerxes did not go out of his way to destroy the temples and holy places of his enemies unless it served his purpose to do so. The pronouncements of the Delphic Oracle had not been entirely hostile to Persia, so Xerxes may have chosen to spare the sanctuary.

Meanwhile, the vast army of Xerxes was lumbering forward across Boeotia. By about 25 August the lead units were in Thebes, accepting the surrender of that great city. Columns of soldiers headed by senior Persian nobles radiated out to the other cities of Boeotia. All received immediate surrender and symbolic gifts of soil and water. Some Persian nobles were no doubt surprised to find themselves being greeted not only by the local Boeotian civic dignitaries, but also by Macedonian officials whom they had last seen some weeks earlier in the entourage of King Alexander of Macedon. These Macedonians smoothly assured the Persians that the cities in which they were living were, and always had been, very friendly to the Persians – so there was no need for any unpleasantness. No doubt the wily Alexander managed to extract some reward for his helpfulness to the Boeotians.

On the journey to Thebes the Persian scouts had rounded up several stragglers from the League army that had marched away from Thermopylae on the morning of 20 August. Most likely these were wounded men who had been unable to keep up the punishing pace of an army in retreat. Several from the Peloponnese were dragged in front of Xerxes and his entourage to be interrogated. They revealed that the army that had fought at Thermopylae was simply an advance guard of the main armies of Sparta and the Peloponnese. This had been sent, they said, because everyone else was too busy to at the Olympic Games watching and competing in athletic contests in honour of the god Zeus. Xerxes was amazed that the

Greeks would go to Olympia rather than try to defend their country and assumed that some fantastically valuable prizes must be on offer. Oh no, came the reply to this question, the only prize is a wreath of olive leaves and the honour of winning. At this, Tritantaechmes, son of Artabanes and a cousin of Xerxes, turned to Mardonius and exclaimed, "Good heavens, Mardonius. What manner of men are these that you have brought us to fight. They compete with each other not for money but for honour." The remark earned Tritantaechmes a stern rebuke from his king. He was probably lucky not to share the fate of his father and be promptly sent home.

While Xerxes was moving his army forward, gathering supplies from Boeotia and no doubt bringing his supply fleet forward, the Greek League was meeting at Corinth to discuss what to do in the light of the defeat at Thermopylae. The fleet, at the insistence of Themistocles of Athens, had sought shelter in the narrow channel between the island of Salamis and the mainland, just southwest of Athens. The army, meanwhile, was somewhere a little north of the Isthmus of Corinth.

The delegates at the League meeting were divided. The Athenians and others from north of the Isthmus wanted to fight the Persians in or near Boeotia. But now that Thermopylae was fallen they could not offer a battlefield that had convincing merits. The Peloponnesians, as previously, wanted to hold the line on the narrow Isthmus, but were as before unable to suggest a way of stopping the Persian fleet simply landing troops behind the defensive line. The vote was nevertheless carried by the Peloponnesians. The army would fall back on the Isthmus and begin building a defensive wall or earthwork, while the fleet would move south to try to guard the coast.

The commander of the Peloponnesian army that had been marching north to join Leonidas was none other than Cleombrotus, the younger brother of Leonidas. Receiving his orders, Cleombrotus set about the task of preparing a defensive position with all the thoroughness shown by his elder brother. With some 30,000 men to hand, he had not only enough labour to build a formidable barrier across the Isthmus but also to destroy the roads in front of the Isthmus. Everything was to be done to make the Persian approach as difficult as possible.

In the fleet, the decision of the League meeting caused fresh outbursts of argument. Eurybiades wanted to abandon the secluded waters of Salamis in favour of ports in the Peloponnese. Presumably he thought that if the fleet were stationed there it stood a better chance of driving off a landing by Persian troops. Themistocles, presumably supported by the men of Aegina, wanted the fleet to stay where it was. He knew that neither Athens nor Attica were yet properly evacuated and that the fleet would be needed to guard the refugees as they fled overseas. Commander Eurybiades had to bow to the will of his most powerful junior commanders if the fleet were to remain intact. It stayed at Salamis.

In Athens and across Attica the entire population was getting ready to flee. Those who lived too far from the capital to make it to the evacuation ships in time fled to the mountains and hoped the Persians did not stay long. Most however, flooded down to the port to be taken to Aegina, Troezen or to Salamis, in accordance with the decree agreed some weeks earlier. The merchant ships of the League states were kept constantly busy shipping the mass of terrified humanity to safety.

The process was hurried along by what seemed to be a direct intervention by the goddess Athene herself. A great snake was said to live beneath the temples of the Acropolis, presumably in caverns or crevices, and to come out at night to patrol the sacred precincts of Athene to make sure the place was safe for the goddess. To ensure that the serpent did no harm to humans, such as the priests and priestesses, a piece of honeycake was left out every evening. By dawn it had always gone, consumed it was said by the snake. But now the honeycake was found uneaten at dawn. The High Priestess of Athene made this public, and many took it to mean that the goddess herself had left Athens. The rush to the ships increased dramatically.

Meanwhile, the Acropolis was being hurriedly fortified. There was some hope that Xerxes might decide to spare the holiest sanctuary of the goddess Athene, to whom he had made such a lavish sacrifice at Troy at the start of the campaign. In case he did not, the walls around the hill were reinforced and repaired, while a sizeable garrison of armed men was installed. The priests and priestesses of Attica carried their sacred treasures and holy relics up to the fortified hill, to be joined by a number of refugees who preferred the protection of the gods to that of the fleet. It seems that these people believed that they could hold out against the vast Persian army for quite some time – long enough for Xerxes to lose interest and move on.

On or about 30 August Xerxes and the forward units of the Persian army reached the borders of Attica. Throughout the march across Boeotia, the men had been kept strictly in line. There had been no looting nor any pillage. The Boeotians were, after all, allies of the Great King and were supplying the army with food. But now the Persian troops were again into enemy territory. They were once more let loose to do their worst. Spreading out across the farmland, fields and woods, the Persian troops found themselves advancing across a deserted land. Neither human nor domestic animal was to be found. Only the empty houses and barns with doors flapping in the wind greeted the forces of the Great King. There was still the odd item left to plunder, so the soldiers stole everything they could, then set fire to what was left. The advance of the army was marked by a slowly spreading pall of black smoke as buildings, crops and vegetation baked dry by the summer sun went up in flames. Xerxes was taking his revenge against Athens – but his vengeful master stroke was yet to come.

On about 2 September the Great King reached the city of Athens itself. The supply fleet put in to make use of the impressive, modern dock facilities. Supplies were unloaded and the army allowed to rest and recuperate. Equipment was repaired and renewed, depleted units reorganised and celebrations held. Xerxes sent a messenger racing back to Persia to announce his triumph. The inhabitants of Susa gave themselves over to a public holiday with all the traditional festivities of victory.

Most of the city of Athens was abandoned and empty, but Xerxes could see that the Acropolis was fortified and manned. It would have to be taken, but this might not be easy. The Acropolis, or "high town", was the ancient heart of the city. It had been chosen by Athene, the legends explained, because it was easily defended. The rock stood about 70 metres above the surrounding plain and was topped by a fairly level area 300 metres long and 150 metres wide. A small spring gave out water near the temple of Athene and her sacred olive tree, giving defenders a secure source of water even in mid-summer.

At this date the defensive strength of the Acropolis depended almost entirely on the natural cliffs that surround it. A stout stone wall had been built around the top of the hill in around 1300BC, in Mycenaean times, but the main purpose of this was to provide a level fighting platform for defenders. In any case, later generations had maintained it only in places where the cliffs were less sheer than elsewhere and might be scaled by skilled climbers.

There were two gates in this ancient wall: a small one to the north and a larger one at the southwest, the only side of the Acropolis where the slope is anything less than precipitous. It was at these two places that the Athenians had built stout wooden walls a few generations before the Persian invasion. These were well maintained and pierced by strong gateways. It was to these wooden walls that the priests of Athene had said the Delphic Oracle had referred when she declared, "The wooden wall only shall not fall, but help you and your children". Now with the Persians at the gates, the wooden wall was barricaded to strengthen it and supplies of food and weapons laid in for a long siege.

Xerxes called for his military engineers and had them study the problems posed by the rock of the Acropolis. Coming from a tradition of warfare that had been skilled in siege tactics for over two millennia, the engineers will have regarded the rock with coolly professional eyes. Their first decision was to set up a fortified camp on the site of the Athenian law courts on the Areopagus Hill. This height faced the southwest corner of the Acropolis, with its wooden wall. Although not as high as the Acropolis itself, the hill gave a good view of the defences. The fortifications were necessary to guard against an Athenian sally. Then the siege could begin.

The attack began with a fusillade of arrows. These were no ordinary arrows, but were tipped with wads of cloth soaked in pitch and set on fire. As we have already seen, the Greeks were not accustomed to siege warfare, nor very proficient at its skills. They had clearly neglected to face the wooden wall with wet hides or to soak it with buckets of water. Within a short time the wall caught fire. By the second day of the siege it was a smoking wreck.

In later centuries, certain rules became formalised about siege warfare. We do not know if these were as hard and fast in Xerxes' day as they later became, but he abided by them nonetheless. Now that a breach had been made in the principal defence, Xerxes sent forward a delegation to ask the defenders to surrender. If they agreed terms could be discussed, though they would inevitably be harsh. If they refused then there would be no mercy shown.

For this mission, Xerxes chose to send those Athenians who had been in exile in Persia and whom he had brought along with the army, presumably to lead a puppet government after he had won his expected victory. Among these was a nobleman named Dicaeus, son of Theocydes. The garrison on Acropolis watched the men picking their way up the hill toward the ashes of the wooden wall. As soon as the delegation began to shout out Xerxes' offer, they were met with hoots of derision and cries of treachery. There would be no surrender.

Xerxes ordered an assault, his men racing up the southwestern slope to clamber over the wreck of the wooden wall. They were met by a hail of javelins, and also by a number of large boulders that were rolled down the slope. The attack faltered, and fell back.

Having failed to take the Acropolis by direct assault on the main entrance, the Persian siege masters looked for another way. They found it in the form of an almost sheer rock face on the north side of the Acropolis, between the shrine of Aglauros and the steep staircase up to the narrow northern gate in the old Mycenaean wall. The cliff face here was steep in the extreme, but specialist climbers among the Persian siege train declared that they could get up it. The Greeks, however, considered it unscalable and had their defences on this stretch of the wall concentrated on the staircase.

Aglauros was the daughter of King Cecrops, the first King of Athens. She was loved by the war god Ares, but she earned the enmity of Athene through her insatiable curiosity. Eventually, Athene sent madness to Aglauros who threw herself off the Acropolis and plunged to her death. The Athenians raised a small shrine over the site of her death. (There is some debate today about the actual site of the Aglaureion.) Superstitious Athenians would have seen something in the link between Athene's anger, the god of war and the site of the new Persian attack.

On the third or fourth night of the siege, a fresh assault force was mustered and marched quietly to hide among the houses close to the foot of the old staircase. Then the expert climbers set to work. Moving stealthily and in silence, the men worked their way up the rockface. As the cool light of dawn was coming up out of the east, the Persians reached the top of their ascent. They can have been only lightly armed, but with the element of surprise they had all they needed. They ran to the gateway at the top of the staircase, killed the guards on duty and flung open the gate.

Up the staircase surged the Persians, hundreds of men streaming in through the open gateway. Some of the defenders tried to barricade themselves into the temple of Athene, with its solid stone walls, but to no avail. The Persians were now swarming all over the Acropolis. They killed everyone. Then, following Xerxes orders, they set fire to all the buildings. At this date most of them were wooden or had wooden roofs. They caught fire easily and a thick column of smoke rose into the morning skies over Athens.

The temple of Athene was utterly destroyed. The stones that survived the fire were torn down and the site levelled. The sacred olive tree was consumed in the flames. Xerxes had begun his invasion by sacrificing to the sacred goddess of Athens, now he showed his contempt for her.

With the sacking of Athens and the destruction of the Acropolis, the Thermopylae campaign may fairly be said to have ended. The armies had marched and countermarched, dug in and manoeuvred, fought and died. Now this phase of the war was over. Xerxes was in Athens and had wreaked his vengeance on his most hated enemy.

It might be thought that the campaign of Thermopylae had been a disaster for the Greeks, and so it must have seemed at the time. But with hindsight the campaign was seen in a very different light. The great lyric poet Pindar wrote a celebratory epic poem just a few years later. Sadly this work has been lost, but one line survives in which he praises the battles as "That great fight where the brave sons of Athens planted the shining cornerstone of freedom". Pindar was an adult during these years of war, so he his judgment of the campaign was informed.

The truth of Pindar's judgement was borne out as war went on. And there was one last act that King Leonidas could do for his country from beyond the grave. The Delphic Oracle, it must be remembered had declared:

"Hear your fate, O dwellers in Sparta of the wide spaces;
Either your famed, great town must be sacked by Perseus's sons,
Or, if that not happen, the whole land of Lacedaemon
Shall mourn the death of a king of the house of Heracles."

The king had died and was being mourned. The city had yet to be saved.

Even as the siege of the Acropolis was proceeding, Xerxes was preparing for the next phase of the war. He needed to conquer the Peloponnese and crush all Greek resistance if he were to add Greece to his empire. As so often before, Xerxes gathered his advisors and senior commanders to consult them before reaching a decision. He began with Demaratus, the exiled king of Sparta. Demaratus identified the problem accurately. "There is a narrow isthmus to the Peloponnese [the Isthmus of Corinth] and on it you will find all the troops from that part of Greece come to resist you. You will have to face bloodier battles than any you have yet witnessed. But if you take my advice, the isthmus and Peloponnesian towns will fall into your hands almost without a blow."

Demaratus suggested that 300 ships should be sent to transport a strong raiding force of soldiers to the southern Peloponnese. With such a strong force active on their own territory, the Spartans would not march to the Isthmus, but would be kept running to and fro trying to drive off the Persian raiders. The other League forces, Demaratus was confident, could be driven off the Isthmus by the Persian army with comparative ease.

However, Xerxes' brother and commander of his fleet, Achaemenes, refused to endorse the plan. He told Xerxes that he had lost so many ships in the storms and the battles off Artemisium that if he detached 300 ships to the southern Peloponnese he would have fewer warships than did the Greek fleet at Salamis. He argued, correctly, that to divide the fleet in this way would be extremely dangerous. The Greeks would be able to come out to attack each portion of the Persian fleet in turn and overwhelm them separately.

Xerxes realised that both men were right. An amphibious operation against the southern Peloponnese would make the fighting at the Isthmus easier, but could not be undertaken while the Greek fleet was intact and at Salamis. First, the fleet of the League had to be destroyed.

The Salamis campaign that followed was complex and involved a series of events that had as much to do with political intrigue as with military actions. What is clear, is that the Greek fleet – and Themistocles in particular – had learned the hard lessons of Artemisium. On 20 August they had fought a long, merciless battle against the Persian fleet. The Greeks had held their own, but this was not good enough. Since the Persians outnumbered them, the Greeks would inevitably lose a war of attrition. Some way had to be found to get an initial advantage over the enemy that would allow the Greeks to deliver a crushing blow before the attrition began.

At Salamis on 20 September, the Greeks managed to induce Achaemenes to divide his fleet, and then to send his main force through a narrow channel. In this channel it was ambushed and destroyed piecemeal by the Greeks. The Persian fleet lost over 200 ships, the Greeks barely 40. After such a mauling, the Persian fleet could not be expected to attack again. In terms of numbers it was probably now about equal to the Greek fleet, but its morale and fighting spirit will have been broken by a succession of defeats at the hands of a numerically inferior enemy. By this time all that could be expected of the remnants of the fleet was that it would protect the merchant ships from Greek attack.

There could now be no sea-borne raid on the Peloponnese. If the war was to be won then the army would have to do it alone. That meant attacking and breaking through whatever defences the League had managed to throw up over the Isthmus of Corinth.

Xerxes sent forward his expert scouts to find out the situation on that narrow neck of land. They found that the land in front of the isthmus had been stripped clean of food, shelter and that even the roads had been torn up and destroyed. The isthmus itself was blocked by a newly completed wall and this was guarded by an army some four times larger than that which had fought at Thermopylae. Worst of all, the army was led by the scarlet-cloaked hoplites of Sparta headed by the brother of the commander at Thermopylae.

When all this was reported back to Xerxes, early in October, he knew that to get into the Peloponnese he was facing a repetition of the fight at Thermopylae. As ever, he did not hesitate. Rather than face such an awful prospect, he folded his tents and began the long march back to Persia. The war would go on, but Greece would not be conquered.

That was the final, great victory of King Leonidas and the heroic men who died with him in the narrow pass of Thermopylae.

The Athenian statesman and military leader Themistocles is honoured by the Spartans after the war ends with a Greek victory.

Epilogue

When he left Greece in October 480BC, Xerxes left behind him a powerful army of about 80,000 men under the command of his son-in-law Mardonius. It was Mardonius who had been the leading advocate of the invasion of Greece in the first place, so it was only fit that he should be given the task of both consolidating the areas already won into a new province of the Persian Empire and, if possible, of defeating the still defiant Greeks of the south.

In the spring of 479BC, the Greek League marched north from the Peloponnese to tackle Mardonius. The two armies met at Plataea and the resulting battle ended in complete defeat for the Persians. Mardonius was killed and over half his army either slaughtered or enslaved. The rest marched back to Persia as fast as they could. There was now no real danger to Greece from Persia. The war, however, was to continue intermittently for generations until it was finally and decisively ended by the conquest of the Persian Empire by Alexander the Great of Macedon in 331BC.

Of the main players in the campaign of Thermopylae, their eventual fates, when known, were mixed.

Achaemenes, brother of Xerxes and commander of the fleet, led his defeated ships back to Cyme soon after the battle of Salamis. The fleet was dispersed, each squadron returning to its home port. Achaemenes returned to his post as Governor of Egypt. The date of his death is not recorded.

Alexander I, King of Macedon, did well out of the campaign. Having successfully convinced both the Persians and League that he was on their side, Alexander was ideally placed to benefit, whoever won. The Persian defeat enabled him to regain complete independence for his kingdom. He reigned prosperously until his death in 450BC, when the throne passed peacefully to his son Perdiccas.

Aristodemus, the Spartan soldier with an eye infection who returned to Sparta rather than join Leonidas in the final defence of Thermopylae, redeemed his honour. At the Battle of Plataea, Aristodemus insisted in fighting in the front rank of the phalanx. He fought with unequalled bravery and was killed in the later stages of the battle.

Artabanus, the experienced uncle of Xerxes who had spoken against the attack on Greece, spent most of the campaign as regent in Susa for the absent monarch. After Xerxes' return he seems to have retained his position at court, but was always resented by Xerxes for having correctly predicted the likely outcome of the expedition. In 465 a man named Artabanus was involved in the murder of Xerxes, though whether this was the same Artabanus, his son or some unrelated nobleman who had the same name is unknown.

Cleombrotus, the younger brother of Leonidas, who commanded the League army defending the Isthmus of Corinth, was appointed regent for Leonidas' infant heir. He died of natural causes in the winter of 480-479BC.

Demaratus, the exiled king of Sparta, returned to Persia with Xerxes. He then went back to being Governor of the wealthy province of Pergamum where he enjoyed a long and successful life. He managed to get his son appointed as governor after his death and the position remained within the family for at least the next 200 years.

Ephialtes, the man from Malis who showed Xerxes the route over the mountain to take Thermopylae from the rear, received a massive payment of gold from the delighted monarch. After the defeat of the Persians at Plataea, the Spartans sent officials north to identify and arrest whoever had betrayed their heroic king Leonidas. It did not take long to identify Ephialtes as the guilty man, but by then he had fled. The Spartans put up a large cash reward for whoever managed to kill the renegade. Some time later, the date is not recorded, Ephialtes was seen and recognised by a man from Trachis named Athenades when he was visiting Anticyra. Athenades killed him on the spot, and raced off to Sparta to claim the reward, which was duly paid.

Eurybiades, the Spartan admiral who was at least nominally in command of the League Fleet, went back to the obscurity from which he had sprung. No more is heard of him.

Themistocles, the Athenian commander and politician who had masterminded the Athenian naval preparations, was supreme after the defeat of Xerxes. He began the rebuilding of Athens and the construction of defensive walls on the Persian pattern. For ten years he dominated the government of Athens, but in 471 was implicated in a corruption scandal and fled abroad. He lived for a while in Argos, then moved to Corfu and on to Epirus. He died at Magnesia in 457, never having returned to Athens.

Xerxes remained King of Kings for another 15 years after the Thermopylae campaign. However, his prestige does not seem ever to have recovered fully from the humiliation of his failure to complete the conquest of Greece. After about 470 he seems to have increasingly given himself over to enjoying the earthly pleasures of the flesh that came with his position. It did not take long for the Persian nobility to tire of a monarch who neglected his duties. In 465BC, Xerxes was murdered by the commander of his own bodyguard and replaced on the throne by his son Artaxerxes I.

As for the memory of King Leonidas of Sparta, he left his throne to his infant son, Plistarchus. At Thermopylae a large stone statue of a lion was raised over the communal grave of Leonidas and his Spartans. On this was fixed a plaque facing the road along which all travellers between Boeotia and Thessaly would pass. It carried one of the most famous inscriptions of the ancient world:

> "Go tell the Spartans, stranger passing by,
> That here, obedient to their laws, we lie."

Bibliography

Of the ancient authors, the following are available in modern translations:

Aeschylus	*The Persians*
Diodorus Siculus	*Works*
Herodotus	*The Histories*
Plutarch	*Lives* (Themistocles)

Of the modern works on the course of the Graeco-Persian Wars or on the conduct of ancient warfare, many are out of print, available only from specialist libraries or otherwise unavailable to the general reader. Of those that should be widely available, the following are recommended:

Mercenaries of the Ancient World, Serge Yalichev, Trans-Atlantic Publications, 1996.
Warfare in the Classical World, John Warry, Salamander Books, 1998
The Persian Army 560-330BC, Nicholas Sekunda, Osprey Publishing, 1992
The Spartan Army, Nicholas Sekunda, Osprey Publishing, 1998
Greek Hoplite 480-323BC, Nicholas Sekunda, Osprey Publishing, 2000
The Greek and Persian Wars 500-323BC, Jack Cassin-Scott, Osprey Publishing, 1977
The Greco-Persian Wars, Peter Green, University of California Press, 1998
The Greek Wars: The Failure of Persia, George Cawkwell, Oxford University Press, 2005
The Spartans: An Epic History, Paul Cartledge, Pan, 2003

For an entertaining (though not particularly accurate) afternoon's viewing there is the 1962 movie *300 Spartans*, director Rudolph Maté, available on DVD.

Maps

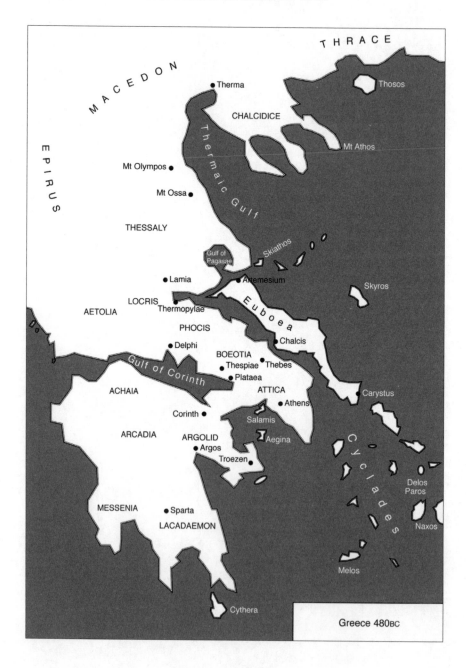

Greece 480BC

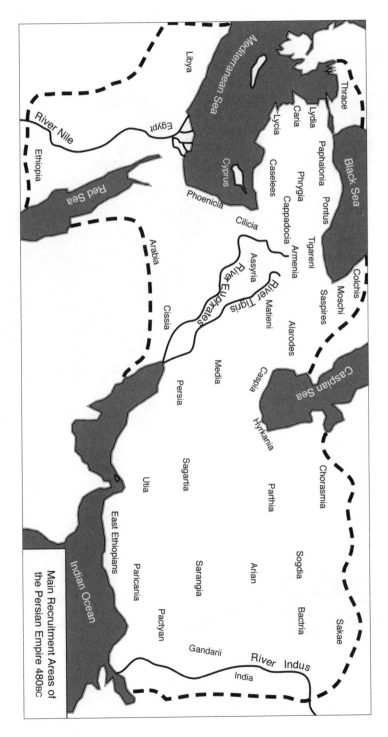

Main Recruitment Areas of
the Persian Empire 480BC

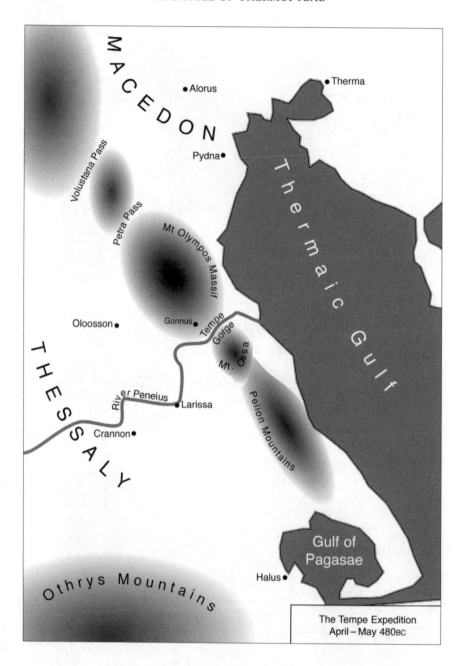

The Tempe Expedition
April – May 480BC

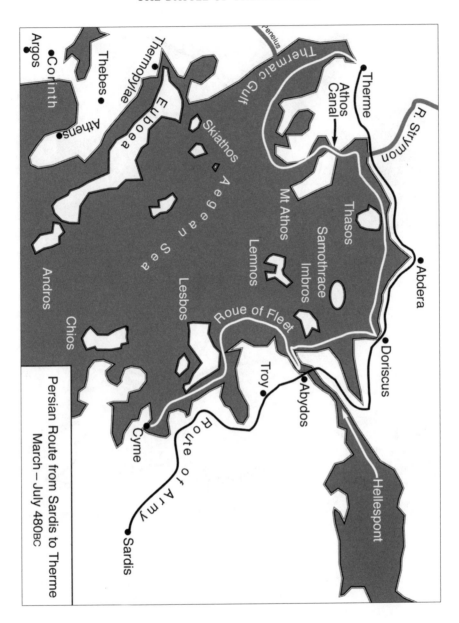

Persian Route from Sardis to Therme
March – July 480BC

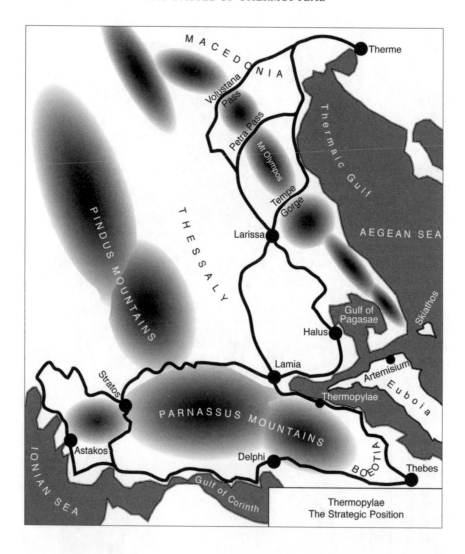

Thermopylae
The Strategic Position

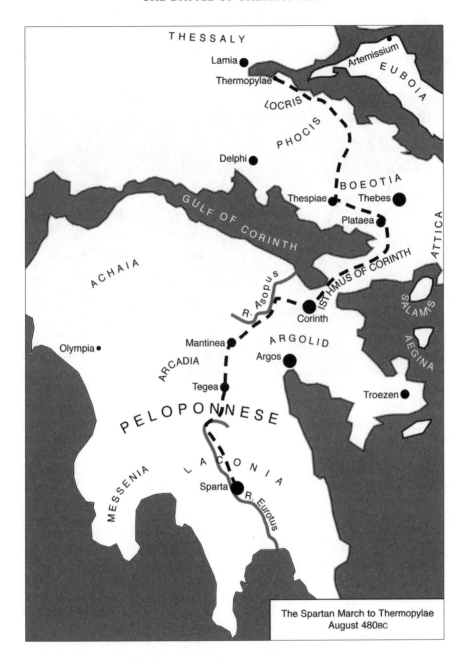

The Spartan March to Thermopylae
August 480BC

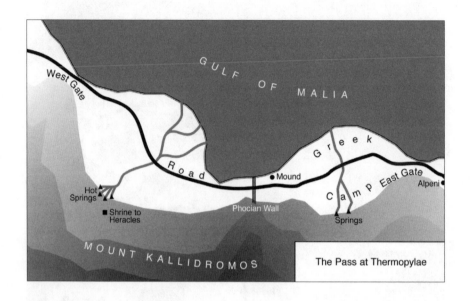

The Pass at Thermopylae

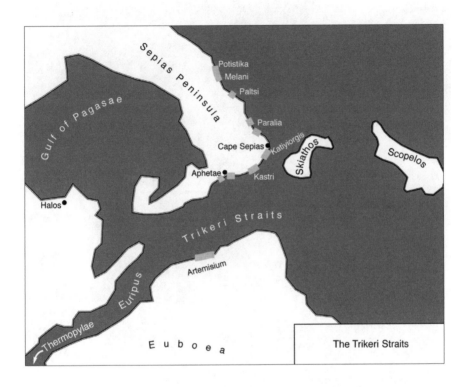

The Trikeri Straits

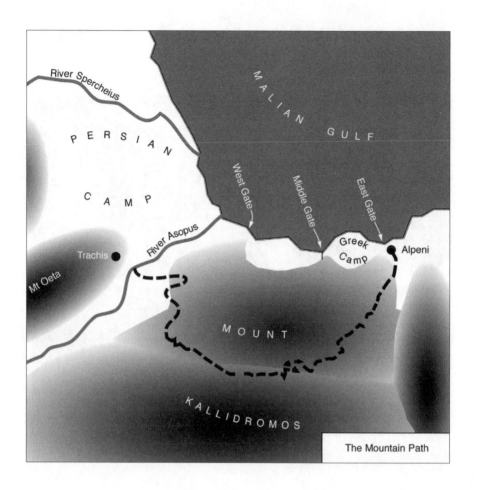

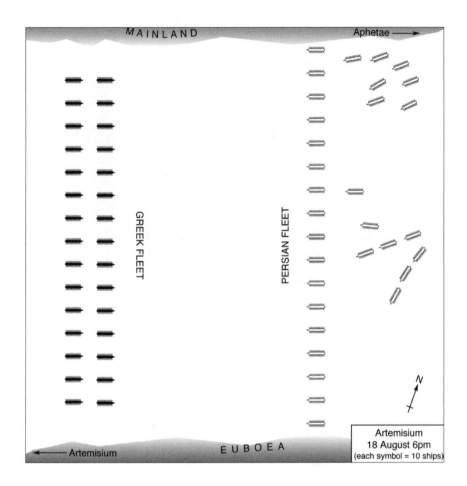

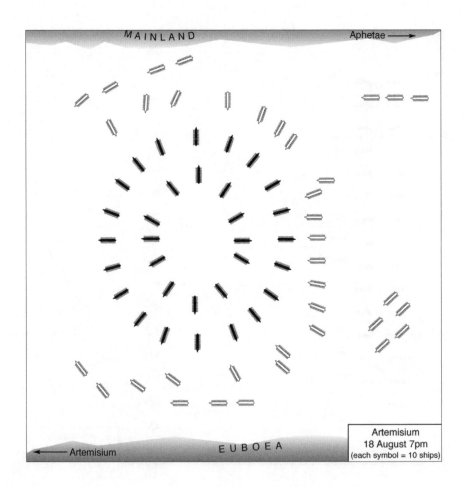

MAINLAND

Aphetae ⟶

EUBOEA

⟵ Artemisium

Artemisium
18 August 7pm
(each symbol = 10 ships)

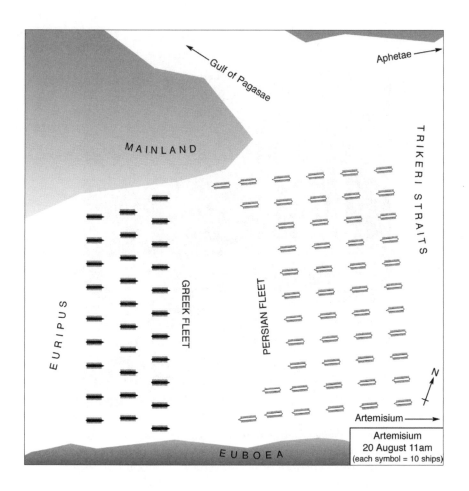

Delphi, with the Theatre and Temple of Apollo beyond and to the left. Athens built a treasury on the slope leading to the Temple to commemorate Athenian victory at the Battle of Marathon. The Gods, as we have seen, could not be 'bought' by such gestures forever. The Persians would return in overwhelming force ten years later.

Picture credits

All illustrations from the author's collection except Library of Congress, Prints and Photographs Division, LC-M31-14552, page 38; LC-USZ62-65913, 49; LC-USZ62-66134, 66; LC-G612-43438, 93; LC-USZ62-65886, 94; LC-USZ62-66132, 105; LC-USZ62-108933, 110; LC-USZ62-65912, 142; LC-USZ62-108913, 200; LC-USZ62-65903, photographic section page 3, below; LC-USZ62-6583, photographic section page 4; LC-USZ62-12756, photographic section page 16, below; LC-M31-13642, 227.

Index

Page references to illustrations are in *italic*.